P9-CQI-652

FERRAN

FERRAN

THE INSIDE STORY OF EL BULLI

AND THE MAN WHO REINVENTED FOOD

COLMAN ANDREWS

GOTHAM
BOOKS

GOTHAM BOOKS
Published by Penguin Group (USA) Inc.
375 Hudson Street, New York, New York 10014, U.S.A.
Penguin Group (Canada), 90 Eglinton Avenue East, Suite 700, Toronto, Ontario M4P 2Y3,
Canada (a division of Pearson Penguin Canada Inc.); Penguin Books Ltd, 80 Strand, London WC2R
0RL, England; Penguin Ireland, 25 St Stephen's Green, Dublin 2, Ireland (a division of Penguin
Books Ltd); Penguin Group (Australia), 250 Camberwell Road, Camberwell, Victoria 3124, Australia
(a division of Pearson Australia Group Pty Ltd); Penguin Books India Pvt Ltd, 11 Community Centre,
Panchsheel Park, New Delhi—110 017, India; Penguin Group (NZ), 67 Apollo Drive, Rosedale, North
Shore 0632, New Zealand (a division of Pearson New Zealand Ltd); Penguin Books (South Africa)
(Pty) Ltd, 24 Sturdee Avenue, Rosebank, Johannesburg 2196, South Africa

Penguin Books Ltd, Registered Offices: 80 Strand, London WC2R 0RL, England

Published by Gotham Books, a member of Penguin Group (USA) Inc.

First printing, October 2010
3 5 7 9 10 8 6 4 2

Copyright © 2010 by Colman Andrews
All rights reserved

Gotham Books and the skyscraper logo are trademarks of Penguin Group (USA) Inc.

LIBRARY OF CONGRESS CATALOGING-IN-PUBLICATION DATA
Andrews, Colman.
Ferran : the inside story of El Bulli and the man who reinvented food / by Colman Andrews.
p. cm.
Includes bibliographical references.
ISBN 978-1-592-40572-5 (hardcover)
1. Adrià, Ferran.   2. Restaurateurs—Spain—Biography.   3. elBulli (Restaurant)—History.
4. Avant-garde (Aesthetics)   I. Title.
TX910.5.A25A53   2010
647.95092—dc22
[B]   2010025124

Printed in the United States of America
Set in Electra LT Std
Designed by [tk]

Without limiting the rights under copyright reserved above, no part of this publication may be
reproduced, stored in or introduced into a retrieval system, or transmitted, in any form, or by any
means (electronic, mechanical, photocopying, recording, or otherwise), without the prior written
permission of both the copyright owner and the above publisher of this book.

The scanning, uploading, and distribution of this book via the Internet or via any other means
without the permission of the publisher is illegal and punishable by law. Please purchase only
authorized electronic editions, and do not participate in or encourage electronic piracy of copyrighted
materials. Your support of the author's rights is appreciated.

While the author has made every effort to provide accurate telephone numbers and Internet
addresses at the time of publication, neither the publisher nor the author assumes any responsibility
for errors, or for changes that occur after publication. Further, the publisher does not have any control
over and does not assume any responsibility for author or third-party Web sites or their content.

Per l'Agustí i na Maria Lluïsa

Més de vint-i-cinc anys d'amistat i de bon menjar—
i només estem començant!

Contents

Author's Note   ix

Introduction   1

1   Ferran Adrià and Why He Matters   13

2   Gorgonzola Mochi and Rabbit Brains   35

3   Dr. and Mrs. Schilling's Mini-Golf   51

4   A Very Good Boy   69

5   Soldado Fernando   79

6   Jumpin' Jack Juli   87

7   Disco-Beach   99

8   Becoming Ferran   111

9   Two Thousand Years of El Bulli   135

10   "The Best Cook on the Planet"   147

11   First, the Concept   165

12   Molecular Gastronomy and the Foam Guy   175

13   A New World   195

14   Anti-Ferran, Santi-Ferran   219

15   In the Kitchen   247

16   Morphing   267

Bibliography   285

Acknowledgments   289

Index   293

Author's Note

No chef in history has been interviewed, written about, and parsed more than Ferran Adrià. Certainly no other chef has so precisely and exhaustively—*obsessively* is probably not too strong a word—chronicled his own professional life and the history of his restaurant, issued so many statements of philosophy, and so freely shared his recipes and the details of his techniques. Every dish the man and his team have created for his legendary restaurant, El Bulli, has been photographed and ordered chronologically, the results appearing in five volumes (more than fifty-three pounds' worth) of "General Catalogue," which run a total of 2,402 pages so far, with more volumes to come. This alone should qualify him for the title of patron saint of professional introspection. A ten-part audiovisual companion to these tomes runs more than eight hours. Another book, *A Day at elBulli*, offers six hundred pages of photographs, not just of finished food but of the people who produce it, the places where it is made and served, and virtually every imaginable aspect of the restaurant and its operation. Much of the material contained in these books (including the catalogue of dishes), and a lot more, also appears on the excellent, multilingual El Bulli Web site, www.elbulli.com.

What my own book does not include, then, is another roster of Ferran's most famous dishes, or a reproduction of his twenty-three-part "Synthesis of elBulli Cuisine," or (with brief exceptions) yet more iterations of his formal statements of culinary philosophy. Instead, I've tried to sketch out, and fill in, a portrait of Ferran Adrià as he hasn't quite been seen before and to retell the oft-told tale of El Bulli from a noncanonical point of view, adding at least some revealing facts that may not already be well-known. I've also attempted to place Ferran and El Bulli in historical and culinary context, to address the more salient criticisms that have been leveled against him, and to both demystify and exalt the man and his accomplishments. Above all, I've tried to tell a good story, one that I hope will interest even those readers who, before picking up this volume, had never heard of Ferran.

I have referred to Ferran Adrià throughout this book by his first name, partly because I feel that—especially after two-plus years of research—I know him well enough to take that liberty; partly to prevent any possible confusion, in certain parts of the book, with his brother, Albert; but mainly because he is one of those personages who have come to be known, to their professional colleagues and a segment of the general public as well, by just one name—like Elvis or Miles or Tiger. Again, to prevent confusion in some passages but also for consistency, I've applied the same usage to Albert Adrià; to Ferran's wife, Isabel; and to his parents, Pepi and Ginés. I've also called Juli Soler by his first name, simply because I can't think of him as anything other than "Juli." The only other person referred to consistently by first name in the pages to come is Marketta Schilling, cofounder of the original El Bulli with her husband, Dr. Hans Schilling. Because both Schillings figure frequently in this book, particularly in the early chapters, I've distinguished between them by referring to them in the same terms nearly everybody who knew them uses: as "Marketta" and "Dr. Schilling," respectively.

As to the name of the restaurant itself and its attendant enterprises, at the beginning of the new millennium "El Bulli" became "elBulli." "We were changing the logo," explains Ferran, "and decided to change and clarify the spelling at the same time, especially since some people were already writing it as one word." This elision of spacing and the insertion of a capital letter midword is a stylistic convention—a device sometimes called "camel case," for the "hump" it introduces—that might work in a logo (think iPod or iPhone) but can be confusing in ordinary text, as when it begins a sentence. For most of its history, anyway, the place was called "El Bulli"; to call it "elBulli" before 2000 would be anachronistic, and to switch back and forth between the two renderings according to the period in question would, again, be confusing. Therefore, unless I'm referring to a book title or to the official name of one of the restaurant's post-2000 enterprises, I have used the form "El Bulli" throughout.

El Bulli is located in the autonomous Spanish community of Catalonia, which has its own language, shared with some surrounding areas: *català*, or Catalan. Catalan, which developed out of Vulgar Latin, is emphatically not a "dialect" of Castilian Spanish but rather a language that evolved separately from, if more or less simultaneously with, it. Today both Spanish and Catalan are among Spain's four legally acknowledged official languages, the others being *euskera* (Basque) and *gallego* (Galician). When Ferran and his friends and associates converse, they do so in both Catalan and Castilian, often toggling between the two with no apparent logic, sometimes within the same sentence. In general, in the pages that follow, I have honored the locality and the culture out of which El Bulli has grown by using the Catalan forms of words and place-names (e.g., Roses instead of Rosas).

Author's Note

All translations, whether from conversation, correspondence, or published sources, and whether from Spanish, Catalan, French, Italian, or, in a few instances, Portuguese or German, are mine, though, since I can claim something approaching fluency in only one and a half of these, I have not hesitated to call on the assistance of friends for whom those are native languages. I have translated for sense rather than literal meaning. Any errors of interpretation—indeed, any errors of any kind in this book—are my responsibility alone.

Finally, though Ferran announced in early 2010 that he would close El Bulli at the end of the 2011 season, reopening it two years later as a foundation, of which a restaurant will be only a part—the details may be found in my last chapter—I have referred to the place in the present tense throughout, since, as this book is published, it is still open in the form in which it has become world famous.

—Colman Andrews
Riverside, Connecticut

"Art is either plagiarism or revolution."

—Attributed to Paul Gauguin

FERRAN

Introduction

"This will be the last book about me. No, really. The last one that I will collaborate with."

—Ferran Adrià, in conversation with the author

My first trip to Spain, in 1984, was a short one. My wife and I were staying in St-Jean-de-Luz, in the French Basque country, and on a whim spun down the autoroute to San Sebastián one day for lunch at some nondescript restaurant in the city's Parte Vieja, or old town, then headed back a few hours later. My first *real* trip to Spain—a trip that changed my professional life (and upended my personal one)—came the following year and began on the other side of the country, when we drove through the Roussillon and across the French border into Catalonia. In doing my homework for that trip, I'd found a reference to the dining room at the Motel Ampurdán (now called the Hotel Empordà) in Figueres, a few miles south of the frontier, describing it as a "highly sophisticated restaurant started by Josep Mercader, founder of the new Catalan cuisine." I hadn't even known there was an *old* Catalan cuisine, but I was intrigued, and the Motel Ampurdán was the first place we stopped at to eat after we'd descended from the Pyrénées.

Walking into the restaurant, I was engulfed by an attractive but exotic aroma that I couldn't quite identify—earthy, sweet, and a little dark, though not in any ominous sense. I later learned that this scent, unique to Catalan cooking, comes from the combination of the *sofregit* (onions and garlic long-cooked in olive oil) and the *picada* (a mortar-ground paste of nuts, garlic, chocolate, and other ingredients)—the two bookends, so to speak, of many traditional Catalan dishes. We sat down and ordered plump anchovy fillets served with little rounds of bread rubbed with tomato and drizzled with olive oil (my introduction to the quintessentially Catalan preparation called *pa amb tomàquet*, or bread with tomato), followed by salt cod croquettes, grilled squid, baby eggplants stuffed with anchovies and fresh herbs, and, finally, a kind of ragout of cuttlefish and pork meatballs, redolent of that room-filling scent. I was captivated: the raw materials were all familiar to me, mostly from meals I'd had in Italy, but the flavors and forms were somehow different, and I definitely wanted to learn (and taste) more.

We drove on to Barcelona after lunch, and over the next few days we ate at a wide range of places, including a couple of contemporary Catalan restaurants, Farín and MG, and a traditionally Catalan hole-in-the-wall in the Gothic Quarter called Quatre Barres. From this brief sampling of local restaurants, I realized that there was something unusual going on here, a kind of accessible, seductive, Mediterranean-style cooking that was virtually unknown in America—and I thought it could make a great story.

Back in the States, I quickly sold an article on the subject to *Metropolitan Home*. Before it was published, my agent took me to breakfast one day in Los Angeles and asked, "What's new in the food world?" I said, "Well, this is probably too obscure for a whole book, but there *is* this little corner of Spain. . . ." "You should write a proposal," she said. I did, and she sold it, and in June 1985 I signed a contract for my first cookbook, to be titled *Catalan Cuisine*. I spent much of the next two years in Catalonia and the culturally related *països catalans*, or Catalan lands—including Valencia, the Balearic Islands, and the Roussillon—exploring tiny villages and cosmopolitan towns, visiting wineries and farms (and taking part in the processing of a just-slaughtered pig), and devouring everything from home-cooked meals to elegant, contemporary-style restaurant dinners. It was in the course of my research that I first ate at a then obscure little restaurant called El Bulli, located pretty much in the middle of nowhere, perched above a cove called Cala Montjoi on a narrow coastal road just outside the Costa Brava town of Roses, twenty miles or so south of the French border.

In those days, El Bulli was isolated in more ways than one. Through the Spanish-born Los Angeles restaurateur and Penedès winemaker Jean Léon, I had been introduced to all manner of food and wine figures and gastronomically inclined locals around Catalonia, but not one of them—and among their number were several of the best-known Barcelona restaurant critics of the era—had ever mentioned El Bulli to me. It was apparently considered too outré, not enough part of the establishment, to merit serious consideration. "Ferran had no pedigree," the Barcelona journalist Pau Arenós explained to me years later. "He belonged to no family of chefs. The critics in those days didn't understand what he was doing. When you're a high priest and know everything, you have no interest in learning."

One exception—a critic who would have scoffed at being called a high priest—was Luis Bettónica, a husky, amiable sort with a raspy voice and a famous fox terrier named Soufflé, known for eating almost anything. Bettónica said to me one day, almost casually, "The next time you're near Roses you might want to try a place called El Bulli, outside of town on a little road that will frighten you a bit. It's an interesting restaurant, with one French chef and one Spanish one." Those chefs were a Lyonnais named Kristian (*sic*) Lutaud and a Catalan

—

3

named Ferran Adrià, both in their early twenties—though Bettónica didn't offer me that information, and it would have meant nothing to me if he had. I took his advice, in any case. I remember crawling up the daunting road in my rented Ford Escort on a sunny summer day. I remember sitting on colorful cushions against a whitewashed wall in a beam-ceilinged dining room. I remember that I had a good lunch. Unfortunately, I don't have the vaguest recollection of anything I ate, though I do remember that it seemed like French nouvelle cuisine, without obvious Catalan accents, so I never asked for any recipes from El Bulli or mentioned it in my book.

After *Catalan Cuisine* was published, I had the idea of following it up with a volume about contemporary cooking all over Spain, and I made several long trips around the country, mostly avoiding Catalonia but sampling the fare at well-regarded "modern" places from San Sebastián to Seville, Alicante to Oviedo. This was several years before the innovative cooking of that young Catalan chef from Cala Montjoi had begun to influence other chefs around the country, and beyond a handful of restaurants in the Basque country and Madrid, I found very little of interest; filet mignon with blueberry sauce seemed to be the emblematic specialty of the Spanish avant-garde in those days.

Disappointed by Spain, I shifted my attentions to Nice and Italy's Ligurian coast instead, eventually producing my next book, *Flavors of the Riviera*, and I didn't think of Catalonia, much less of El Bulli, again for years. The next time I heard anything about the place and first heard Ferran mentioned by name was in the early nineties, when news of a daring and original "new" restaurant in some hidden Spanish coastal town started filtering through the American food community. Vaguely recalling my one meal there, I wasn't sure what all the fuss was about.

I finally met Ferran in 1998, about a year and a half after his restaurant had received its third Michelin star—which has been called "the quietest third star ever," because it seemed to go almost unno-

—

4

ticed, even in Spain itself—but slightly before he was to become an internationally known culinary icon. I'd come to know another young Spanish chef, José Andrés, when he worked in New York in the early nineties at the short-lived Manhattan incarnation of Barcelona's stylish Eldorado Petit. Andrés had worked at El Bulli in the late eighties and become a friend of Ferran's, and when Ferran was coming through New York Andrés thought we should get acquainted. "Ferran is *very* important," he assured me. "He is going to be very famous." The three of us had lunch at Quilty's, a good little restaurant, now long gone, near my old office in SoHo—my choice. On my recommendation, Ferran—who struck me as an unexceptional-looking fellow, low-key in manner, with none of the swagger I'd seen in the French three-star chefs I knew—had the white corn soup; I don't remember what else any of us ate, but at least one of us must have had a hamburger. "Ferran was a little annoyed by that lunch," Andrés told me years later. "He said, 'I'm in New York for only a few days and he takes us to a burger place?'"(One of these days I'll have to tell the woman who was chef there, Katy Sparks, that she once cooked—a burger?—for Ferran Adrià without knowing it. She'll probably kill me.)

However he may have felt about the menu, Ferran told me as we ate that he knew and liked my book on Catalan cooking, which had subsequently been published in Spain in both Spanish- and Catalan-language editions; he was later quoted somewhere as calling it his "bedside reading." He and Andrés and I went on to have a good, long, far-ranging conversation, about not just food but also politics, business, and sports, and Ferran and I agreed to keep in touch.

I saw him again, and met his younger brother and frequent collaborator, Albert, in 2003. It was off-season for the restaurant, and learning that I was coming to Barcelona, he invited me to visit the famous El Bulli Taller, or workshop, just off the Ramblas in Barcelona. The brothers showed me around, and Albert gave me a quick demonstration of the technique of spherification. Then we all headed

—

down to Barceloneta, the former fishermen's quarter by the city's old port, to a restaurant called Julius (now gone), where we had a lunch of fried calamari, baby cuttlefish sautéed in the traditional Catalan fashion with garlic and parsley, and cast-iron cauldrons of rice cooked with assorted seafood—exactly the kind of food Ferran likes to eat the most, he said. (This came as a revelation to me.) Somewhere in the midst of talk about the quality of Mediterranean seafood—very high, in Ferran's opinion, though for some things the Atlantic coast couldn't be beat—and the use of chemical additives in food ("What's wrong with chemicals?" he asked), he teased me about coming back to El Bulli. "We've changed a little bit since 1985," he said.

In September 2006, I finally managed, going with my then girlfriend (now my wife), Erin Walker, and her mother and stepfather in honor of his birthday. When we went to meet Ferran in the kitchen upon our arrival—a ritual for all the guests—he embraced me like a long-lost friend. Then we sat down and he served us thirty-three courses—by turns dazzling, interesting, and not our thing—including such house classics, all of them in that first category, as spherified green olives (intense olive juice enclosed in a skin of olive juice, shaped and cured like real olives), melon caviar (also spherified, looking exactly like perfect salmon roe and served in little caviar tins labeled Caviar ImitaciónelBulli), hibiscus "paper" with cassis and eucalyptus, frozen Parmigiano with muesli (the latter served in small plastic pouches), and tomato soup with virtual ham (a clear broth tasting vividly of tomatoes, with strips of gelatin somehow imbued with all the flavor of the best *jamón ibérico*).

I had the chance to see and talk with Ferran twice more that year: in October, in New York, where he joined such other Spanish culinary luminaries as Juan Mari Arzak, Joan Roca, Quique Dacosta, Dany García, and Paco Torreblanca at the French Culinary Institute's program "Spain's Ten: Cocina de Vanguardia"; and again in November, at greater length, at the Culinary Institute of America's hugely

ambitious, highly successful "Spain and the World Table" program at
its Greystone campus in the Napa Valley, where I gave a sort of unofficial keynote address.

It was at the C.I.A. that I first started thinking about writing
something on Ferran, and the idea of doing a book about him gradually took shape. The following year, I began to chase him, both directly, through a stream of e-mail messages, and indirectly, with the
help of José Andrés, who spoke with Ferran frequently and often saw
him in Spain. Let me do a book about you, I pleaded. A biography,
or not a biography; a portrait. An explication and appreciation of who
you are and how you got that way and what you do and why. Something that nobody has ever quite done, despite all the hundreds of
thousands of words that have appeared in print already—by you and
about you. I'm too busy, he'd reply. I'm not old enough to be the subject of a biography. There are too many books about me already.

I persisted. Andrés persisted on my behalf. "You know," he warned
me at one point, "Ferran is funny. If he thinks this is my idea or your
idea, he will maybe not be so eager to say yes. He has to think that it
is his idea." Still, we both kept at it—and finally, after eight or nine
months, Ferran relented, sort of: "Okay," he e-mailed me one day.
"The best thing is that the next time you're in Barcelona, we'll talk."
I replied at once, before he had a chance to change his mind. "I have
to go to Paris in a few weeks on a quick business trip," I told him, "and
I'll come through Barcelona on my way home." Then I booked a
flight straight to the Catalan capital—there was no business trip to
Paris—where he had agreed to meet me for dinner at Inopia, the lively,
traditional-style tapas bar that Albert had opened not long before in a
plebeian neighborhood near the Plaça d'Espanya. (Inopia, in both
Spanish and Catalan, means poverty or scarcity, though Albert defines it as "when a person loses his concentration and finds himself
simultaneously in a state of total blankness and satisfaction.")

Inopia is brightly lit and all black and white and cartoony inside, with mirrors autographed by local celebrities and the names of dishes and drinks written on walls and columns and sometimes illustrated in a Wham! Pow! style. It is wildly popular, and it is the only tapas bar I have ever seen with a velvet rope—actually, a plastic band—at the entrance to limit the number of people inside. (There are always just enough to give the place a buzz, but not so many that you're likely to get an elbow in your croquetas.) When I arrived, Ferran was sitting at one end of a communal table elevated from the room on a platform to the right of the door. With him was his wife, Isabel, whom he'd brought along because she speaks English, as he does not—and also, I suspect, to help him assess my suitability as his biographer. (My Spanish isn't good enough to handle serious interviews; my Catalan is slightly better, but most of my conversations with Ferran have been conducted in French, in which we are both fluent.)

As soon as I sat down, the food started coming. It was straightforward, without the slightest hint of Bulli-esque elaboration, and it was terrific: fat white asparagus from Valladolid; four or five kinds of perfect olives; an abundance of *jamón ibérico* from Guijuelo in Salamanca, draped on the plate in almost floral curls; a refined interpretation of *esqueixada*, the Catalan salad of shredded raw salt cod; tiny segments of fried artichoke bottoms; fried *boquerones* (fresh anchovies); grilled *pa amb tomàquet* with plump salt-cured anchovies from Santander; and simply grilled sweet little shrimp seasoned with nothing more than olive oil and salt—all washed down with clean, crisp, simple Catalan white wine for Isabel and me, beer for Ferran. As we ate, I saw him do something for which he is famous: after picking up a piece of Guijuelo ham and eating it, instead of wiping the fat from his fingers, he rubbed it on his lips, waited a moment, then licked it off. This is one of his favorite indulgences. "Nothing tastes like *ibérico* fat at body temperature," he announced.

Then he asked our waiter to send the chef out from the tiny Inopia kitchen. When he appeared, Ferran asked him to bring us a few more grilled shrimp, this time with only salt, no olive oil. They arrived quickly, and we tried them. Ferran nodded his head in approval; without the olive oil, they were even sweeter than the first batch had been, with purer flavor. "Now bring me twelve or fourteen raw shrimp," he asked. I wondered whether we were about to have an impromptu sashimi course, but no; this was a lesson for the chef. Ferran picked up the shrimp one by one and examined them as the chef watched closely. "This one's good," he said. "So's this one. This one, yes. This one . . . maybe." Finally, he picked up the smallest shrimp on the plate, a sorry specimen by comparison, limp and a little pale. "No," he announced. The chef nodded and took the plate back to the kitchen. "To understand me," Ferran said when he'd left, "you have to understand why I love food like this."

I do understand, I said, and I understand the connection between this food and what you create at El Bulli: As unusual and unexpected as it is, your cuisine has the same kind of purity of flavor that this simple cooking does. He nodded. I started my sales pitch, addressing Isabel as well as Ferran. I will do all the work on this, I assured him. I won't get in your way. Just give me access to what you're doing and to your friends and colleagues, and you'll hardly know I'm there. It's time to do this, I continued. If I don't write this book about you, somebody else will, and they probably won't know Catalan cooking and French culinary history as well as I do. This launched a conversation about nouvelle cuisine, Ferran's first great inspiration. I told him about a few of my experiences: my meals at nouvelle cuisine shrines like Troisgros and Alain Chapel; the long conversations I'd had with legends like Michel Guérard and Jacques Maximin; my journeys to Girardet in Switzerland and the meal Girardet himself had cooked for me in his house after he'd prematurely sold his restaurant. . . . Then I added, "You know, I went to three-star restaurants in France *before* nouvelle cuisine." I described to him the sole Albert at Maxim's, the perfect roasted woodcock at the lamented Garin. It may have been my imagination, but I had the feeling that at that moment he started to take my idea seriously. ("Ferran falls in love with things little by little," the filmmaker David Pujol, who has worked with him extensively, later told me.)

Ferran likes pen and paper. He scribbles and sketches, makes lists, connects words and images with arrows. Even in his Barcelona workshop, which is full of laptop computers, he uses notebooks and scratch pads and pins scraps of paper to the walls. Now, he grabbed an Inopia place mat, turned it over, and started filling it with boxes. "When would your book come out?" he asked. I gave him a rough estimate. "Okay," he said. The boxes on the place mat became other books and nonbook projects: two more this year, three next year, one so far the year after that . . . Ultimately, he came to a blank space. "Your book would be here," he said. I nodded. He nodded back. Was this his capitulation?

It had occurred to me, as Ferran was constructing his chart of future activities, that maybe I should discreetly take the place mat— which by now was stained with olive oil and wine—when we left. Whatever happened, I thought, it would be a nice souvenir of the evening. Ferran was way ahead of me. As we finished our meal, he quickly scrawled his name across the bottom of the sheet, folded it in half, and handed it to me. Of *course* I'd want it. Then he said, "Okay. The first thing for you to do is to come spend a week at El Bulli." I was in.

At the very moment we were sitting at Inopia eating *ibérico* ham and grilled shrimp, as I learned the next day, a chef named Santi Santamaria—the first chef in Catalonia to earn three Michelin stars and a man whose path had been crossing Ferran's for decades—was accepting an award in Madrid for a controversial book he'd written, called *La cocina al desnudo* (Cuisine Stripped Bare). A polemic on the state of haute cuisine, and of food in Spain in general, the book denounces Ferran for selling out to commercial food interests and for endangering the health of his customers through the use of "additives"—and in accepting his prize, Santamaria had repeated and amplified his charges. Not everybody, I realized, worshipped Ferran.

It occurred to me at that point, in fact, that Ferran's story was probably going to be a good deal more complex than I had imagined. I was right. Over the course of my subsequent research, as I spent countless hours with Ferran and his family and closest associates, interviewed scores of his friends and critics and a number of his fellow chefs, lurked endlessly around El Bulli and the Taller, and read many thousands of words in assorted languages about the man and his restaurant, I found myself constantly surprised, intrigued, amazed, and charmed. And I soon learned never to assume that I knew the whole story until I had gotten it from Ferran's own mouth—if even then. Thus when he unexpectedly announced, just after I had finished the first draft of this book, that he planned to close El Bulli for two years at the end of the 2011 season and reopen it two years later in some vaguely mysterious altered form, I wasn't exactly taken aback. I did realize, though, that wherever my book ended up, the last chapter of the story of Ferran Adrià and El Bulli was not likely to be written for a very long time.

1

Ferran Adrià and Why He Matters

"In Ferran Adrià's brain is the combination to unlock the culinary door of the third millennium."

—Pau Arenós, *Els genis del foc: Qui son, com creen i què cuinen 10 xefs catalans d'avantguarda*

Hailed as a genius and a prophet by fellow chefs, worshipped (if often misunderstood) by critics and lay diners alike, imitated and paid homage to in restaurant kitchens all over the world, Ferran Adrià is easily the most influential serious chef of the late twentieth and early twenty-first centuries. Quite simply, he changed the game. Anybody cooking haute—or even *moyenne*—cuisine professionally today has to pay attention to him, either directly or by extension, like it or not. And some don't like it. Besides being the most influential chef alive, Ferran is also the most controversial. He has been called pretentious, a charlatan, an enemy of good sense and real food; he has been parodied, insulted, condemned for intellectual dishonesty and nutritional malfeasance. There's no effective way to answer such charges. You either buy what Ferran does, or you don't. Even if you don't, though— even if you believe the worst about him—the creative and conceptual breakthroughs he has made over the past two-plus decades are almost certainly going to have an effect, eventually if not tomorrow, on at least some of what ends up on your plate, even at the most modest of restaurants, even at home.

Ferran doesn't look like a prophet *or* a charlatan; he looks like an ordinary guy. He is of modest height—about five foot six—with sturdy shoulders and a compact torso. (He had a teddy-bear tummy when I first started spending time with him but lost about thirty-five pounds over the next year or so by doing daily exercises and eating lighter meals.) He has bristly graying hair retreating casually back from his broad forehead. His eyes are close set, brown, and penetrating; when he gets excited, which is often, they grow wide and bright, as if someone has bumped up the rheostat, and dart back and forth almost frenetically. His eyebrows are thick and dark, and he raises them frequently when he's making a point. His face can become so expressive and his gestures so extravagant, in fact, that I sometimes find myself thinking that he could have been a great physical comedian; I can almost see him doing slapstick. One day when he was trying to decide whether or not to share a delicate observation with me, he began to argue back and forth with himself with such animation that I couldn't help picturing Donald Duck with the good angel on one shoulder and the bad angel on the other, contesting for his virtue.

Ferran dresses simply, distractedly. When he's not in chef's whites, he favors jeans and shirts and jackets in grays and browns. He wears athletic shoes, not particularly expensive ones. He'd rather spend his money on a bottle of champagne than a pair of shoes, he once told me, because he'll always remember the champagne but will forget the shoes. When he does wear whites, it's not one of those celebrity-chef chef's coats with his name embroidered across the front in haloed multicolored script. He seems to put on whatever's handy. One night it might bear the name of Lavazza coffee (for which he consults); another night it could be the logo—two red chopsticks—of Dos Palillos, the Asian tapas bar opened in Barcelona by his former head chef Albert Raurich; for some months in 2009 he wore a jacket commemorating the hundredth anniversary of the naming of the Costa Brava.

Ferran's personal austerity is well-known. "I need very little money to live," he told me one day. "I need less than you do. I'm not at all materialistic." He collects not fine art or rare books but logo pens and pencils from hotels he has stayed in when he travels (he has more than five hundred of them). He doesn't drive a fancy car. "Ferran once said that he could buy a Ferrari," Albert Raurich told me, "but that El Bulli was his Ferrari. The truth is that for years he had no car at all. I used to drive him around. He gets that simplicity from his father, Ginés. Ginés had an old, falling-apart Fiat for years. One day Ferran offered to buy him a Mercedes. No, said Ginés. Maybe a new Fiat if you want to, but what would I do with a Mercedes?" Finally, in 2008, Ferran got a car of his own: his wife gave him a little two-door Suzuki for his birthday; he didn't want anything larger or more elaborate. Raurich told me that the car had no air-conditioning and that "Ferran's air-conditioning is to drive without his shirt, with the windows down." (I loved that image, but Ferran says his car does indeed have air-conditioning of the conventional sort.)

The Argentine-born, Paris-based journalist Óscar Caballero, a cultural correspondent for the big Barcelona daily *La Vanguardia*, tells another story about Ferran's modest tastes: "Every time he came to town," says Caballero, "he liked to stay at a little thirty-euro hotel in Montparnasse, the Pavillon Bleu. When Gosset Champagne brought him to Paris—with twenty-five cooks!—to create a cocktail for them, they booked a fancy hotel for Ferran and a simpler one for the others, but Ferran said, 'No, we'll all stay at the Pavillon Bleu.' They said, 'Oh, is that a new boutique hotel? We don't know it.' Ferran thought that was very funny."

Ferran rarely talks about his private life, and over the many months when I was researching this book, while he disclosed every aspect of his professional existence to me, he never once invited me home. "I'm a very comfortable person," he once told his journalist friend Pau Arenós. "[A] calm person who doesn't like to complicate the lives of others and doesn't like them to complicate mine. Professionally I'm very cold and calculating, but privately I'm warm. What's more, I'm a little timid." When Ferran agreed—with some reluctance, I think—to let me talk with his parents, he brought them to the Taller for our meeting. "My private life isn't interesting," he says. "I lead a normal life. I eat normally. I don't wake up and say, 'I have to have the best possible bread for breakfast, the best possible butter.' Everything that's special is connected to my work."

Ferran has a curious way of speaking, a gruff vocal thickness that can make him hard to understand in any language. As Arthur Lubow put it in *The New York Times Magazine*, his voice "hisses and sputters like a severed electrical line." In 2010, Ferran revealed to *La Vanguardia* that people had sometimes offered to help him improve his diction. "I told them that I have always been like this," he said, "and life has gone well for me. If I worked at something else, maybe I would need to be able to speak better, but I have no interest in changing." The sculptor Xavier Medina-Campeny, who knows Ferran well, has an interesting explanation for the way he sounds: "His tongue is bigger than ours," he says. "He literally has a larger tongue than normal, with more papillae [taste buds]. That's why he speaks the way he does." If this is true—I've never summoned up the nerve to ask Ferran whether I can peer into his mouth—I wonder if it might also affect the way he tastes food. Do more receptors give him a more acute perception of sweet and sour, bitter, salty, and umami? That might explain a lot.

Being around Ferran can be exhausting. He talks fast. He can be almost electrically intense. He always seems to be thinking of three or maybe ten things at a time. He's way ahead of you. Sometimes you have the impression that the world is moving too slowly for him.

———

There is an air of almost naïve enthusiasm about Ferran on some occasions. If he thinks you don't quite believe something he has said, he gets a look of real concern on his face, wags his finger, and says, "No, no, no, no. It's true." The Barcelona pastry chef Christian Escribà, whom Ferran describes as his best friend, says, "Ferran is always excited about something. He's forever finding a new product and saying, 'Here, Christian, try this, it's the best in the world!'" When I watched him on the stage as part of a panel discussion on "molecular gastronomy" (a term he loathes) at the Madrid Fusión gastronomic conference in 2009, Ferran seemed forever on the edge of his chair, impatient, ready to jump in—like the smartest kid in the class madly waving his hand and saying, "Teacher, teacher! I know! I know!" Sometimes, in contrast, he gets a bored look on his face, suddenly skipping into distraction—*inopia?*—for a moment or two, occasionally scowling as if something is not right and he is figuring out what it is. Then he will rebound with tremendous energy, more animated than ever, focused again.

When he's giving a talk or a demonstration, Ferran will often prowl and pounce and sometimes practically leap around the stage, as if gravity itself were an annoyance to him and he wished he could fly off into space just to demonstrate a point with the drama it deserves. He captivates audiences, charms them, gives them their money's worth. He claims to be beyond ego, and maybe he is. I've seen him come offstage after one of his presentations, the applause still echoing in the auditorium, and ask, with a creased brow, "Was that okay? Did they like it?" And he seems authentically amazed and not at all self-aggrandizing when he says, earnestly, "You know, it's much more difficult to be creative today than it was ten years ago" or "For a chef to make something new in 2008, after centuries of cuisine, that is incredible." He retains the ability to surprise himself, apparently genuinely and with something like humility. On the other hand, I've heard him deflect difficult questions with a politician's skill, offering an articulate and sensible answer to something that hasn't really been asked; one specialty food supplier who has known him for more than a decade says that, when it comes to confronting certain kinds of controversy, "Ferran is the best matador in Spain."

Ferran's friends and colleagues think the world of him. The first word almost everybody uses, when asked what his best qualities are, is *generosity*. Thomas Keller elaborates: "In every way, Ferran is there for you," he says, "and he's absolutely sincere about it, with no hesitation. What's his is yours. Outside of maybe giving a reservation to a friend of mine, he'll do whatever I ask." ("A friend," Ferran once told a reporter, "is someone who will never ask for something he shouldn't.") Kim Yorio of YC Media, the public relations expert who accompanied him on his 2008 book tour in the United States and Canada, saw a different kind of generosity in Ferran: "He understood when the people around him were not with the program," she says, "and still gave as much as he could to them. He spent time with everyone, gave everybody his card, really tried to answer everybody's questions. He was so appreciative of everyone's efforts, right down to the person unwrapping the books from the shrink-wrap."

Above all, Ferran is well-known for sharing his culinary techniques and recipes: Though he doesn't like explaining to his customers what goes on in his kitchen—because he wants them to approach his food with an open mind, he says, susceptible to its magic—he has no secrets from his fellow chefs or students. If he figures out how to do something, he wants his counterparts to be able to do it too, if they're interested. He also shares whatever glory accrues to him. The filmmaker David Pujol says, "He is so quick to give other people credit for their contributions to his food that sometimes you start to think, well, what did *you* do?" What he did, of course, was plenty—not least providing the environment in which those other people could make those contributions.

Ferran is a Spaniard, in the sense that he is a citizen of Spain, but to comprehend his personality and the nature of his achieve-ments fully, one must remember that he is also—perhaps most of all—a Catalan. Catalonia is one of Spain's seventeen autonomous communities, covering just under 12,500 square miles of farmland, seacoast, mountains, and cities in the far northeastern corner of the country, bordered by the Mediterranean, the Pyrénées (with France on the far side), and the communities of Aragón and Valencia. It is a wealthy area, one rich in art and architecture. Barcelona, the region's capital, is the largest city in Spain. Two thousand years ago, the region was occupied by Celtiberian tribes; in later centuries, the Phocaean Greeks, the Carthaginians, the Romans, and the Moors, in succes-sion, conquered and settled in various parts of the area, and assorted barbarian hordes passed through; all left genetic and cultural traces, and most also influenced the cuisine.

Catalans have a reputation for being industrious, sober, thrifty, and maybe sometimes a little blockheaded, but they are also known for their unpredictability, their independence, their flights of fancy, their artistic nature, and their tendency to rebel against authority (a ten-dency that, not surprisingly, has brought them into frequent conflict with the central government in Madrid over the centuries). If those two sets of characteristics seem contradictory, Catalans will tell you that that's the whole point. They're proud of the two sides of their national character, and they have terms, not easily translatable, for the qualities that inspire them: *seny*, which is more or less common sense tempered with ancestral wisdom and a measure of moral rectitude (this is a bit like what the Scots would call *nous*), and *rauxa*, which is something like wildness, foolishness, or abandon. It would be oversimplifying, but not wholly incorrect, to say that these qualities represent the Apollo-nian and the Dionysian, respectively.

An abundance of *rauxa* is often ascribed to "crazy" Catalans like Salvador Dalí and Antoni Gaudí, and to a lesser extent Joan Miró and Ricardo Bofill. It is ideally counterbalanced, however, by *seny*. Miró, in fact, once told *Partisan Review*, "We Catalans believe you must always plant your feet firmly on the ground if you want to be able to jump up in the air." This isn't far from something Ferran said to me one evening in the kitchen at El Bulli: "We must be very organized in order to be anarchic." In the way he channels the zany passion of his creativity into precisely planned and highly regulated production, in fact, I think Ferran embodies the yin-yang contrast of *seny* and *rauxa* about as well as any Catalan alive today.

Ferran can be philosophical: "Eating is a very complex thing," he once said, "but because we eat every day, we don't want to see it that way. Imagine for a moment that food wasn't a physiological need; what would our relationship with food be then? We really need to think about eating, because eating and breathing are the only two things we do from the moment we are born to the moment we die." Questions like these are central to the way Ferran thinks about food: Do we eat only for physical nourishment? If so, why do we sometimes take such care with the non-nutritional particulars? We know why we eat, but why do we dine? To paraphrase John Ciardi, how does a dinner mean?

On one occasion, Ferran rather cryptically remarked, "Why do we have coffee and then an egg at breakfast, while at lunch we eat the egg and then have the coffee? If you understand that, you can do avant-garde cooking." What he meant—I think—was that if it occurs to you to notice such contradictions in the way we eat, you'll be more likely to question the common culinary wisdom and then be able to imagine ways to countermand it. Ferran wants us to eat with our brains.

Avant-garde—or, to use the Spanish term, *vanguardia*—cooking is what Ferran Adrià devotes most of his professional life to; he might well be said to have invented the genre, in fact, taking haute cuisine beyond the merely contemporary into a whole new realm. The originality and derring-do with which he has done so lead some observers to assume that he's a fantasist, a creator of culinary science fiction, unmoored from tradition and trafficking in the exotic and unrecognizable for its own sake. Not so.

Bob Noto is not a chef or a food journalist—he's a tool manufacturer from Turin—but he has a particularly lucid appreciation of what Ferran is up to. He certainly has the experience: Noto and his wife, Antonella, are El Bulli's best customers, having eaten at the restaurant on more than seventy-five occasions since their first visit, in 1993. (The couple have privately published a catalogue of every dish Ferran has ever served them, under the title—clever, if in questionable taste— "Bullimia"; my copy, which goes only as far as late 2008, lists 1,222 items.) The Notos had an epiphany the first time they ate Ferran's food, Bob Noto told me one evening on the restaurant's terrace: "At our first taste of our first appetizer, a granita of tomato, we said, 'This is a genius.' It had the DNA, the soul of the tomato. In this one dish was all the philosophy of El Bulli. They take the best tomato in the world and work with temperature and texture and technique, but you will always have a tomato. It is not a copy but a transformation. People who say they don't understand El Bulli haven't eaten here. This is the restaurant where the flavors are the purest in the world."

■ ■ ■

Ferran took over the kitchen at El Bulli in 1987, at the age of twenty-five, and almost immediately began cooking what was, by all accounts, some of the most exciting and original food in Spain. Until 2003, however, he remained something of a cult figure, little known outside Catalonia and not always appreciated even there. The well-traveled American food writer Mark Bittman once wrote that he'd never heard Ferran's name until 1996, when somebody casually mentioned it to him on the street in Barcelona.

The first major article about Ferran in the United States was a piece written by the Hispanophile food and wine writer Gerry Dawes for the chef-centered magazine *Food Arts* in late 1997; in reference to what became Ferran's first famous culinary creation, it was headlined "Foam, Foam on the Range." Ferran's profile in Spain became more prominent in 1999, when he was named Chef of the Year by the glossy *Spain Gourmetour* magazine and appeared on the cover of the weekend magazine of *El País*, Spain's best-selling daily. This was the first time many Spaniards had ever heard of him. But it was a seven-thousand-word cover story built around Ferran in *The New York Times Magazine*, in late summer of 2003, that changed everything. Above the headline "The Nueva Nouvelle Cuisine: How Spain Became the New France" Ferran appeared, looking somber, dark, and misleadingly thin—almost sepulchral—and holding out, like a witch offering a poisoned apple, a small bowl from which rose a beehive of "carrot air with essence of mandarin." The effect was electric. "Before *The New York Times*," says Ferran, "my success was only in the culinary world. Before the *Times*, there was only the restaurant. Since the *Times*, there has been the myth."

By the time they'd finished breakfast, American food lovers knew who Ferran was, and a good many of them immediately decided that they wanted to go to his restaurant. Almost overnight, reservations at El Bulli became all but impossible to obtain; for decades, the restaurant had struggled to fill seats, and suddenly getting a table at the restaurant, for those who cared about such things, became the equivalent of a sports fan's nabbing 50-yard-line tickets for the Super Bowl—except that the latter could be bought, if price were no object, and a place at El Bulli could not. Getting into El Bulli became more or less impossible but not impossible in the same way that it's "impossible" to get into whatever restaurant *The New York Times* has just given four stars to on a Saturday night. El Bulli serves dinner—or occasionally lunch instead of dinner, but never both in one day—for about 160 days out of every 365. There are fifteen tables in the two small dining rooms, capable of holding comfortably a total of about fifty people per meal. That works out to a maximum of eight thousand diners every season. In 2002, according to *The New York Times*, more than three hundred thousand would-be customers tried to get in. By 2008, Ferran was routinely quoting the number as two million. I'm not sure that's possible: even if you assume that each request covers four diners on average, for the restaurant simply to read or listen to that many requests—they'd work out to more than 1,350 a day, 365 days a year— it would need a full-time, year-round call center and/or secretarial staff, which it patently doesn't have. But the point is that the number of people dying to eat at El Bulli clearly exceeds the number of available chairs by an extraordinary margin. And after Ferran announced that he planned to close the restaurant temporarily for two years and reopen it in a very different form, all bets—even long shots—were off. (If you hadn't been to El Bulli by the time that announcement was made, in January 2010, chances were pretty good that you weren't going to make it.)

The acclaim continued. In 2004, Ferran was on the cover of the first edition of the newly redesigned *Le Monde* magazine, widely seen all over France, and shared the cover of *Time* as one of the "100 Most Influential People in the World." In 2006, the British-based *Restaurant* magazine dubbed El Bulli the world's best restaurant, an honor it held for the next four years (it was displaced in 2010 by El Bulli alumnus René Redzepi's Noma in Copenhagen, with El Bulli moving down to second place). Today, Ferran is not just a chef showered with accolades, he's a full-scale international media celebrity. He is the target—and, let's admit it, the beneficiary—of almost unimaginable hype. He is an icon, an idol. He is, as he says, a myth.

"Ferran forever altered the world of haute cuisine," says the Barcelona restaurant critic Carmen Casas. "Before him, haute cuisine was a cuisine of repetition. Since he has done what he has done, it has become a language to explain things, to share experiences—a powerful thing. It's *very* important that he began to consider cuisine as a language, as a means to communicate." Ferran likes that conceit—cuisine as language. At the *New York Times* "Times Talk" event, sharing a stage with Anthony Bourdain and Eric Asimov in Manhattan in October 2008, he told the overflow audience, "When you cook, you create a conversation with the diner. With avant-garde cooking, you create a new language for this conversation. To do that, your first job is to create a new alphabet. Then you can make words, then you can make sentences. As a diner, you have to be willing to try to understand this new language." He realizes that not everyone will make the effort, but that doesn't bother him. "Avant-garde cuisine will always belong to the minority," he added. "There's nothing wrong with that. Jazz belongs to the minority too, and it's wonderful."

What, exactly, has Ferran done? Twenty-five years ago, it could have been argued that everything imaginable in cooking had pretty much been tried. Aside from certain combinations of ingredients that would have been unachievable or at least unlikely in an earlier era, there was really nothing new under the salamander. Every viable technique had been attempted, every philosophical notion of cuisine had been proposed, in one form or another—if not by the Greeks or Romans, then by Carême or Escoffier; if not by them, then by Marinetti or (more seriously) by the giants of France's nouvelle cuisine in the 1970s or the happily anarchistic young chefs of Australia and America in the 1980s and beyond, with their multicultural influences and their refreshing independence from hidebound tradition. Granted, every genuinely talented chef brought something slightly different to the table, some expression of his or her own character—but let's face it: Ultimately all that was left to do was some fine-tuning, some personalization.

Today, thanks almost entirely to Ferran and his disciples, that is no longer true. Everything, it turns out, had *not* been done before. Forced to memorize fundamental techniques and classic dishes at his first kitchen job, Ferran went on to teach himself the principles of

French nouvelle and post-nouvelle cuisine, immersed himself in those idioms and mastered them, and then came out the other side. He had the inspiration and the innate ability to reimagine the most basic culinary processes, expanding the vocabulary of the kitchen beyond our wildest imaginations. It was as if he had said to himself, Okay, this is what food is, as we have always known it; this is what cooking is; this is what constitutes cuisine. Now, what else could these things be? As a result, in ways that we have not yet even begun to comprehend fully, the possibilities of preparation and consumption have changed. He asks us—permits us—to look at what we eat and, by extension, at the physical world in general, in a new way, without preconceptions.

The time I've spent around Ferran—having long conversations with him and watching him work and seeing his interactions with his colleagues and tasting his food and cataloguing the reactions of diners and his fellow chefs—has left me convinced that he is an authentic genius. I think he is one of those rare creative life forces—a Picasso, a Le Corbusier, a Charlie Parker—who have completely rewritten the rules of their chosen art form, presenting new possibilities previously not only undiscovered but undreamed of. Ferran's greatest accomplishment, it could be argued, isn't even in the remarkable specifics of what he went on to create in his techniques and combinations but rather in the fact that he had the inspiration and the courage to imagine the possibility of such creation in the first place. He has upended the stockpots, snuffed out the wood-fired grill, let the larder run wild—and in the process turned dining into a kind of subversive fun.

Ultimately, Ferran has reinvented food. Working with such techniques as caramelization, liquefaction, emulsification, ultra-low-temperature freezing, "spherification," and the production of food-based "foams" and "airs," among many other things, he has done nothing less than alter the basic characteristics of food's forms and flavors. The purity and authenticity of flavor is paramount to him, but it is not his only concern. "Taste," he wrote in a sort of manifesto he published in 2006, "is not the only sense that can be stimulated: touch can also be played with (contrasts of temperatures and textures), as well as smell [and] sight (colors, shapes, trompe l'oeil, etc.). . . ." Perhaps even more important to him is what he likes to call a "sixth sense," which to him involves the emotional reactions diners have to what they eat: childhood memories stimulated, echoes of favorite foods heard, cultural baggage of all kinds unpacked or rummaged through.

Some of Ferran's most successful and beguiling creations, which speak directly to this sixth sense, are the result of culinary "deconstruction," which involves the breaking down of familiar dishes into their constituent parts, changing the physical identity of at least some of those parts, and then reassembling the pieces in new ways, so that the dishes take on different forms while retaining sensory connections with their models. Ferran once explained this process as identifying and emphasizing the character of every ingredient but still keeping the character of the whole. The term *deconstruction* was coined by the French philosopher Jacques Derrida in the context of philosophy and literary criticism and later adapted to postmodern architecture. Ferran originally called his technique *descomposición*, but he borrowed the more elegant term at the suggestion of a young Italian architecture student, a cousin of the aforementioned Bob Noto's. Both the word and the concept are now commonplace in restaurant kitchens all over the world.

Ferran's first deconstruction was his take on an everyday Spanish favorite called *arroz a la cubana*, which is simply white rice with tomato sauce accompanied by a fried egg and sometimes a fried plantain or banana. In Ferran's reimagining of it, it became rice with a tomato granita, poached quail eggs coated in vanilla oil, and a plantain wrapped in bacon. Another deconstruction remade chicken curry into curry ice cream with chicken sauce, apple gelatin, and coconut soup. (When he once served them this dish, says Ferran, a couple of his friends joked,

"Breast or thigh?") Reminiscing about his mother's *tortilla española* (potato omelette), a dish he considers to be a culinary touchstone, he and one of his chefs at the time, Marc Singla, had the idea of recasting it as a layered construction of potato foam, onion purée, and egg white sabayon, scattered with deep-fried potato crumbs. (Ferran still attaches Singla's name to the dish when he reproduces it.)

Ferran tampered with another of Spain's great culinary institutions by inventing a "Kellogg's paella," made out of puffed rice (think Rice Krispies) fried with saffron and mixed with tomato powder, shrimp powder, and raw shrimp and served with an ampule of intense brown shrimp extract to be squeezed directly into the mouth. A bite of the enhanced cereal combined with a squirt of the shrimp essence, say those who tasted the dish—Ferran no longer makes it—delivered a vivid sensation of paella flavor.

The amazing thing about these deconstructions is that, besides being witty and tasty, they had a way of illuminating the originals on which they were based, putting them into a new perspective and even potentially enhancing our future appreciation of them—a bit the way a good remix might do with a familiar song. "And Ferran didn't deconstruct just traditional dishes," says the Barcelona chef Isidre Soler, who spent a year in the El Bulli kitchen at the height of the deconstruction phase. "He'd make up entirely new combinations of ingredients and then deconstruct *them*."

Ferran has done a lot more, though, than just take apart and reassemble familiar dishes and introduce new devices and techniques into the kitchen. Along the way, he has redefined the whole restaurant experience. One of his most revolutionary acts, at least in terms of European haute cuisine, was something as simple as doing away with bread at the table (diners at El Bulli get their first bites set in front of them at almost the moment they sit down, so there's no need for something to nibble on) and then banishing such "essentials" of the genre as the cheese tray, the dessert trolley, and the à la carte menu. Beyond that, he has blurred the line between savory and sweet, appetizer and main course, main course and dessert, and introduced new terminology to describe the stages of a meal—in the process devising a whole "cold cuisine" based on frozen savory preparations. He involves his customers in the creative process, sending out dishes that are meant to be finished in the dining room by the diners themselves. He has introduced the concept of chef-created cocktails—playful variations on the classics (the mojito, the margarita, the gin and tonic) that become part of the meal instead of palate-dulling precursors. "The cuisine of El Bulli is opera," Ferran remarked to me one day, "not theater like at most restaurants. It is spectacle."

His fellow chefs tend to speak of Ferran as a kind of creative savior. "He taught us that there were many ways to change," says Joan Roca, chef and co-owner of the three-star restaurant El Celler de Can Roca in Girona, who did a *stage* (a short unpaid apprenticeship) at El Bulli in 1989. "He opened the door, he gave us freedom. His greatest influence isn't in recipes or techniques but in giving us the idea that anything is possible." Carme Ruscalleda of Sant Pau in Sant Pol de Mar, another Catalan three-star chef, says, "Ferran's message is that if the results are good, anything goes. How liberating!" The avant-garde Milanese chef Carlo Cracco, observing El Bulli from a greater distance, says simply, "Since Ferran, every chef has felt free to create new things."

Ferran's influence is seen everywhere in Spain today, not just in affluent Madrid and in Catalonia and the Basque country, which have always been the country's culinary capitals, but in contemporary restaurants with forward-thinking chefs in virtually every region of the country, from La Mancha to Andalusia to Galicia, even down to the Canary Islands. Thanks to Ferran, wrote the journalist Anya von Bremzen, "everyone in Spain can make frozen foie gras dust." (It may be argued whether that is a good thing or not.) Ferran's friend the pastry chef Christian Escribà maintains that his impact goes beyond the

professional sphere. "Ferran has helped make 'chef' a desirable voca-
tion in Spain," he says. "Kids used to dream of becoming a singer or a
football player or a race car driver, but now they add chef to the list."

Spain marks just the beginning; Ferran's ideas, variously translated, find expression today not only in England and France and Italy
but also in Japan and China and Australia, in Peru and Mexico, and,
most definitely, in America. Ferran's good friend and onetime employee José Andrés gives the United States its nearest approximation
of El Bulli's food, with innovations of his own, at his Minibar in
Washington, D.C., and Bazaar in Los Angeles. Chefs like Wylie Dufresne of WD-50 in New York City and Grant Achatz of Alinea and
Homar Cantu of Moto, both in Chicago, go off in different directions,
but they wouldn't be doing what they do—probably wouldn't be allowed by their customers to do it—were it not for Ferran's example.
Even comparatively elder statesmen of American cuisine like Thomas
Keller and Charlie Trotter, whose own styles were well developed
before Ferran became known in this country, have borrowed and
adapted and taken inspiration from him—and substances whose use
in cuisine Ferran has made famous, like liquid nitrogen, xanthan, and
agar, are now commonplace in serious American restaurant kitchens.
There's even at least one Adrià-affected chef in Moscow: Anatoly
Komm of Varvary restaurant, who serves borscht in the form of spherified beet juice and pelmeni coated in an emulsion of chicken broth
with beet-and-horseradish ice cream on the side.

It doesn't all happen at fancy restaurants, either. Aki Kamozawa
and H. Alexander Talbot own a consulting business called Ideas in
Food, LLC, in Levittown, Pennsylvania, through which they offer
culinary workshops to both professionals and non-pros with titles
like "Specific Hydrocolloids and Their Uses," "Hands On with Liquid Nitrogen," and "Compression and Exploration with a Vacuum
Sealer"—topics that would have sounded like nonsense, at least in a
culinary context, before Ferran. In Bellevue, Washington, a former

chief technology officer at Microsoft, Nathan Myhrvold, has set up a culinary laboratory equipped with the latest equipment—including devices of his own invention—and is working with a staff of fifteen to produce a definitive, 1,500-page book on avant-garde cooking techniques, which will have an introduction by Ferran. A home vacuum-cooking unit called SousVide Supreme, a version of an important tool in Ferran-inspired kitchens, is now available to amateur cooks for less than four hundred dollars. An enterprise called ThinkGeek sells a "Molecular Gastronomy Starter Set," including "everything you need to get started in spherification, thickeners and foaming agents" (somebody at ThinkGeek used the kit to produce Jolt Cola "caviar"). The French-based Gourmet Academy has marketed a similar kit aimed at children of ten years and older—a culinary version of the old chemistry sets with which kids of my generation used to wreak havoc in the basement on Christmas afternoons—complete with agar, carrageenan, coconut and lemon flavorings, pipettes, flasks and beakers, and a recipe book.

Even if you've never been to Spain or never eaten in a Michelin-starred restaurant, Ferran's innovations—or the innovations of others that were made possible by Ferran's—have probably already filtered down to you. The general public, even that segment that dines out regularly in fine restaurants, may not have known who Ferran was until very recently, but chefs around Spain did, and they have taken inspiration and borrowed techniques from him for years. Chefs from elsewhere who encountered Ferran's creations secondhand in modern Spanish restaurants, I'm certain, often adopted them without realizing where they'd come from. I suspect that there are a great many Ferran-influenced chefs who aren't even aware of the debt they owe to him.

Beyond all that, if you've ever had a familiar dish remade in a form different from the usual (a soup presented as a salad, say); if you've encountered commonplace foodstuffs with unexpected textures (oversize spheres of dense-looking chocolate that melt in your mouth; whipped cream that's somehow lighter than air) or found your plate garnished with food in the form of paper or film or with a savory foam; if you've ever confronted a contemporary menu that has no clear separation between appetizers and main courses, then you have probably tasted something of Ferran. In June 2009, the 1,400-unit international ice cream chain Cold Stone Creamery introduced two flavors of nonmelting ice cream; that's Ferran, too, if only distantly. In 2006, a Virginia-based company called Cuisine Solutions, Inc., unveiled a line of naturally flavored frozen foam bases at the National Restaurant Association Show in Chicago. According to a news report at the time, "The chef simply pours a thawed and heated (or cool) bag of the selected foam base into a canister whip with a nitrous oxide charger and dispenses atop the food." Can Ruby Tuesday's spherified chicken wings with blue cheese foam be far behind?

Interest in Ferran and other avant-garde Spanish chefs has had another unexpected side effect—one that delights Ferran: Chefs and lay diners alike, drawn to Spain by its *vanguardia* cuisine and forced to consider it as a serious food destination by dint of its sheer energy and novelty, have been discovering traditional Spanish cooking along the way, as well as the great wealth of natural raw materials and food products—cheeses, olive oils, olives and almonds, the exquisite Spanish ham, and so on—that the country produces. If there's a new tapas bar in your town, or arbequina olive oil in your pantry, or Manchego cheese on your deli sandwich, Ferran probably deserves some of the credit. It's little wonder that, in 2010, Turespaña, the Spanish government tourism office, named Ferran its international ambassador, with plans to send him around the world promoting not just Spanish gastronomy—traditional as well as avant-garde—but Spain as a whole. "Cuisine is the only cultural sector in which the Spanish are the world leaders," Ferran points out. "Do you realize what that's worth?" He'd like to see ten thousand tapas bars around the world, he adds, "just as

---

there are now ten thousand pizzerias." (His figure is a little off, by the way; there are an estimated 61,000 pizzerias in the United States alone.)

Ferran himself seems more vexed than flattered by the extent of his sway. At the gastronomic exhibition Madrid Fusión in 2009, he mused, "We are caught up in a madness for the new, and it's because of me." One afternoon at the Taller, he told me, "I don't feel like 'the best chef in the world.' What does that mean, anyway? It's a horror, a nightmare, what's happened. With nouvelle cuisine, you had ten or twelve influential chefs even at the beginning, and younger chefs could take a little from Guérard, a little from Chapel, a little from Bocuse, and so on. Now there is only El Bulli. It is the only influence. I understand that that influence is too strong, too much of a monopoly, but what can I do?"

What indeed. "Ferran was a wake-up call for every chef in the world," says Fabrizio Aielli, the Venetian-born chef who ran the popular Goldoni restaurants in Washington, D.C., before opening Sea Salt in Naples, Florida, and whose own food is far from avant-garde. "Even the ones who said, 'Oh, I don't believe in what he's doing' ended up trying some of his ideas." The author-chef Anthony Bourdain makes the same point, saying, "many of the same chefs who've been sneering at the very idea of Ferran now shamelessly crib his ideas, peeling off the more applicable concepts to use in their more conventional menus." It would be easier to identify areas of modern professional cooking that have *not* been influenced by Ferran, directly or indirectly, than those that have. Even chefs who disdain everything he stands for (or think they do) have been touched by him, if only in the sense that his all-pervasiveness has sometimes galvanized them to move in the opposite direction.

At least one Ferran-like character has shown up in popular fiction. In Peter Schechter's thriller *Pipeline*, the villainous Russian oligarch Viktor Zhironovsky invites his newly appointed underling Daniel Uggin to lunch in his private dining room. The menu bears the signature of "Juan-Esteban Arcos, the world-famous Spanish chef and producer of avant-garde, experimental delicacies in his small restaurant north of Barcelona." The text goes on, "In the past years, Arcos had been fawned over as the world's most original gastronome by prestigious international foodie magazines; his restaurant had a two-year waiting list . . ." The menu he designs for Zhironovsky includes "seaweed tagliatelle with Bay of Biscay scallops, a cappuccino of foamed duck liver, and seared tuna made into a Tower of Babel with golden beets and salted jicama." The food, in fact, sounds rather pedestrian, and not very Ferran-esque. It is a tribute to Ferran to say that even a novelist capable of fabricating the most improbable plots and completely unfettered by practical concerns can't be as imaginative in the kitchen as Ferran can.

2

Gorgonzola Mochi and Rabbit Brains

"If you're not capable of a little sorcery, you shouldn't bother cooking."

—Colette, *Prisons et paradis*

This is what I had the second-to-last time I ate at El Bulli, in order:

Sake sorbet with yuzu foam and tonic. Tart and bracing—a kind of pale sorbet soda in a tall glass. Woke my palate right up.

Nori-trias. Black nori seaweed made crisp and crackly, like pâte feuilleté, then folded around black sesame butter—sort of a peanut butter cracker elevated to perfection, with an Asian accent.

"Easter egg" of frozen coconut milk with curry powder. A large white globe of frozen coconut milk, almost like a thin layer of firm frosting. A server cracked it open at the table and sprinkled on the curry powder. It was to be eaten in shards. Strange but good, and tasting purely and intensely of coconut.

Passion fruit "orchid." Thin slices of the fruit turned into three crisp, bright yellow-orange petals with a sweet carpel of hazelnuts and passion fruit essence—as fragrant and flowery as an orchid itself.

Pine nut bonbons. Racy-looking bittersweet chocolate globes, each with a single pine nut extending from it like a nipple. Earthy and only faintly sweet, and very tasty.

Gominola of shiso. Vinegary little sour plum candies with a strong taste of minty shiso leaves, round and deep garnet red in color, jellied and a little chewy in texture. Not my thing. (*Gominola* is Spanish for Gummi bear.)

Galetas of tomato and Parmigiano. Medium-thin cookies, one of each ingredient and very *true* to its flavor. I would have liked a few more of both.

Amaranth with hazelnut oil. A little round of pan-toasted amaranth leaves anointed with hazelnut oil. Nutty and ethereal.

Miso turrón with walnuts. Extraordinary, like a real *turrón* (halvah-like Spanish nougat) but cold, salty, and sweet.

Peking crêpes and crab and soya wontons. The former were like fried soup dumplings with impossibly thin skins, filled with liquefied sesame with a touch of heat; the latter were sweet and salty, with some peppery micro sprouts on top for texture. I could have eaten a plateful of either.

Braç de gitano and beet essence. The *braç de gitano* (literally, Gypsy's arm), traditionally a rolled sponge cake filled with cream, was here made with a featherweight beet meringue filled with whipped yogurt, encased in a thin, sweet, yogurt-based shell. Alongside it came one of the restaurant's funny little spoons—mostly bowl, with just a wisp of handle—full of very concentrated beet reduction. The reduction flooded the palate with intensity; the "Gypsy's arm" was like a soft echo of the initial statement.

A single grilled strawberry flavored with gin and juniper. Just what it sounds like. Didn't do a thing for me.

Chervil tea. Served tableside by one of the chefs, who came out and performed a kind of tea ceremony. Two chrome bowls on wooden stands were placed on the table; into these he spooned a fine powder of dried chervil, then whisked in very hot (but not boiling) water. We were instructed to drink from the bowls. The tea was strong—curious, because chervil is such a mild herb—and bitter. It tasted like medicine, vaguely punitive.

Gorgonzola mochi. A creamy little morsel, snowy white and glistening, in which the traditional Japanese pounded rice paste had somehow been turned into a skin so delicate that it almost broke on the way to the mouth; inside was a subtly blue cheese–flavored liquid (rice milk?). Gone in one satisfying bite—a bite particularly welcome after that chervil tea.

Black sesame sponge cake. A sponge so light in texture that it seemed to countermand some basic law of physics, with a creamy, savory miso paste interior. Perfect balance of salty and sweet. Remarkable.

Oyster leaf with vinegar dew. The gray-green leaves of *Mertensia maritima*, which have the texture of a succulent, were known popularly as lungwort before the menu writers got ahold of them. Their new name is no cheat, however; they really do taste like oysters. The presentation here was a single leaf per person, each bearing a few drops of amber-hued shallot vinegar. It was very pretty, like something in a jewelry ad, but I didn't find it particularly appealing.

Razor clam Laurencia. A single raw razor clam on the half shell, the other half shell filled with a concoction of ponzu jelly and crunchy, slightly iodine-y red Laurencia seaweed—very Chinese tasting. Not bad.

Umeboshi. Ferran's version of the traditional sour-salty Japanese pickled plums. These were wrapped in nori seaweed, moistened with plum juice and green and bitter almond oils, and served in more of those almost handleless spoons. Strong flavors, not entirely pleasant.

Parmesan dumplings with tallarines. Mildly cheese-flavored soft dough wrapped around barely cooked sea-bright miniature clams. Very good.

Baby cuttlefish with pesto ravioli. Three triangular pale green ravioli— the pesto was "spherified," forming both the ravioli wrapper and the filling—with a lightly cooked little cuttlefish; dots of its ink accented the plate. Lots of fun and just plain delicious.

Mandarin flower sorbet with pumpkin oil, pumpkin seeds, and mandarin seeds. A dramatic transition from the previous two dishes; a frozen custard, not very sweet, served in a hollowed-out white cube. Attractive fragrances; nice textural asides from the seeds. Pretty appealing.

Spherified Parmigiano gnocchi. Very light "pasta" with a pronounced Parmigiano flavor, but the sauce of concentrated hazelnut oil overpowered it; my palate couldn't make the two elements meld.

Anchovy with truffle. The anchovy was a real one, and there was a bit of mangosteen to offset the salt, but the "truffle" was truffle oil, a substance whose gassy, artificial character always ruins food for me. Good anchovies are one of Spain's great food treasures; they don't need truffle oil or tropical fruit.

Tomatoes and basil. A wonderful example of how Ferran can reinterpret familiar flavors with humor and imagination and come up with something that both echoes the original and takes the basic concept into another realm. Confit cherry tomatoes, dehydrated and injected with olive oil, looked like chocolate-glazed profiteroles (they were coated in black olive oil with dots of balsamic vinegar); with them were fake "olives" fashioned out of puréed Japanese black garlic, and "basil leaves" made of dried caramelized mango coated with basil water powder. A triumph, fooling the eye, delighting the taste buds.

Coco with caviar. A yin-yang presentation of coconut milk and thickened coconut water topped with three small spoonfuls of real caviar. Appealing in an off-the-wall sort of way.

Lulo. This is a high-acid tropical fruit from Colombia (*Solanum quitoense*), with a citrusy, faintly metallic character. It had been concentrated into a kind of firm jelly and was served with little clouds of whipped yogurt and dots of unsweetened cacao. Interesting—I almost want to say thought-provoking.

"Tagliatelle." Usually served atop the lulo, but in this case a separate course: a coil of noodles made not from flour but from frozen foie gras fat, dusted with crystals of salt. Really out there—a love-it-or-hate-it proposition. I loved it. Don't tell my cardiologist.

Veal tendon. Like some slow-braised red-cooked Chinese meat dish, rich and very flavorful, served in a tarragon-scented broth, then followed quickly by a small, tiny-handled spoon of bone marrow soup. Really good.

Abalone. Thin-sliced baby abalone, the pieces interleaved with wisps of ham fat, surrounded by lots of other stuff: black Codium seaweed, ginger jelly, golden enoki stems cooked like *fideus* noodles (the thin, short pasta beloved in Catalonia), hazelnut oil . . . Interesting flavors and textural contrasts, but there was just too much going on; I could never get the dish in focus.

Soup of mango and begonia flower tea. Thin, aromatic fruit punch. Okay.

"Nenúfars." A soup, based on elderflower syrup, that looked like a tiny, yellowish lily pond; the pond was inset with "water lilies" (that's what the dish's name means in Catalan) of nasturtium leaf and (very bitter) Australian finger lime and with brittle-like cashew rock and little pink and white flowers of some kind preserved in sugar. Floral and sharp. Didn't love it, didn't hate it.

Pork tail. Sweet meat, mahogany in color, crunchy and superb, alongside a ham soup with melon, cilantro, jasmine drops, and carnation flowers. The overall effect in the mouth was of an elegant evocation of prosciutto and melon.

Green walnuts with endive. An almost recognizable version of the classic salad, with a jumble of soft, herbaceous walnuts glazed in Roquefort, out of which rose a bud of red-tinged Belgian endive upended like a rocket about to be launched. On one side of the plate was a small dot of passion fruit purée to be eaten at the end; that sounded a little too precious to me, but the sweet acidity actually provided a nice finish to the dish.

Sea anemone 2008. Just your everyday mix of sea anemone, raw rabbit brains, oysters, and calamondin (a sour-sweet Southeast Asian citrus) in lukewarm dill broth. I wouldn't go as far as one blog entry I later happened across, which described this creation as "Vile. Vomitous. Nightmare!" But I found it so utterly unpleasant and cacophonous that I wondered for a moment whether Ferran had gone off the rails. It made my teeth ache. One of the stagiares later told me that the revered Basque chef Juan Mari Arzak—one of Ferran's closest friends and a frequent visitor to El Bulli—went into the kitchen after being served this dish one night and asked Ferran what had possessed him. "It's just terrible!" he reportedly exclaimed. Ferran, said the stagiare, started to laugh.

Game canapé. Duck foie gras and hare sauce made into a paste and spread on a bitter cacao cracker. Very good, despite the ghost of truffle oil in the background.

Flower canapé. A bar of meringue topped with tiny but pungent yellow-green Sichuan pepper blossoms and two or three other kinds of minuscule flowers. Neither refreshing nor very flavorful. I could easily have skipped it.

Honey caramel. A crisp wafer of caramelized honey and sunflower seeds glistening with bitter arbutus honey. Brilliant, a perfect confection.

Elderberry juice. Just that, with honey water jelly stirred in. It tasted like bubble bath.

"Autumn landscape." Sculpture on a plate, an evocative scene built from spice bread, licorice, frozen chocolate powder, and cherry sorbet, all excellent and all in surprising harmony. A truly memorable dessert, beautiful to look at and a joy to eat.

Morphings. What would be called *mignardises* in a French restaurant or *pequeñas locuras* (little follies) in Spain, something to go with the coffee—in this case, twenty-five or thirty little candies and confections, most of them chocolate, presented in a beautiful, dark-wood treasure chest (sometimes jokingly referred to as the "Caja [box or strongbox] Willy Wonka"). I managed a few, including a dark-chocolate-framed mint leaf, a chocolate flavored with eucalyptus, an airy but crisp chocolate-yogurt sponge, a bit of freeze-dried peach coated in dark chocolate, and a couple of branches of chocolate "coral," given color by sour cherry powder. All were impeccable.

The experience of dining at El Bulli begins, long before the sake sorbet or its equivalent, with the road that leads there. Almost everyone who has gone to the restaurant, especially those who braved the trek in earlier days, seems to have commented on the precipitous approach to Cala Montjoi. Like the food at the other end, the road inspires metaphor. In his book *elBulli des de dins* (El Bulli from Within), for instance, Xavier Moret writes that heading up it is like entering, "without wanting to, into another dimension, or into the next screen of a computer game . . ." For decades, the road was little more than a dirt path, rutted and rocky, curving mercilessly, unlit, free of guardrails, full of potholes that gaped wider after every rain; it was petrifying to travel if there was a Tramuntana—the strong, dry wind that blows down from the Pyrénées, so powerful it is said to have overturned a train on one occasion—and all but impassable after a storm.

"When I started driving there after I'd first been hired at El Bulli," recalls Jean-Paul Vinay, who was the restaurant's chef from 1981 to

1984, "I thought I must be lost. There can't be a restaurant here, I said to myself. You can't imagine what the road was like then. I crashed two cars in my years there." Vinay's predecessor, Jean-Louis Neichel, used to haul buckets of beach sand up from the cove to fill in the potholes—a temporary measure that had to be endlessly repeated in the winter. "The road was horrible but wonderful," says the restaurant critic Carmen Casas—a sentiment early fans of the restaurant often echoed. It was as if the drive to Cala Montjoi were a rite of passage, a task to be completed before the treasures at the other end became accessible.

How bad is the road today? It's a veritable superhighway compared with what it once was, but it can still pose a challenge, especially after dark—a fact that accounts for the stream of Roses taxicabs flowing up and down the road at the start and the end of the dinner hour. (Occasionally an intrepid visitor will charter a small fishing boat in Roses and arrive by water; the tricky part is to stay dry between the boat and the restaurant.) That said, the paving is good now: the city of Roses began laying down asphalt in 1995, proceeding in three phases and completing a new road in 2000. There are now several places to turn around or pull off if necessary, and the road is wide enough to let two cars going in opposite directions pass each other, barely.

Nonetheless, the trip from Roses to Cala Montjoi—it takes twenty to thirty minutes, depending on how confidently you drive—remains something of an adventure. The climb starts slowly, sloping up past vacation houses and small apartment blocks on both sides. Soon the landscape grows spare and a little rugged (the promontory, said to be some 450 million years old, has been part of a *parc naturel* since 1998), with fields and hillocks covered in thick scrub accented here and there by olive trees and clumps of agave. The road passes by patches of grapevines (these belong to one of the region's best wineries, Celler Espelt) and an old stone house with a ruined tower, then runs through dense stands of pine as it descends into the cove. There are now guardrails here and there, but much of the shoulder on both sides is unprotected, and the drop down to the rocks and then the sea is often sheer; if your brakes fail on the wrong curve on your way back down from dinner late at night, you probably will have eaten your last spherified olive. By the time you get to the road sign bearing a single exclamation point, you might wonder what took them so long.

When you finally arrive at El Bulli, the appearance of the restaurant itself seems almost pedestrian. The exterior of this temple of the avant-garde suggests some rural inn or roadside trattoria. The structure is part local stone, part smartly whitewashed adobe covered here and there in vines; a rim of terra-cotta tiles lines the edge of the flat roof, and dry stone walls define one side of the steps up to the entrance. The word *hacienda* suggests itself—and in fact, one early name for the place was Hacienda El Bulli (the term was later banished because it sounded "too Marbella," too faux-rustic). Around the restaurant grow agave, cactus, pittosporum, pine and eucalyptus trees, tall cypresses, stocky palms. Below the restaurant is Cala Montjoi, a pretty little cove with a broad sand beach and a camping resort at the far end.

The rural look continues inside, but with urbane accents. To the left of the entryway is an open terrace with a stone floor and an archway giving onto the cove; to the right is the very modern kitchen, partly visible. The two dining rooms have whitewashed walls and ceilings crossed with dark wood beams, interrupted here and there by stone columns and half walls. A miscellany of art, good and bad, contemporary and otherwise, crowds the place. The fifteen tables are cloaked in white linen, flanked by tapestry-back chairs and set with long-stem wineglasses, thick folded white napkins, and custom-designed white oblong chargers with a bas-relief pattern that seems to echo the shape of the cove below. There is no silverware on the tables: Ferran's food is almost never eaten with conventional forks or spoons, and whatever implements are needed are brought seconds before each course arrives. A few more tables sit on the terrace, but these are used mostly for the leisurely enjoyment of apéritifs and after-dinner coffee, drinks, and cigars; if parties are seated outdoors for dinner, a table is always left open for them indoors, too, in case the Tramuntana suddenly blows up.

The welcome at El Bulli—what the French call the *accueil*—is warm and professional. Guests are greeted, then led straight into the kitchen for a ritual introduction to Ferran. Oohing and aahing generally ensues, and most people seem to want to say something to Ferran, whether or not they have a language in common with him, even if it's just to comment on how beautiful the kitchen is or how much they've looked forward to coming here. Someone in almost every group takes a picture or asks one of the staff to snap one of them with Ferran. He is a good sport about it, posing, smiling, allowing arms to be thrown briefly around his shoulders. The ritual observed, guests sometimes choose to have an apéritif on the terrace or else are taken straight to their table. Once they're seated, the show begins. There isn't a whiff of pretension about the service or a hint of overfamiliarity. The tone is perfect. Sitting there in this fabled dining room on a comfortable chair or banquette at a commodious table, the diner feels superbly taken care of, cosseted, privileged. The only surprises, the only unexpected moments, of the evening will come from the food—and those will be momentous ones.

There used to be an à la carte menu at El Bulli, but since 2002 only a multicourse tasting menu has been offered, on the theory that (as Ferran has said) "how you eat is as important as what you eat." El Bulli, he points out, was the first three-star restaurant to discard the à la carte menu. "From the moment we did," he says, "people no longer chose what they were going to eat: It was we who chose for them." Ferran's friend Vicente Todolí, the Valencian-born director of the Tate Modern in London, maintains that it is this menu, not its separate components, that defines Ferran's genius. "As with the great photographers, like Walker Evans," he says, "the sequence is as important as the individual parts. Ferran's menus are organic. They have a kind of seamlessness, which is one thing that I think defines great creators."

The exact number of courses on an El Bulli menu varies. It is generally at least thirty and no more than thirty-five, though Ferran sometimes gets carried away and keeps going beyond that; this might seem excessive, but it isn't as overwhelming as it sounds, as many of the courses consist of no more than a single bite, and they keep coming at a steady but manageable tempo. The particulars of the food vary not only from season to season but sometimes from night to night. Diners are asked when they obtain their reservations and usually again when they sit down whether they have any food allergies or strong dislikes. ("You have no problem with shellfish?" "Will you eat rabbit brains?" "Are sea urchins all right?") One of the first things Ferran and his chefs do every morning when they assemble in the kitchen is to plot out the menus for each table; no two are ever exactly alike. Ferran is particularly concerned that he never serve repeat customers—a handful of fortunate souls who manage to dine here more than once a year—the same things twice. As a result, there are typically about sixty different items prepared every evening, though the kitchen is said to have a repertoire of about fifteen hundred in all. On an average evening, these items typically utilize about two hundred different ingredients, about three-quarters of them from Spain, the rest sourced internationally. According to *A Day at El Bulli*, the raw materials for each individual menu weigh about three pounds in their natural state and translate to about a pound and a half of food on the table per person.

The structure of the menu has evolved over the years, but currently it is divided into "cocktails" (which may take a solid or a semi-solid form), snacks (canapés and the like, mostly finger food, mostly savory but sometimes sweet or ambiguous), tapas dishes (small servings, many involving seafood or offal—meat is a rarity here—to be eaten with cutlery), avant-desserts (transitional bits that may combine sweet and savory elements), desserts, and, finally, morphings. (When pronounced with a Cockney accent, a British guest once pointed out, "morphings" can be taken as a nicely descriptive pun.) In 2009, the tariff, without wine, was 230 euros, about $340, per person—expensive, but certainly not the most you can pay in a three-star restaurant.

The Italian futurist writer and poet Filippo Tommaso Marinetti could have been describing certain qualities of the El Bulli tasting menu when he wrote, in 1932, that for him the perfect meal required "[a]bsolute originality in the food . . . the abolition of the knife and fork . . . [and] the creation of simultaneous and changing canapés which contain ten, twenty flavors to be tasted in a few seconds. . . ." (He also described dishes one can almost imagine encountering on that menu, among them marinated eel stuffed with frozen Milanese minestrone and anchovy-stuffed dates, and mysterious caramel balls, "each one filled with something different . . . so that the diners cannot guess which flavor will enter the mouth next.")

The experience of dining at El Bulli is, in any case, so unusual, so unexpected if you've never had it before, that it tends to inspire vivid responses even from those who are intimately familiar with great food. When I asked Thomas Keller what he thought the first time he dined at the restaurant, he replied, "My first impression was . . . WOW! You're just *amazed*." Wolfgang Puck told me, "I thought it was as if you hadn't seen New York City for two hundred years and then you saw it today. It was that different from anything I could imagine." Anthony Bourdain once admitted, "I came to El Bulli with a hostile attitude, as someone who associated cooking with exposing protein to flame," but he went on to say, "When I ate the food, I felt fear, delight, confusion, real joy. The world changed. For a chef, it was like Eric Clapton coming out of hearing Jimi Hendrix for the first time. What do you do now?"

The journalist Óscar Caballero expressed his own feelings about the place like this: "Dining at El Bulli is like losing your virginity. When it happens, you are transformed. Until then, you think it's the devil." After *his* dinner at El Bulli, Giles Coren, restaurant critic for *The Times* in London, played with the same metaphor: "Ferran Adrià did not feed us," he wrote. "He deflowered us. He took our innocence, and left us elated, confused and melancholy." Coren, it might be noted, won the *Literary Review's* 2005 Bad Sex in Fiction award for his novel *Winkler.* The prize for purple prose, however, goes to *New York* magazine's art critic, Jerry Saltz, who wrote, after dining at El Bulli, "I was very ashamed to see Ferran . . . : [W]e had shared something so intimate that I was horrified that the lights were back on and that we were together . . . I feel like he knows my body, and I know his body . . ." Hey, I know it's a remarkable experience but, er, down, boy.

■ ■ ■

This is what I had the last time I ate at El Bulli:

I don't remember.

Or, rather, I don't remember very many specifics. I didn't take notes. I made the conscious decision to just eat (and drink) what was put in front of me and savor it as much as I could. I wanted to have an impressionistic experience instead of an analytical one. Thinking back on the meal now, I can recall a dozen or so offerings in detail, out of forty-six. ("Ferran has planned just a *crazy* menu for you tonight," the maître d'hôtel Lluís García told me; as opposed to his usual sane ones?)

The courses I do recall are the following, not necessarily in this order: a small cactus leaf impregnated with tequila, triple sec, and lime juice—Ferran's version of the margarita, great fun and very tasty; simply (and barely) steamed local baby shrimp, without a touch of trickery, very light but intense in flavor; a sphere like the coconut "egg" I'd had before but this time made of Gorgonzola with powdered nutmeg (I think) sprinkled over it; "lentils" concocted from sesame and butter, as earthy as the real thing; chicken-skin canapés, perfect little mouthfuls; intense pigeon consommé served in a brandy snifter with a cacao cracker on the side—a wonderful combination; something to do with eel and cherimoya, interesting; mochi with persimmon sorbet, strange but good; some sort of cep dish that I didn't like very much; a conversation-stopping combination of artichoke leaves and white Ecuadoran rose petals—I couldn't decide whether I liked it or not; wild hare (in place of rabbit) brains—I made the obvious joke—in what tasted like a reduction of the classic sauce for *lièvre à la royale*, just delicious (Ferran uses hare's and rabbit's brains so often, it's a wonder there's a sentient lapine left in Catalonia); a remarkable dessert called "pond," a paper-thin sheet of ice frozen over a bowl, sprinkled with brown sugar, powdered matcha green tea, and powdered peppermint, to be broken and eaten in shards. . . .

Beyond that, in general, I recall, there were lots of nuts, both real and reconstructed—pine nuts, pistachios, peanuts. Sesame seeds appeared more than once. There seemed to be fruit or flowers or both with many of the courses. There were evocations of Japan (miso, soy milk, yuzu) and some items that had, in the words of the English restaurant critic A. A. Gill, "that strange cardboard and plastic taste that the Japanese love." Many dishes had a bitter note, even those that were otherwise sweet or mild, as if Ferran had no intention of letting the diner off too easily.

Some of what I had, I do remember, was brilliant. Some was fascinating. Some slipped by too quickly to make much of an impression. Two or three things I frankly didn't want to finish. I got up from the table thinking that what I'd just had wasn't so much a meal as some kind of all-stops-out multisensory performance piece, an encounter with the unknown or the unfamiliar, using sight, smell, taste, and touch to sidestep, with balletic precision, any reasonable expectations I might have sat down with.

Did it bother me that not every morsel I tasted at this, the "best restaurant in the world," presided over by "the world's greatest chef," absolutely delighted me? No, not at all. I wasn't here looking for comfort food. As Anthony Bourdain once said, "You don't go to El Bulli because you want chicken that night." I didn't expect a progression of crowd-pleasers. I knew before sitting down that this meal would be more roller coaster than Ferris wheel, more trek-through-the-rainforest than suite-at-the-Four-Seasons. If Ferran is sometimes difficult to understand when he speaks, he can be even more so in his culinary conversations with the diner—but that's the whole point. The most important thing to Ferran—and, by extension, to those who are open to the magic he creates—is not that the food he presents lives up to reasonable expectations but that it turns those expectations upside down. There is much pleasure to be had from a meal at El Bulli, but the most important thing about it is that it is always unique.

3

Dr. and Mrs. Schilling's Mini-Golf

"El Bulli was already one of the best restaurants in Spain before I did my first stage there."

—Ferran Adrià, in conversation with the author

A century ago, Gelsenkirchen, near Essen in western Germany, was the most important coal-mining town in Europe; it was known as "the city of a thousand fires" after the mine gases that ignited there spontaneously every day. Because it was an important industrial center—there were oil refineries in the region, too—it was bombed frequently by the Allies during World War II. It was also the site of a forced-labor camp for women, administered from Buchenwald, and it must have still been a very grim place indeed when Hans Schilling and Margareta Schönova were married there on December 7, 1946.

Schilling was a German doctor who practiced both conventional and homeopathic medicine in Gelsenkirchen; his homeopathic specialty was iridology, a pseudoscientific discipline, which enjoyed a vogue in early-twentieth-century Germany, that purports to diagnose illness through examination of the iris of the eye. His bride was a stateless Czech, "German by adoption," born—as she later told Spanish interviewers—in 1919 in Drassau (apparently the small town now called Drásov, in southern Moravia) and educated in Prague. Her wedding documents identify her as not Margareta but Marqueta Schönova de Schilling; she later took the name Marketa or Marketta (she signed it both ways), ultimately coming to prefer the latter spelling.

Photographs of the couple toward the end of their first decade of marriage show a lean, handsome young man, with a Roman nose, wavy hair, and a close-cropped beard, and a sturdy-looking, attractive blonde with a broad face and a determined mien. Dr. Schilling wasn't exactly wealthy, but his practice was fairly lucrative, and the couple were—as Óscar Caballero once put it—"victims of the virus of gastronomy." They started to take vacations around Germany and through France and neighboring countries, shaping their itineraries with the help of the *Guide Michelin*. In the 1950s, the Schillings began to visit Spain's Mediterranean coast—"I wanted to leave cities behind for personal reasons," Marketta later said—driving up and down through countryside that was then mostly undeveloped, towing a *rulot*, or caravan, in which they'd cook and spend the night. Sharing the caravan were always a couple of *bouledogues françaises* (French bulldogs), exemplars of a small but muscular bat-eared breed with a chirping bark that Marketta doted on.

One day, on the outskirts of Roses, the Schillings by chance headed up a narrow dirt road, mined with potholes, and found that they couldn't turn around with the caravan behind them. They pressed on and finally arrived in a little cove that they later learned was called Cala Montjoi. The land behind the beach and the hills on either side of the cove were barren of trees, covered with nothing but low scrub, and the only structure was a small guardhouse for the Guardia Civil, Spain's military police, who came through the area periodically to look for smugglers and probably also to make sure that the German and

Italian scuba divers and sunbathers who seemed to like the little Montjoi beach didn't have designs on any nearby military installations.

Marketta, Ferran once wrote, was "passionate for the drama of landscapes," and she and her husband fell in love with the place immediately. Dr. Schilling later told an interviewer, "The war had ended only a few years before. The discovery of this sea, this unspoiled coastline . . . When we arrived, there was nothing for miles around. We managed to locate the owner of this piece of land [on the southern end of the cove, where El Bulli now stands] and we sat here on a rock and asked the cost." In 1957 the Schillings bought a five-and-a-half-acre plot above the cove, transected by the sorry road, for 15,000 pesetas, less than four hundred dollars at the time—to be paid half down, half the following year. "There was little money then," the doctor said, "but money was worth something."

Soon after the purchase had been completed, the Schillings began to build a house, in the whitewashed Spanish Mediterranean style, complete with arches and a small tower, on a rise on the inland side of the road. They did the work themselves—"Every stone was touched by our hands," the doctor always said—with the assistance of a jack-of-all-trades from Córdoba named José Lozano, known as Joselillo. Lozano had been doing his military service at Punta Falconera, on the tip of the promontory between Roses and Cala Montjoi, and had heard about the "German couple" who had bought land on the cove. (Ferran says there were early rumors that Marketta was a German spy.) He made the trek and asked them for work; they needed help and gladly hired him. Always deeply tanned, with a broad, expressive face, he was of modest size but muscular, and for decades he did much of the manual labor around the property.

While they were working on their house, Dr. Schilling applied for a permit from the town of Roses to build bungalows and open a medical center for the aged on the site, but his application was turned down.

Then he had a very different notion. Perhaps, he thought, the spot would be a good place for one of those mini-golf courses that were a popular amusement along the coast; once people got on the road to Cala Montjoi, he reasoned, they—like the Schillings themselves—would find it impossible to turn around and so would continue on to the cove. Why not give them something to do when they arrived? Marketta protested that the spot was too windy, but her husband persisted, and on June 7, 1961, "Don Juan Schilling" was granted a city permit for the mini-golf, signed by the mayor of Roses. Later the same year, he left Marketta and returned to Germany, where he took up with his housekeeper, a younger woman named Erna—Don Juan indeed.

That was hardly the end of Dr. Schilling's involvement with Cala Montjoi, however. Marketta remained in the new house, and her husband came back frequently and continued to take part in the development of the property. In 1962, Lozano constructed a reed shack, labeled simply Chiringuito (the word is Spanish for beach-side bar), overlooking the cove, and Marketta started to serve sand-wiches, Coke, and beer to the sunbathers and scuba divers. (The original structure sat where the restaurant's reception desk and an unused stone fireplace are now.) Marketta had been right about the mini-golf course: It was never a success. Few non-beachgoers found their way to the end of the road, and it was too hot to play in the summer anyway and impossible to hit a golf ball when the Tramuntana blew. Instead of generating income, the attraction cost money almost constantly for upkeep and repair. "We had to pay, pay, pay," Marketta said late in her life. In 1963, to offset expenses, she decided to upgrade the shack. Lozano installed a grill, and the menu was expanded to include gazpacho and simply grilled chicken and fish. A new sign outside read "Bar Alemany" (Catalan for "German Bar"). Marketta cooked, with the help of Joselillo. The Guardia Civil wasn't always pleased—anything that encouraged foreigners to linger around the cove made their job more difficult—but as one of Marketta's friends told the *Diari de Girona* after her death, "The personality of Marketta always fixed things, to the point that those on foot patrol would take refuge in her house when the weather was bad."

Dr. Schilling continued to return at least two or three times a year, driving down from Germany in his white Mercedes with Erna, stashing her in a hotel room in Roses, then coming to stay in Cala Montjoi (he slept upstairs, Marketta on the ground floor). Marketta's friend Feggy Bonodo, who worked briefly as a waitress at the *chiringuito*, once noted that "Marketta was separated, but not abandoned." When the doctor sent word that he was coming to the property, Marketta would always say, "My husband is coming." The Schillings maintained such an amiable relationship, in fact, that a chef who worked at El Bulli in the early eighties told me that he never even realized that they weren't still together until someone mentioned it.

At some point, being serious food lovers, the Schillings began to fantasize about having a real restaurant in their remote corner of the Costa Brava—perhaps one day even an establishment that was, as the Michelin guide puts it, "worth a detour." In 1964, with that in mind, the Schillings hired a crew to turn the glorified *chiringuito* into a "grill room," with an outdoor grill, a small indoor kitchen, a terrace dining room and outdoor bar, and a few modest guest rooms. The new place was clearly more than a *bar alemany*, and Marketta decided to rename it after her pet bulldogs—by this time, she had four or five—using a French slang term for the breed, *bulli*. One early sign read "Bully-Bar," but another got it right with "Bulli-Bar"—and the place was soon dubbed Rotisserie Hacienda El Bulli. The bulldog head on a dark ochre background that's inset into the wall just to the left of the entrance to El Bulli today comes from one of the original Bulli-Bar signs. (In French, *bulli* would be pronounced "boo-LEE," but today everybody says it the Spanish way, as "BOOL-yee." As for the common mispronunciation "bool-YEE," neither Spanish nor French, it can probably be traced to the author of *Fodor's Guide to Barcelona*, George Semler; somebody told him years ago that *Bulli* was spelled with an accent, as *Bullí*, he says, and he set it down that way in *Fodor's*, where it remained uncorrected for about five years.)

Though the Schillings hired a Swiss dining room director, Otto Müller, for the new place, Marketta continued to supervise the cooking, and the restaurant remained casual. Before lunchtime every day, one of the kitchen boys would take menus down to the beach to try to rustle up customers, and photographs from the era show young women in bathing suits and men in swimming trunks or shirtless in white slacks, almost all of them with dark tans, lounging on the terrace, smoking, nibbling, sipping tall drinks; one shot shows a man clad only in shorts and sandals tending something on the grill—apparently one of the regulars pitching in.

One early celebrity customer was the British Pop artist Richard Hamilton, who had bought a house just up the coast in Cadaqués, the fishing village where both Miró and Picasso spent time and where Dalí lived part-time at Port Lligat. Hamilton remembers visiting the restaurant for the first time at some point in the mid-sixties with Marcel Duchamp and his wife and his own young son, Roderick. The menu was still very simple and traditional, and Hamilton remembers that Roderick ordered *botifarra* (Catalan pork sausage) and white beans; this became the young man's favorite meal and was all he'd ever order when he visited.

The trip to Cala Montjoi took Hamilton less than half an hour by water in his inflatable Zodiac, and he became a regular guest, sometimes arriving soaking wet. "They had a nice toilet," he told an interviewer recently, "so I would go in and squeeze the water out of my shirt and put it on again." A few years after Hamilton began coming to the restaurant, an attractive young woman apparently fell into the water while clambering out of a small boat near the shore, with a loud splash that was heard on the terrace; a few minutes later, she appeared at the door draped in a sheet someone had found for her, and she ate lunch with her companions in that garb while her dress dried on a chair in the sun. Other visitors of the period remember washing the beach sand off with that hose outside El Bulli before tramping through the arched doorway and out onto the terrace.

Did Dalí—to whom Ferran is sometimes compared—ever visit El Bulli? Marketta always maintained that he had come several times, but there's no proof of his visits. Catherine Moore, widow of Dalí's long-time agent, Captain John Peter Moore, told me that she was reasonably certain he never had. The Moores surely would have known, because they were themselves regular customers of the restaurant. They had a house near Dalí's in Port Lligat, and they used to cruise down to Cala Montjoi for dinner on their yacht, whose decks were usually crowded, it is said, with young, bikini-clad lovelies. According to restaurant lore, as soon as he'd dropped anchor, the captain would call up to the dining room with a megaphone and announce how many guests he had on board. Because there were often ten or twelve, and the yacht's tender held only two or three at a time, it would sometimes take two hours before everyone had assembled in the restaurant. The Moores were also famous for arriving at El Bulli with a pet ocelot. "His name was Babou," says Mrs. Moore, "and he was perfectly behaved—a gentleman on a leash."

Dalí did have an interest in food. He once proposed that "the most philosophic organs a man possesses are his jaws," and in 1971 he published a cookbook called *Les dîners de Gala* (named in honor of his wife). Ferran didn't become aware of the volume until many years later, of course, and though the recipes are given in conventional-looking form, it is difficult to imagine his or anyone else's essaying Dalí's snail saltimbocca with calf's liver; his "avocado toast," consisting of avocado and lamb's brains with minced almonds, cayenne, and tequila on rye toast; or his "frog cream"—a soufflé of curried cauliflower with boneless frogs' legs, some on little skewers *inside* the soufflé, with a larger brochette of frogs' legs coated in egg and bread crumbs, then fried, sticking up in the middle. Looking at Dalí's painting of limp vertical fried eggs, though, you realize that Ferran could probably achieve that effect through some of his hydrocolloidal magic if he wanted to. It's either a pity or a blessing that the two men never met and collaborated.

The Schillings brought in El Bulli's first real chef, a German named Fritz Kreis, in 1967, and both food and service grew more elaborate. At Dr. Schilling's suggestion, waiters began to flambé desserts in the dining room—and they began to dress up. On one of his drives to Cala Montjoi, the doctor passed by a restaurant somewhere in Alsace that was going out of business and bought from it a large stock of folkloric-looking waiter's jackets, in colors including bright green, red, brown, orange, and three shades of blue, with embroidered floral-pattern plunging V-necks. These became a tradition at El Bulli and were still being worn as late as 1998—a jarring note, neither rustic like the furnishings nor contemporary, as the food had by then become.

Kreis was replaced after a year by another German, Manfred Hüschelrath, who lasted for two years before being supplanted by a Dutch chef, Octaaf "Oki" Bouillard. Under Bouillard, the menu grew ever more refined and turned toward French cuisine, and the presentation became more elaborate; among the dishes of the era were sea bass flambéed with fennel, entrecôte with sauce béarnaise, and beef Stroganoff. José Lozano took it upon himself, with no objection from Marketta, to dismantle the remains of the now derelict mini-golf course, and the restaurant was expanded over part of the land it had occupied, assuming more or less the shape it has today.

Dr. Schilling stayed in touch from Gelsenkirchen, offering support and advice, but it wasn't easy; there was no telephone at El Bulli, so when he wanted to communicate with Marketta or the chef, he would send a telegram fixing an appointment for a call several days later at the Hotel Moderno in Roses. When he did come, winding his way down to the Costa Brava slowly through France, stopping at great restaurants along the way, he always approved of the progress Marketta had made in his absence, and he encouraged yet further refinements. And he always brought things with him when he arrived—rare wines and spirits, new kitchen implements, new recipes and ideas. Photographs from the early seventies portray Marketta with a slightly imperious expression and a hint of mischief in her eyes; Dr. Schilling, by this time balding and filling out, looks self-confident and proud.

■ ■ ■

Generalissimo Francisco Franco died in 1975—ending, as Carmen Casas has written, forty years of "curtailing all initiatives towards cultural progress, of which gastronomy and cooking are part." Franco's effects on the restaurant business were of course the least of it. From the end of the Spanish Civil War in 1936 until his demise, Franco and his government ruled Spain through intimidation, imprisonment, and torture, and the execution, official or otherwise, of dissidents—all, he would have said, to protect the values he held dear, which included conservative Catholicism, anti-communism, and Spanish nationalism, in the most traditional and jingoistic sense. Under Franco's direction, the Guardia Civil imposed draconian justice—petty thieves were routinely beaten—and enforced puritanical laws that seem comical today (male bathers, for instance, could be arrested for going "topless" on the beach—though this was rarely a problem at Cala Montjoi; it was simply too remote). Thousands of professionals in every field fled the country when Franco took power, casting the country into a kind of new Dark Ages; many of those who remained were thrown out of work or demoted to menial positions. Trade unions and political parties were outlawed, the press was heavily censored, and regional culture and language were supressed, most strongly in the Basque country and Catalonia, supposedly in the interests of promoting Spanish unity.

The public use of Spain's non-Castilian languages was banned, as was the christening of newborns with non-Castilian names; the Castilian *Ignacio* was fine, for instance, while the Basque *Iñaki* or the Catalan *Ignasi* were not. An infamous poster slapped up around Barcelona read (in Castilian Spanish) "Catalans! Don't bark! Speak Christian!" Older Barcelonans remember when the castle on Montjuïc, the hill where many of the city's museums and recreational facilities are now located, was a prison filled with political prisoners—some of whom never emerged. When I first started going to Barcelona in the early eighties, there were still locals who wouldn't walk in front of the Policía Nacional headquarters on the Via Laetana, which had reportedly been a chamber of horrors. (A good friend of mine, now a prominent attorney, was once taken there—he doesn't offer any details—and says that passing by the place still gives him chills.) It has been said that Franco prolonged the nineteenth century in Spain by seventy-five years.

In the late fifties, facing the possibility of state bankruptcy and under increasing pressure from its allies to modernize its economy and end its isolationist policies, Spain began to revive. A new breed of economists, known as the technocrats, called for extensive reforms— with unexpected success. Economic liberalization drew international investment to Spain (low taxes and the fact that the Spanish work force was forbidden to strike certainly helped), and there was a huge population shift as blue-collar laborers from poorer parts of the country flocked to the cities to work in the new enterprises. Spain even began to produce its own car, the SEAT 600, based on Italy's Fiat 600, and this became a symbol of the country's so-called Desarrollo (meaning expansion or development)—the "Spanish Miracle" that turned its economy into the second-fastest-growing one in the world after Japan's. As its borders opened increasingly to the rest of the world, even the old prohibitions on non-Castilian languages were eased.

It was Franco's death, though, that changed everything. Almost overnight, Spain found political and social freedom; prosperity spread;

regional culture and language were reborn; the arts flourished. In 1982, the long-reviled (and long illegal) Socialist Party came to power. And, along with everything else, something that might be called contemporary Spanish cuisine began to emerge, influenced of course by France, but also fueled by a quickly growing sense of regional identity and new pride in Spanish products and traditions.

Jean-Louis Neichel's timing was perfect: He became chef at El Bulli the year that Franco died, the year that Spain breathed a sigh of relief and opened the doors and windows—the year that anything began to seem possible. And almost at once, he elevated the restaurant to an entirely new level. Today a compact, round-faced, white-haired man with overflowing energy and an engaging smile—he could play a grown-up version of one of Santa's elves—Neichel was born in the Alsatian capital of Strasbourg, studied cooking at the Colmar–Ribeauvillé hotel school, and then worked in a number of celebrated kitchens in France and Germany. After he'd hired him and brought him to Cala Montjoi, says Neichel, Dr. Schilling posed a question: "Why not make El Bulli a gastronomic restaurant?" Neichel replied, "Yes, why not?" And that is exactly what he proceeded to do.

Neichel remembers the doctor with great affection. "Marketta was the heart of the place," he tells me when I visit him late one afternoon at his handsome eponymous Barcelona restaurant, which he has run since the early eighties, "but it was Dr. Schilling who really knew what was happening in good restaurants around Europe, and he was the one who decided everything. He was so generous. The Schillings didn't have any children, and El Bulli was his child and his lover. He didn't care about profits. We would make money in the summer, when we were open seven days and nights a week, then lose it in the winter when sometimes nobody would come for days at a time. He didn't care. He always said, 'We have to make it better.' He was the ideal boss."

In July of 1975, the *Gault/Millau* magazine, in what was probably the first official acknowledgment of El Bulli's existence by a French publication, reviewed El Bulli and gave it a score of 14/20—calling the place *la grande surprise de la Costa Brava*. The review didn't mention Neichel by name, but it singled out for praise his chicken-liver mousse with crayfish coulis, crayfish salad with truffles, and chicken steamed in a pig's bladder. These dishes were strictly French—but that didn't stop the food-loving Catalan novelist Manuel Vásquez Montalbán (author of, among many other books, a definitive work called *L'art del menjar a Catalunya*—The Art of Eating in Catalonia) from declaring that "Neichel revolutionized Catalan cuisine."

What is Catalan cuisine? It's a highly original idiom, with characteristics that seem both medieval and contemporary—specifically its use of sweet and savory elements together (many sauces are subtly flavored with chocolate or with "sweet" spices like cinnamon and nutmeg; fruit is frequently combined with poultry or meat) and its juxtaposition of diverse foodstuffs within the same dish. The latter device is best illustrated by the class of dishes known collectively as *mar i muntanya*, sea and mountain, the simplest expression of which is a kind of ragoût of chicken and shrimp, though other versions get much more complicated (one, for example, mixes rabbit, snails, monkfish, cuttlefish, and shrimp). The word "baroque" is sometimes used to describe the more elaborate concoctions of the Catalan kitchen. At the same time, there is a measure of simplicity and purity in the region's cuisine: Many varieties of seafood and some other items, for instance, are simply sautéed in olive oil—almost stir-fried—with nothing more than minced garlic and parsley. The most emblematic Catalan preparation of all is arguably pa amb tomàquet, literally bread with tomato, which is nothing more than bread (often toasted or grilled) rubbed with a halved tomato and seasoned with olive oil and salt, to be eaten by itself or with anchovies, ham, or other accompaniments. (I had to laugh when one writer noted, as an example of Ferran's unbridled imagination, that he had created a daring presentation of bread with chocolate, olive oil, and sea salt; pa amb tomàquet with a piece of chocolate, as Ferran would be the first to tell you, has been the traditional after-school snack of Catalan children for many generations.)

At El Bulli, Neichel devised what must surely be one of the first examples of a non-traditional mar i muntanya, adding sea urchin and the locally favored sea cucumbers known as espardenyes to the traditional chicken and shrimp. He also integrated into his cooking regional ingredients like fish and shellfish from the market in Roses, olive oil from Tarragona, and truffles from the mountain town of Vic. The Barcelona restaurant critic Carmen Casas remembers being surprised by Neichel's Mediterranean-inspired innovation of preserving those truffles in that oil—something a more conventional French chef would have considered heresy. When Dr. Schilling brought a sorbet maker across the border tied to the roof of his car—it was apparently one of the first in Spain—Neichel made sorbet from wild thyme plucked in the hills above the restaurant. (The machine lasted and was in constant use until the late eighties, when it was supplanted by a more sophisticated model using newer technology.)

In 1976, justifying his employer's faith in him, Neichel won El Bulli its first-ever Michelin star. "Dr. Schilling was happy about the star," Neichel later remembered, "but not for long, because he immediately began thinking of a second one." In any case, the accolade had little immediate effect on the restaurant. Isolated and out of the Spanish culinary mainstream, El Bulli was full only in mid-summer, when vacationers from the far side of the Pyrénées, many of them with the red Michelin guide in hand, found their way there. Neichel had little time for relaxation, though, even when he wasn't cooking. Marketta gave him full responsibility for the restaurant: He ran the dining room as well as the kitchen, and because this was still very much a shoestring operation, he also did everything else that needed doing. The ever-faithful José Lozano was in charge of cutting flowers for the tables and foraging mussels and sea urchins—a rarity on Spanish tables in that era—from the rocks of Cala Montjoi, but Neichel helped with the gardening, and both men took the garbage downhill to Roses and repaired the road when it got washed out.

"We built El Bulli little by little," says Neichel. "There were no lights in the parking lot, for instance, so I drove up to Figueres and bought thirty meters of cable and a big lamp and hung it up on a tall tree." Big saltwater crayfish of excellent quality were fished off the Cap de Creus, just north of the cove, but Neichel didn't buy them because he didn't have a *vivier*, a tank in which to store them live. He and Lozano solved the problem by constructing a cement cistern outside the kitchen door and rigging a hose leading down to the sea, so that water circulated with every surge of the tide. "Then," Neichel tells me, "we could buy twenty, thirty, forty kilos of crayfish at a time and have them always ready. The tank was completely open, but the Guardia Civil was still around, and nobody ever stole any."

The telephone was a much more ambitious project. "For four years," Neichel explains, "El Bulli had a phone number, but no phone. To reserve a table, people had to send a letter or drive here." Finally, in 1977, he and Dr. Schilling convinced the phone company to run a line from Roses to Cala Montjoi. "It was very expensive," he continues. "Seven kilometers of cable for one customer." Once the line reached the restaurant, he realized that it had to be extended to Marketta's house, across the road. Neichel and Lozano dug a ditch more than three hundred feet long through rocky soil, uphill, to connect her. Then it dawned on them that when the phone rang, there was no way to know whether the call was for El Bulli or Marketta. "We had to dig another trench," he tells me, "for a line connected to a bell. Then we could have a signal—one beep for the laundry, two for Marketta, three for the neighbors who rented the place next door, four for the restaurant."

Because El Bulli was so far from Roses, suppliers wouldn't deliver, so every Monday, when the restaurant was closed, Neichel would drive down to Barcelona to buy supplies, or cross the French border and shop in Perpignan. "Whenever I'd come back from France with my trunk full of food and wine that was unavailable in Spain," he tells me, "the Guardia Civil would stop me at the frontier and stick their noses in the trunk. 'I smell cheese,' one would say. 'Oh, you have three nice cheeses. One must be for me. Thank you.' Or 'That's nice French cognac. You have two bottles. I'll take one.' I knew this would happen, of course, so I always brought one extra of everything, and they weren't too greedy."

El Bulli was pricey by local standards. "Our menu was three hundred fifty pesetas [just over six dollars] per person," says Neichel, "when in a regular restaurant in Roses you could eat for a hundred pesetas. Some Spanish snobs started coming—'Oh, they have French cognac, French champagne!'—but the people of the town thought we were too expensive. 'Oh, only foreign people go there,' they'd say. 'The people are crazy, and there's a sexy blonde . . .'"

The sexy blonde, of course, was Marketta. "Marketta was a bit of a hippie," Neichel says. "A hippie de luxe. She was more modern and sexy than the Spanish girls, and very pretty." (Neichel seems to start blushing a little as he says this.) "She loved Cadaqués, Cadaqués was a bit like Ibiza, very Bohemian. She'd say, 'Let's go there to shop.' I'd drive her and she'd buy hippie clothes in a little shop, and very tight jeans. Then she always wanted to go have coffee at the Bar Marítim. There was another bar that was more intellectual [presumably the Meliton, where Marcel Duchamp and John Cage once played chess], but the Marítim was more hippie, and she preferred that." Marketta's good friend Silvia Breur later told the *Diari de Girona* that she was "very different from the other women of her time, because she was very simple but at the same time very enterprising and had a very strong character, which in Spain in the sixties—when women were subordinate to men in every way—was a little surprising."

It was also Neichel who brought to El Bulli a conveyance that was to become part of the restaurant's folklore. The few guest rooms of the old Hacienda had long since been turned into staff quarters, but even so, Neichel tells me, "We didn't have room for everybody who worked there to stay overnight at the restaurant. And of course in those days the young people didn't have cars, maybe just little motos, maybe not even that, so it was hard for them to travel back and forth to Roses." Neichel may or may not have realized that the Schillings had first arrived in Cala Montjoi about two decades earlier in a caravan, long since vanished, but, he says, "I knew that Dutch tourists loved traveling and staying in caravans, and they used to drive them down from Holland in July and then leave them for the next summer when they went back home a month or two later. I had an idea, and I found a caravan at the campground in Empuriabrava that had gotten too old to ever make the trip back on the autoroute. I bought it from a Dutch guy for five thousand pesetas [about eighty-eight dollars] and towed it back to the restaurant. There's a steep driveway that goes down to the back of the kitchen, just before you come to the main entrance, and that's where we parked it, just across from the garbage bins."

The caravan, a dirty shade of white, had running water but no heat, so it turned out to be more useful as a dormitory in the warmer weather. "Sometimes four or five people slept in it," remembers Neichel. Along with water, he adds, the beer and the whisky and the gin and tonic flowed freely. Sometimes when they'd quit for the day and didn't feel like going into Roses, the staff would gather in the caravan to drink and play poker. It became known as "the casino." Of course, the caravan was in poor repair when Neichel bought it, and it didn't weather well. By the time Neichel's successor, Jean-Paul Vinay, got to El Bulli, the windows were covered with plywood. When the Tramuntana blew, one of *his* successors, Kristian Lutaud, remembers, the caravan rocked back and forth. "But I loved it because it was apart," he says. "Independent."

So many three-star restaurants, in France and elsewhere, seem to have grown out of pedestrian family-run cafés and bistros, defined by drudgery and tradition, blossoming into gastronomic glory only after some talented son or grandson had gone off to learn the chef's trade and then returned to take over his forebears' establishment and lead it step by step into the Michelin firmament. I'm pretty sure that the easygoing "hippie de luxe" beginnings of El Bulli—its beach-bar origins—had at least some residual influence on the eccentric and unfettered creativity that have characterized its later years.

A Very Good Boy

"*A genius is the one most like himself.*"

—Thelonious Monk, unpublished notebooks

Fernando Adrià Acosta was born on May 14, 1962, in the barrio of Santa Eulàlia in Hospitalet de Llobregat, a crowded, demographically diverse municipality immediately southwest of Barcelona. Though often described as a suburb of the Catalan capital, and contiguous with it, Hospitalet is in fact an independent city, the second largest in Catalonia and the twelfth largest in Spain. *L'Hospitalet no és Barcelona*—Hospitalet isn't Barcelona—is something of a local slogan, in fact, even screened onto souvenir T-shirts.

Hospitalet is an old Catalan word for hostel, and the village that grew up here in the Middle Ages was named for a famous inn for religious pilgrims attached to the church of Santa Eulàlia de Provençana. The village grew steadily over the centuries and expanded dramatically with the Spanish economic boom of the early 1960s, becoming one of the most densely populated cities in Europe. Job-seeking immigrants from poorer parts of Spain flooded Hospitalet, many of them from Andalusia, the birthplace of tapas.

When a reporter for *Diari de L'Hospitalet*, the local newspaper, asked Ferran not long ago what food influences, if any, he had drawn from his hometown, he quickly replied, "First of all, the taste for tapas." He also spoke fondly of the town tradition of the Sunday afternoon *"vermut,"* or "vermouth," meaning not literally the flavored wine of that name but the custom of stopping at a tapas bar for a *pica pica* (snack) and a glass of something cold. When asked where he liked to eat in Hospitalet today, he replied, "Any Andalusian tapas bar. They're magical." (His favorite is Casa Juan, famous for its tripe.)

Ferran's mother, Josefa Acosta Sanchez, known as Pepi, was born in Barcelona to an Andalusian mother and a father from Murcia. His father, Ginés Adrià Muñoz, comes from the Catalan town of Vilalba dels Arcs (Villalba de los Arcos in Spanish), about fifty miles west of the old Roman capital of Tarragona—a city where the Adrià name is common—but *his* mother, too, was from Murcia.

Pepi and Ginés met and married in Hospitalet, moving into one floor of a gray seven-story house on a narrow urban street lightened by a row of small tamarisk trees with metallic green needles. They have never moved. "People from the neighborhood say, 'Why are you still living here? Why don't you have a villa?'" Pepi tells me one day. "A lot of people don't even believe that we're the parents of Ferran Adrià because we don't have a big mansion and a big car. But why should we? We're simple people. We don't have to change our lives." Ferran and Albert still have their rooms at the house, too, and, until Ferran and his wife, Isabel, took a modest apartment of their own in an unfashionable neighborhood of Barcelona, he slept there whenever he was in the city.

Pepi is a calm, elegantly coiffed woman (she once helped out in a friend's beauty salon, next door to her house) with a quiet manner and warm, kind eyes. Ginés is sturdy looking and outgoing, with a face full of character, an apparently permanent tan, and a big, unself-conscious laugh; he looks like a good guy to have a beer with. Retired now, he worked as an *estucador*, or plasterer—which trade, especially during the housing boom of the 1960s, provided a comfortable living.

"Ferran was a very good boy," says Pepi. So, she quickly adds, was his brother, Albert, born in 1969. "They had good relations as brothers," she continues. "They never fought. When one talked, the other would listen. We never had any problems with them."

"They were different," Ginés reminds her.

"Oh, yes," says Pepi, "the boys were very different. Both were very calm, but Ferran was very affectionate, and from the start he had a brilliant memory. Albert was always a little cooler, and he doesn't have such a good memory. Sometimes he says things and then doesn't remember. 'We'll eat together tomorrow,' he'll say, and then he doesn't come. It's just that he forgot that he'd said that." The boys both left home at an early age—Ferran at seventeen, Albert at fifteen—but, says Pepi, "Even though they left, they have always remained part of the family. The concept of family is very strong with them."

A photograph of the brothers as youngsters shows them sitting at the table at home, looking rather bored, in front of anonymous-looking fried food of some kind. What, in fact, did the world's greatest chef and his brother eat growing up? I posed this question more than once to both Ferran and Albert. If you ask Ferran what his favorite meal was as a child, he usually says, "Steak and potatoes." He once claimed that he didn't discover his mouth until he was twenty. Albert, on the other hand, says, "We were always interested in eating. Every weekend our parents took us out, always to modest but good restaurants." (Ginés remembers particularly that they'd go to a place that specialized in lamb chops grilled over hot coals.) Albert also has vivid memories of a simple meal his father served every Sunday: "He'd put out salt cod with the skin and salt scraped off, but not soaked, and dump a bag of raw favas from the garden onto the table. My mother would bring out olives, capers, and tomatoes from the garden. Everybody made his own lunch."

I got a different story from Pepi. "As a child," she told me, "Albert didn't like to eat much. He was never as interested in food as Ferran was. Ferran didn't object all the time to what I served like Albert did. On the other hand, Ferran never went into the kitchen, and Albert did." She confirmed the simplicity of their diet: "We ate normally," Pepi remembered. "Steak, fried potatoes, spaghetti with tomato sauce—but I had to take the seeds out of the tomatoes. Albert hated the seeds."

"Our mother made very good stews," counters Albert. "Anything she could cook in a pot was excellent. Otherwise, as a cook, she was hopeless. Her pasta was horrible, dry and overcooked." (When Pepi mentioned the seeds, I thought immediately of a dish I'd had at El Bulli in 2006, a plate dotted with nothing but smears of pulp-dampened seeds of eight or ten kinds of vegetables; I thought it was very silly.) Tomato salad was also a staple. According to the German writer Manfred Weber-Lamberdière, who has written a book about Ferran that its subject calls "not always accurate," "Tomatoes were sacred to [Pepi] because it was that way in Murcia, where her family comes from."

"Neither boy liked garbanzos," Pepi continues, "and Albert wouldn't eat peas." Ferran adds bell peppers to the list. He still can't stand them, he says. "There's no reason. I just don't like them. I don't like morcilla [blood sausage] either." His wife told me, though, that Ferran loves spicy chiles and also the mild Basque frying peppers called guernikas and the pimientos de padrón of Galicia, which are mostly mild with an occasional hot one—about one in twelve, tradition says. (Ferran also, as I learned firsthand while lunching with him and Isabel one day, can eat food that is very hot in temperature; he popped a just-served little Chinese dumpling into his mouth happily, but when I did the same, my mouth was scalded. "Ferran likes food that way," his wife told me, just a little too late.)

Ferran has said that his most evocative childhood food memory is of his mother's tortilla española; whether or not it was the perfect classic potato omelette, he can't say, but he has a romantic image of it. "The boys liked eggs and tortillas better than soups," Pepi confirms. They probably also ate yogurt and related milk products, which first came into popularity when Ferran and Albert were young (the pioneering Danone firm was founded in Barcelona). Ferran liked licorice, and has confessed a "guilty pleasure" affection for Bollycao, a chocolate-filled Spanish relative of the infamous Hostess Twinkie. It has been said that as a boy, Ferran always had stains on his sweater from the chocolate, or from his mother's stew.

■ ■ ■

From the age of three until he was thirteen, Ferran attended the Colegio Casal dels Àngels, an elementary school near his house. A big institutional-looking place with an immense black cast-iron exterior staircase, it is directly across the street from Santa Eulàlia's covered market. I asked Ferran if he used to wander through the market before or after school, and he said no, but that he used to go there all the time with his mother. He claims to have no specific food memories of the place, though; "Above all," he says, "it reminds me of my mother and our neighbors."

Ferran was an athletic boy, wiry and energetic, and he started playing soccer for the local youth team, Joventut de l'Hospitalet. In 1975, he transferred to another school in the neighborhood, a parochial institution in a nondescript brick and concrete building next to the church of San Isidre. By this time, he was playing midfield for Santa Eulàlia Football Club, and getting increasingly serious about the possibility of a soccer career. He once told an interviewer that as a young man he had "wanted to be Cruyff, not Robuchon"—a reference to the legendary Dutch footballer Johan Cruyff, then playing for FC Barcelona. He also had an aptitude for mathematics, and in 1977, deciding that he would study business when he got to university, he enrolled in a preparatory program in professional administrative training at the Instituto Politécnico Virgen de la Merced (now known as the Institut d'Educació Secundària Mare de Déu de la Mercè), amidst the cranes and stacked cargo containers of Barcelona's Zona Franca, the city's massive commercial port area, which abuts l'Hospitalet. He did well in his studies, but was also a precocious habitué of the local discos, and apparently more or less lived for Thursday nights—there was no school on Fridays—when a long weekend of revelry began. After three years at the school, he dropped out. "If you asked me why," he says, "I couldn't tell you. It was just a decision I made one day." He had no immediate plans, other than to continue playing soccer and to get a job so that he could make enough money to spend the summer in Ibiza, the "party island" in the Balearics, off the Spanish coast.

His parents didn't seem particularly bothered by Ferran's intentions. Ginés, in fact, found Ferran a job: He had an old friend named Miquel Moy—they'd done their military service together—who was the chef at the Hotel Playafels, a comparatively upscale seaside property facing the long beach of Castelldefels, eight or ten miles southwest of the Barcelona airport. "Miquel and I went to a bar to have a beer one day," Ginés told me, "and I said to him, 'My son has quit school and needs to find a job. Maybe he would like to work at your hotel.'" Miquel replied that he could find him something to do in the kitchen. "I said, 'Miquel, I have to warn you: Fernando doesn't know anything about cooking at all.' At that moment, Fernando arrived at the bar. I explained that Miquel had agreed to hire him if he wanted the position, and he said, 'Okay, let's go.' That surprised me because he'd never shown the least bit of interest in the kitchen."

"The idea of working in a kitchen was nothing thrilling to me," Ferran told me one afternoon on the terrace at El Bulli, adding that he could have just as happily taken a job in a factory or an auto shop. "It was just a means to an end." At what point, I asked him, did he have his epiphany, realizing that he wanted to be a chef? "There was no one point when that happened," he replied. "It was very gradual. It took years." Astonishingly, I thought, considering the authority and originality with which he was apparently cooking as early as 1987, he added that it wasn't until 1990—when he and the dining room director Juli Soler bought El Bulli—that he really felt that he had to be a chef. "Up to that point," he said, "I still could have done any other kind of work."

■ ■ ■

Still lean and full of nervous energy, and sporting what might be described as a Catalan afro, Ferran reported to Moy's kitchen on June fifteenth, 1980—a Sunday. This was significant: "They wanted me to work on Sundays," says Ferran, "and Sunday was the day we played soccer, so I had to choose between the job and the playing field." He went to his soccer coach to ask frankly what his chances would be as a professional athlete, and was told that Third Division was probably the best he could hope for. That helped him make up his mind— though today he says, "If I had been more serious about soccer, I wouldn't be where I am today."

Ferran started as a *fregador*—a clean-up guy, a dishwasher—and that's what he was for about three months. Then, little by little, Moy let him start helping with some of the cooking. "This wasn't some saloon," Ferran told an Italian interviewer. "Miquel made tournedos Rossini, paella, things like that, and he worked like a slave. He was incredibly demanding of himself and everyone else. I've never met another chef who yelled so much or got angry so often. If you deviated only a little bit from what was for him the right way to do something, he'd start roaring terribly. He also demanded the utmost punctuality. If you arrived five minutes late, the heavens would open!" The first food Ferran ever cooked by himself for other people was a stew of flank steak and potatoes that he prepared one evening for the staff meal.

Moy was a good all-around chef in the old style, who had learned his craft in traditional Spanish kitchens. His bible was *El práctico*, a collection of 6,500 recipes from Spain, France, and elsewhere, written by two Argentinian chefs, Ramon Rabaso and Fernando Aneiros, and originally published in 1895. Moy gave a copy of the book to his young charge and challenged him to learn as many of the recipes as possible by heart. Ferran still has the book; I saw it one day, its red binding cracked and faded, on his desk at his Barcelona workshop.

He did most of his studying just before starting work, Ferran recalls. He didn't have time at night. When he got off work every evening, he'd go out with his co-workers to bars and discos, drinking beer or vodka until all hours of the morning. As the writer Xavier Moret puts it, Ferran was *molt amic de la festa*—a good friend of the party. "Under Moy," Ferran later remembered, "we could be up until eight a.m., but an hour later, we had to be in shape up to work normally and seriously. The rule was to arrive on time and stay right till the end." When he came in badly hungover one day, Moy asked him how to make a coulibiac—a complex French-inspired Russian dish of stuffed whole salmon wrapped in pastry. He passed the test. Years later, when he was in charge of his own kitchen at El Bulli, Ferran made his own chefs study *El práctico* to learn the classics. "He'd come into the kitchen in the morning and see you standing there," remembers his friend and protégé José Andrés, "and he'd say, 'Sauce Choron,' and you had to tell him how to make it." Andrés laughs and adds, "He still does that. I was giving a class with Ferran and translating for him at the Culinary Institute of America in Hyde Park, New York, in 2006, and he mentioned sauce américaine, and right away he turned to me and said 'José, what's in a sauce américaine? Who invented it?'"

One day, Ginés told me, "Miquel called me and said, 'Please take your son back, because now this boy knows more than me.'" He'd earned enough money by then, anyway, and in early March 1981, after nine months in Moy's kitchen, Ferran left to fulfill his dream of a long vacation in Ibiza. He had a month or so of leisure there and then, needing more money, talked himself into a job in the kitchen at a mid-range resort hotel called the Club Cala Llenya. After four months of cooking and partying and spending time on the beach in Ibiza, he went back home. He spent the next ten months doing brief stages in a succession of restaurants: a traditional-style place called El Suquet; a tapas bar inside Barcelona's El Bingo gaming parlor; Castell Arnau, a conference and party venue in a fourteenth-century villa in Sabadell, northwest of the city; a place called Martinica, back in town, where Ferran had what he calls his first contact with "modern cooking"; and finally, for two weeks, Finisterre, an elegant, old-style restaurant then considered to be among the city's best. At that point, he probably would have found himself a regular kitchen job—but he got drafted into the navy.

■ ■ ■

Ginés says that his son's culinary creations are, for him, "one of life's little pleasures"—which sounds like extravagant praise coming from this no-nonsense workingman. "We are very proud of Ferran, and of Albert, too," he says. Ginés and Pepi aren't regulars at El Bulli, however. "The first time we went to the restaurant," Pepi tells me, "I was a critic. I said to Ferran, 'You have to add something here, you should leave this out.' I don't remember what I ate, but probably it was salmon, which I'd never had before. I didn't like it very much." When they went on another occasion, she says, they sat at the chef's table in the kitchen. "But it was a very tense service," she recalls, "and Ferran was shouting. I was very worried, and didn't enjoy the meal. I was suffering all the time."

Ginés adds that the last time they ate at the restaurant, they thought it was very good. "There were a lot of dishes," he adds. "I remember we had quail eggs. It was simpler than today. There were more sauces, a piece of fish, a piece of meat. You could tell what things were more

---

easily." They haven't been back for five or six years, they tell me. "We go sometimes to visit Ferran, but not to eat," explains Pepi. "There is no room. We understand the problem with the tables." She adds, "I don't even have all of Ferran's books. He always gives me one when it comes out, but if he needs it for something, he takes it and it never gets replaced. Probably I have only two or three of them."

Both Ginés and Pepi still seem a little surprised by the celebrity their sons have achieved. But, says Ginés, "Today, people see only their success. What we know, as their parents, is that behind it all, they worked hard, very hard."

Soldado Fernando

"Some of the best chefs in Spain today came through me."

—Jorge Marin, former head butler to
Admiral Ángel Liberal Lucini,
in conversation with the author

In late September of 1982, when he was twenty, Ferran was drafted into Spain's then-obligatory military service and posted to the country's principal Mediterranean naval base, in Cartagena. His heart must have sunk when he learned of his posting: The other branches of the Spanish armed forces required fourteen-month tours of duty at the time, but for the navy, it was eighteen months. Nonetheless, there were frequent leaves—recruits had twenty or thirty days off for every forty to sixty days on duty—and Cartagena was a pleasant enough place. A sunny walled town of Carthaginian origins (hence its name) south of Valencia on the coast of Murcia—a region to which Ferran had family ties—it had been the seat of Spanish naval power since the eighteenth century, and later became a prosperous mining capital, and its city center was full of attractive fin-de-siècle buildings and had a stylish, faintly raffish air. There were also plenty of bars.

In the instructional barracks to which he was initially assigned, Ferran, fresh from the kitchen at Finisterre in Barcelona, volunteered for cook's duty, and spent a month preparing vast amounts of simple food for his fellow sailors. "We made potato tortillas for three thousand people," he later remembered, "with fresh eggs." It was in the barracks kitchen that Jorge Marin found him. Marin was the civilian *mayordomo*, or head butler, for the household of the base commander, the Barcelona-born Admiral Ángel Liberal Lucini. Lucini liked good food, and Marin was his talent scout. "About a thousand new recruits came here every three months," explains Marin, today a smartly dressed, avuncular gentleman who runs a small bar near one of Cartagena's main squares, when we meet for coffee in a café near his establishment. "I'd always ask them, 'Who among you has worked as a cook? Who has worked as a waiter?' And then I'd ask if they would be happy to be a cook or a waiter for the admiral. I never wanted to force them. It was important to find good cooks. You have to remember that until fairly recently, real cuisine in Spain was only for the nobility, and after them, the military ate the best."

Ferran quickly admitted that he'd had professional cooking experience. "I gave all the would-be cooks some tests," Marin continues. "'Where are you from? Do you know how to make a vichyssoise, a sauce béarnaise, poached eggs, consommé, mayonnaise, paella, canelones . . . ?' I'd rate the boys 'Bien,' 'Normal,' or 'Malo.' Fernando— that was his name then, and I'll always think of him that way, or by his nickname, Nando—was 'Bien.' He did very well on his test."

The admiral's residence was in an eighteenth-century palace in the center of town. The kitchen staff entered from a side street and climbed a back staircase to the second-floor kitchen. The staff entrance was well-situated: a few doors down was the Bar Salvador, where Ferran and his friends could usually be found after work. "Being in the kitchen was a good life for the boys," says Marin. "They had the freedom of teenagers." He adds that "Fernando always had long hair, while everyone else was neatly shorn. And he was always trying things in the kitchen, experimenting, dirtying dishes and then putting them in the washing-up." A photograph of Ferran from his navy days shows a wiry young man with a scraggly haircut (the afro has subsided), a faint moustache, and penetrating eyes staring straight at the camera; they seem to express simultaneously fearlessness, alertness, and a hint of surprise.

When he first went to work for the admiral, Ferran says, he thought it was a cushy posting, but he quickly realized that he not only had to think up new menus every day for the admiral's family, but also to conceive and execute serious banquets for visiting dignitaries. He had already learned the discipline of the professional kitchen, and now to that was added military discipline. "I hate to tell you what was implied when the two were put together," he later wrote. He also had to learn financial restraint. The admiral paid for his family meals himself, and, Ferran has said, it often seemed as though "the budget was in inverse proportion to the number of diners."

Three months after Ferran's arrival, in early 1983, the next wave of recruits appeared in Cartagena. One of them was Fermí Puig. Puig (pronounced approximately "pooch"), today the chef at two popular Barcelona restaurants, the elegant Drolma and the casual, traditional-style Petit Comité, came from Granollers, just northeast of Barcelona, where his family was in the business of packing and selling preserved truffles and wild mushrooms. Like Ferran, he had quit school young and gone to work in a restaurant, in his case as a waiter at MG in Barcelona, run by the pioneering "new Catalan" chef Montse Guillén. After a couple of months in the dining room, he decided that he'd rather be in the kitchen, so he called an old friend named Juli Soler. Since early 1981, Soler had been running the dining room at a French restaurant near Roses called El Bulli, and Puig asked if he could come up as a kitchen stagiare. Juli said okay. "My very first day in the kitchen," Puig recalls, "I had to skin one hundred fifty sole and pluck seventy-five ducks. I worked until four in the morning."

Puig quickly became part of the El Bulli family, and to improve his kitchen skills, he began devouring the Sacred Writ of France's nouvelle cuisine: a series of volumes by the genre's founding chefs, put out by the Parisian publisher Robert Laffont—among them *La cuisine c'est beaucoup plus que des recettes* by Alain Chapel, *La cuisine du marché* by Paul Bocuse, and *La grande cuisine minceur* by Michel Guérard.

Though he was three years older than Ferran, Puig had somehow avoided his compulsory military service—but the government caught up with him in Cala Montjoi, and he, too, was posted to Cartagena. When Jorge Marin addressed Puig's group of recruits looking for fresh kitchen staff, Puig was front and center. "As well as Fernando did on his test," Marin tells me, "Fermin was even better, because he'd read all the books. He knew things like how to remove the fat from a big pot of consommé by putting a hose down at the bottom and draining off the liquid. He could explain everything theoretically."

Puig quickly joined Ferran in the admiral's kitchen. "Ferran and I hit it off and became friends," says Puig. "He had no experience in haute cuisine, but I had all those Robert Laffont books with me, and we'd go through them to find dishes to make for the special occasions. We cooked things like sirloin Mary Stuart with grape sauce, noisettes of lamb with basil, Bocuse's *loup en croûte*, Guérard's *huré de saumon*. . . ."

"Fernando knew the practice, Fermín knew the theory," says Marin. "Together, they were the best. Fernando was the hands of Fermín." (For just an instant, when Marin said this, I had an image of Remy the rat sitting in Linguini the kitchen boy's toque and controlling his cooking in *Ratatouille*—an image that probably came to mind at least partly because Ferran voiced one of the minor characters, a diner asking for sweetbreads, in the Spanish version of the film; Guy Savoy played the part in the French edition.)

Marin remembers the huré de saumon—salmon "headcheese," in fact a kind of terrine of salmon with eggs and green peppercorns in a rich aspic—very well. "One night they were making this dish for a banquet the next day. It got late, and Fernando said to me, 'Go home, we'll take care of it.' The next morning at eight, I arrived to find Fernando asleep on the sofa. The other cooks said, 'Don't get mad at him. He worked until four A.M.' Apparently, he hadn't liked the way the huré looked, so he went back to the recipe, and maybe even telephoned Guérard, I don't know, and made it all over again. It was a big success, by the way."

On another occasion, Ferran and Puig bought a huge fish of some kind at the market, a monster weighing twenty pounds or more. The admiral's wife took one look at it resting on the kitchen shelf and left the room without a word. The two chefs decapitated the fish, cleaned it, and trimmed it into manageable shape. It ended up about one-third its original size. Marin was angry and accused the two of saving some for themselves. At that moment, the admiral's wife walked back through the kitchen and said, "Thank God someone had the sense to arrange this terrible fish. It looked like a sofa!" She later told an interviewer that she'd always had confidence in Ferran and Puig, even when they prepared modern dishes that she'd never heard of.

Ferran's bibliography lists *El sabor del Mediterráneo*, published in Barcelona in 1993, as his first book. It was certainly his first conventionally published one, but while he was working for the admiral, Ferran spent months working with Puig and the admiral's pastry chef on a collection of recipes meant as a gift for the admiral's wife. Composed on an old Olivetti typewriter, it had no title or index or page numbers. It included recipes for dishes the team had served at official banquets, but also some "daydreams"—recipes for dishes Ferran had never had the materials (or possibly the nerve) to prepare. One of these was paupiettes (thin rolls) of crayfish with bacon and a sauce of garlic, fish fumet, *glace de viande* (concentrated veal or beef stock), olive oil, and cream. "Ferran included imaginary dishes in the book," confirms Puig. "He thought up dishes that we had never cooked, in other words, things that had never been heard of before in any kitchen, and we wrote the recipes." Two copies of the book were made, and someone ran off three more surreptitiously. Neither Ferran nor Puig kept one, but a copy was presented to Ferran at a reunion of the old navy crew in 2008.

Though they worked hard, especially for official banquets—Puig says that on at least one occasion, Marin called Ferran back from leave to cook for an important dignitary—the two young Catalans enjoyed privileged status on the base. The admiral and his wife treated them like family, says Puig. They shared the lowest rank in the Spanish armed forces, *soldado* (soldier), but they had their own apartment, with television, apart from the regular barracks, and were exempt from drills and military busy-work. "Nobody would touch the admiral's chefs," remembers Puig. "We dressed as chefs, not sailors. We used to order one of the admiral's cars and a driver to take us to the market. When other sailors would see the car coming down the street with the flags flying, they'd stand at attention—but it was only us." They became celebrities at the market, and always concluded their purchases with a sandwich at some friendly stand and a bottle or two of beer. Along with their friend and colleague Ramiro Buj, the admiral's pastry chef, they became known as "the Mambo Kings." Sometimes, Puig admits, they took advantage of the situation. "More than once we were almost 'exiled to Maó,'" he says—a navy term for being banished to a far-off post for insubordination. (Maó, or Mahon, is the capital of Minorca in the Balearic Islands.)

On occasion, says Puig, either he or Ferran would climb through the transom into Marin's office with an empty bottle of the cheap Spanish whisky they usually drank, and fill it with Chivas Regal from the admiral's store, and then later sip their booty openly in their room. Marin noticed, but let them get away with it. He also gave them work on the side: The admiral and his family had a house on a tiny island across from La Manga del Mar Menor, about twenty miles east of Cartagena, and Ferran and Puig and two or three waiters would accompany them when they went to stay there. Marin owned a disco nearby, and when they were off duty with the admiral, they'd go and work for him, cooking burgers and pizza for hungry teenagers until five or six in the morning—"making money, drinking, looking for girls," says Puig—and then fall asleep on couches in the back. "We were nobody," Puig tells me, "but we were human, passionate, and always ready to learn."

As the time approached for Ferran to take his summer leave, he began making plans to go home to Hospitalet de Llobregat. Puig had another idea. "Whether it was a case of the new boy trying to impress the old hand," Ferran has written, "or just a way to share experiences outside the military, Fermí tried to convince me that I should spend my break doing a stage at the restaurant he'd worked at, El Bulli." Puig called Juli and asked him to take Ferran on for a month as a favor. "It was evident that he was a very good cook," Puig says, "and I really thought it would be good for him and for the restaurant if he went." Ferran's first reaction was that he had no intention of spending his vacation in another kitchen. But it has two stars in the *Guide Michelin*, Puig said, and it's one of the best restaurants in Spain. Ferran barely knew what the *Guide Michelin* was, and remained unimpressed. Then Puig pointed out that there was a beautiful beach just outside the doors of the restaurant, and that pretty girls came there from all over Europe, and Ferran began to consider the idea—and finally relented.

Puig's leave came at a different time, so Ferran was on his own, but following his friend's instructions, he made his way to Roses and showed up at a waterfront bar called La Sirena. One of the El Bulli waiters met him there and drove him up the road to Cala Montjoi. It was little more than a "goat track" in those days, Ferran remembers, and not at all the kind of thoroughfare that would lead to a fancy restaurant, and he began to seriously consider the possibility that Puig was playing some elaborate practical joke on him.

Arriving at El Bulli, Ferran was remanded to the kitchen, and the care of chef Jean-Paul Vinay. He acquitted himself well. "That month," Ferran has written, "was highly intense in all senses of the word. . . . [T]here was the work itself, stimulating and new, but also the nights out in Roses. Professionally speaking, the stint in El Bulli was a real immersion in the world of haute cuisine, since it was the first time I had heard of all the trappings of this world: the critics, the running of a restaurant, gourmet guides, and so on." After he'd been at El Bulli for three weeks, says Puig, "Juli called to say, 'Hey, Fermí, no offense, but that guy you sent, Fernando, he's much better than you.'" Ferran returned to Cartagena with an agreement to come to work full-time at El Bulli when he finished his military service.

Jumpin' Jack Juli

*"[Juli is] vital and positive, king of the art of improvisa-
tion, who can, from nothing, make something great and
magical."*

—Xavier Sagristà, *Entre mar i muntanya:
Apunts de cuina a l'Empordà*

Juli Soler: Director of the dining room at El Bulli since 1981. Co-
owner of the place, with Ferran, since 1990. Winner of numerous
prizes as best maître d'hôtel in Spain, best maître d'hôtel in Europe.
Co-author of at least eight El Bulli books. The restaurant's reluctant
financial manager, personnel wrangler, and detail man. Alter ego,
henchman, sounding board, and professional helpmeet to the world's
greatest chef. Without Juli Soler, there would be no El Bulli as we
know it today, and probably no Ferran Adrià.

■ ■ ■

September 2008. Juli and I have just had a good lunch—*jamón ibérico*
and rice with lobster—at Mar y Sol in Roses, during which we talked
about his past and many other things. Over coffee, I mention the new
billboard I've just noticed as you enter the town: a huge portrait of

Ferran, above the legend "Roses Celebrates the Best Restaurant in the World." Juli smiles and shakes his head. "The best restaurant in the world? I say El Bulli is the best restaurant in Cala Montjoi. What does 'best' mean? There are only two kinds of restaurants, good and bad. And there are only two kinds of cuisine, good and bad." Then he stands up and says, "Come on."

He is driving me back along the waterfront in his off-white Voyager to my hotel two coves over. We've barely pulled out of our parking space when he punches on the CD player. On come the Rolling Stones, *loud*, singing "Stupid Girl." I look over at Juli. He has a big, dark smile on his face and is grooving to the music, rocking back and forth, slapping his hands on the steering wheel in rhythm with Charlie Watts. As Jagger sings, "I'm not talkin' about the kind of clothes she wears," he points theatrically to a badly dressed tourist crossing the street in front of us. "This saved my life!" he yells over the beat. "This song?" I yell back. He shakes his head. "No, *music*! Music saved my life! Music makes life worthwhile!" Well, yes—but if music saved Juli Soler's life, he saved El Bulli's, more than once.

Juli Soler Lobo was born in 1949 in Terrassa, a onetime textile manufacturing capital about fifteen miles northwest of Barcelona. His father, also named Juli, was head waiter in the dining room of a small spa hotel in the area, and the younger Juli's first job, at the age of ten, was as an apprentice waiter there. He worked at several other local restaurants over the next few years, and then, when he was sixteen, got a job in Barcelona in the dining room of what he calls "the best restaurant in Spain" at the time—Reno, a superbly run old-style establishment that for years set the standard in the Catalan capital.

In 1966, Juli went back to work for his father, who had taken over the employee canteen at an electrical company near Terrassa. Their contract required them to feed breakfast and lunch five days a week to five hundred workers for ten pesetas (less than twenty cents) apiece, and Juli later said that this was where he first learned the importance of keeping tight control of expenses. He liked the job, though, because it left his evenings and weekends free, leaving him plenty of time for . . . music.

He practically lived in the discos and jazz clubs of Terrassa and other nearby towns. He even became a DJ in a couple of them in the late sixties, and then, in 1972, after he completed his military service, he opened a record shop in Terrassa called Transformer—after Lou Reed's breakthrough album—buying LPs tax-free in Andorra and driving them discreetly back home in the trunk of his car. After he closed the shop in 1978, he helped his friend Ramon Parellada open a combination disco, music club, and restaurant in Granollers called La Sila, which offered live performances of jazz, rock, folk, blues, and traditional Catalan music. (This is where Granollers native Fermí Puig first met Juli and became his friend.) He made a tentative beginning as a concert promoter, arranging an appearance in Terrassa by the acclaimed American jazz and fusion bassist Stanley Clarke. The Rolling Stones, he has said, were the soundtrack of his life; somebody dubbed him "Jumpin' Jack Juli." Then, suddenly, in 1980, he says, he decided that he'd had enough, that he was burnt out on the scene. "Stop the show!" he says (in English). "I left it all, like *that*. I wanted to change my life."

Meanwhile, back at Cala Montjoi, Jean-Louis Neichel had decided to quit El Bulli when it closed for its annual two-month vacation in January, to open a restaurant of his own in Barcelona. "I wanted to do something for myself," Neichel explains. "I kept asking Dr. Schilling to sell or lease the restaurant to me, and he always refused." Neichel had been restaurant director as well as chef, so his departure would leave vacancies to be filled in both the kitchen and the front of the house. His sous-chef, Yves Krämer, agreed to keep things going in the kitchen, and Marketta started looking for someone to run the dining room.

After Juli stopped the show, he took a vacation in Roses, staying with his friend Silvia Breuer, who owned the town's Barbarossa jazz club and disco. Breuer had known Marketta since 1968, and she and Juli had dined once at El Bulli. When Juli told her that he wanted to do something different with his life, she had the inspiration—knowing that he'd worked in restaurants as a young man—to recommend him to Marketta. He and Marketta met over coffee and he agreed to come to the restaurant for an interview with Dr. Schilling.

"My interview was set for noon on the day after Christmas," as Juli later recounted, "and on Christmas night, as usual, I did well for myself. The next morning I had planned to get up at ten to go to El Bulli, but punctuality isn't my strong suit, and I slept for two more hours. Finally, I started for Cala Montjoi. I had no car, so I began to walk. I was wearing a sheepskin coat and even though it was late December, the sun was hot. I went two kilometers, then another two, and the road got steeper and steeper. I had run out of breath when a car came around the bend and stopped and gave me a ride." When he arrived, he found the Schillings waiting impatiently for him, about to sample Neichel's New Year's Eve dinner menu. They invited him to join them, and the three settled down to a sophisticated meal of pâté de foie gras with a mousse of local thrushes; warm terrine of fresh truffles, saltwater crayfish, and sea urchins; and rare, lightly smoked Barbarie duck. As they ate, says Juli, "Dr. Schilling told me that he wanted to bring the best of Europe to El Bulli, all the newest things from all the top restaurants, and that he wanted his customers to be comfortable and happy. He cared more about that, he said, than he did about making money. He told me that it was his policy to send or take his staff to tour restaurants around the continent—not just the ones he wanted to emulate, but also those that did things badly, so that his people could appreciate the difference. I liked that. That's the only reason I went to work for El Bulli."

Juli admitted to Dr. Schilling that he had had little experience of top-class restaurants or fine wines. Since the restaurant was about to close for two months for its annual vacation, the doctor suggested that Juli should use the time to travel around France, Belgium, and Germany, at his expense, eating and observing. As a part of the experience, the doctor arranged for Juli to do a one-month stage in the dining room at one of his favorite restaurants, the two-star L'Orangerie in Düsseldorf. Every Sunday, when the place was closed, the doctor would pick up Juli and take him out to other restaurants, pointing out details of service or presentation and saying, "This, one must do" or "This, one must not do." One day at L'Orangerie, somebody from Pink Floyd, who were doing a concert in town, called to make a reservation for dinner after the show. The restaurant would ordinarily have been closed by the time they wanted to come in, says Juli. "But I told the owner we should stay open, that this would be great publicity. I don't think he really knew who they were, but he finally agreed. They came with a large group, and the owner said, 'I should ask them to sign a menu, but I don't know which ones are the musicians.' I said, 'Don't worry, I'll take care of it.' There were stories in all the newspapers the next day, and it was very good for the restaurant."

His exposure to fine restaurants away from Cala Montjoi helped Juli understand the problems and challenges he would face back home, he says, and he returned to El Bulli ready to take charge. He immediately named Yves Krämer as Neichel's official successor in the kitchen—and then confronted his first crisis. The seasonal opening coincided with Holy Week, and El Bulli was packed with customers not only from the surrounding area and Barcelona but from Germany and France. They'd even hung a "Reservations Only" sign on the door, which was a rare occurrence. A group from Perpignan arrived one day, and said, "We have noticed that you're no longer in the Michelin guide." This was news to Juli and Marketta. They hadn't been notified by Michelin and they didn't have a copy of the new edition at the restaurant. After the service that day, Juli drove to Figueres and found one in a bookshop. It was true: no El Bulli. The Michelin star had helped draw diners from France and beyond, and had also brought the restaurant to the attention of some of those Spanish "snobs" Jean-Louis Neichel mentioned—so being omitted was a serious matter.

Juli thought it was vital to act fast and decisively. "I went to Marketta, and said, 'We have to go to Paris,'" he tells me. Marketta rarely left Cala Montjoi, but she realized that this was important, so the day after Easter Sunday, she, Juli, and Yves Krämer drove up toward the French capital. Not wanting to miss an opportunity to expand his experience of top restaurants, Juli routed them through Burgundy, where they stopped for dinner and the night at the three-star Lameloise in Chagny. In Paris the next morning, they found their way to the Michelin offices and Juli went into a phone booth across the street, called, and said, "I'd like to make an appointment to discuss our restaurant." "What day would you like?" they asked. "We're at the door," Juli replied. A representative of the guide agreed to see them, and offered an explanation: Because El Bulli had closed down for its annual winter break in mid-January, when the guide was being prepared, somebody—obviously somebody who hadn't been following the past patterns of the place very closely—assumed that it had closed for good. There was nothing to be done in 1981, but Michelin promised to send an inspector back to the restaurant and to consider reinstating the star in the next year's edition. A few months later, a man who had lunched alone at the restaurant came up to Juli after paying his check and said, "Look, don't hit me—I'm a Michelin inspector." He asked for a tour of the place, and asked Juli some questions. When he left, Juli felt confident that El Bulli's star would be restored.

Yves Krämer was an old-style cook, a workhorse, who could do anything in the kitchen—but Dr. Schilling found his food less than inspiring, and only a few months after Juli had installed him as chef, he asked Juli to bring on a new, more contemporary-minded sous-chef. This was Jean-Paul Vinay, a young man who had done stages at Michel Guérard and at Jacqueline Fénix in Paris, and was a chef de partie—in charge of one station in the kitchen—at the well-respected Chez Nandron in Lyon when the doctor encountered him. Dr. Schilling also engaged Vinay's girlfriend, Annick Janin, a pastry chef who was working at another Lyon restaurant, La Tour Rose. "We came for the beach," Vinay told me. "I love the sea. I thought of this new job as a vacation."

"Vinay brought a lot to the kitchen in terms of organization and precision," Juli later said, "and he was a representative of French modernity." He was also, it quickly became apparent, a very good chef. After he had worked under Krämer for a few months, Juli called both chefs into his office and, with Dr. Schilling's blessing, told them that he wanted them to switch places, with Krämer becoming Vinay's sous-chef. Krämer shrugged and agreed. Juli's instinct was a good one, and the kitchen started humming. In 1982, Michelin gave El Bulli its star back. In 1983, the restaurant got its second one—making Vinay, then only twenty-six, the youngest two-star chef in Europe.

In April of that year, on Vinay's recommendation, Dr. Schilling hired yet another young French chef, a Lyonnais named Kristian Lutaud, who had worked at the celebrated Troisgros. Again, Juli reorganized the kitchen, with Lutaud taking Krämer's sous-chef position, and Krämer moving down another rung—"a strange situation," says Lutaud today. (Krämer left after about a year and went to work as Jean-Louis Neichel's chef de cuisine in Barcelona; he died suddenly several years later.) The same year, the Schillings decided to enclose a portion of the restaurant's sprawling open terrace, constructing a second dining room with a ceiling crossed by ancient wood beams salvaged from an old house and windows offering dazzling views of the Mediterranean.

Though Vinay used as many local products as he could, and included an occasional Spanish- or Catalan-style dish in his menus (one of them, for instance, lists an adobo of cuttlefish and pigs' feet—pure Catalonia), the cooking at El Bulli during this period was mostly modern French. The menus included such dishes as duck terrine with truffle aspic, trout mousse with rosemary cream, civet of Roses crayfish, oysters in red wine, frogs' legs and watercress soup, scallops with ceps, roast turbot with orange sauce, salmon baked in gray salt, rabbit saddle with parsley broth, and chartreuse of pigeon. The periodical *El Cinco Días* noted that a visit to El Bulli was "an obligatory experience to know French cuisine, and without crossing the border."

Lutaud maintains that, without question, Vinay was the best classically trained French chef in Spain in that era. Janin, meanwhile, was by this time producing what was by all accounts a spectacular array of desserts every day, earning El Bulli a reputation for having what might have been Spain's best pastry cart (two carts, in fact, to hold all the treasures). The three—Vinay and Janin (who had gotten married by this time) and Lutaud—were clearly a formidable team.

Despite the quality of its food and its two Michelin stars, however, the restaurant struggled through much of the year. "Outside of the summer months," Fermí Puig remembers, "there wasn't a lot to do at El Bulli. We were closed from January fifteenth to March fifteenth, but for many weeks before we closed every year and for the first few months after we reopened, it was very slow. We spent a lot of time playing soccer in the campgrounds or fishing for crabs—or just 'catching flies.' I remember nights of sitting around the radio with Marketta and Juli listening to a soccer match, waiting for somebody to come to the door. There was one couple that lived nearby, and there were nights when they were our only customers. At some point in the evening, if even they hadn't shown up, we'd say to Marketta, 'Señora, I don't think they're coming tonight,' and she'd tell us to close up. Sometimes, one of the waiters would sneak outside around nine or nine-thirty and turn out the lights without telling her, just to make sure we didn't have any late visitors. Those nights, we just cooked for ourselves and Marketta, and made 'meals for the children'—Marketta's dogs."

Juli sometimes used an interesting technique to juggle what customers there were: When people would call for a reservation on, say, a Wednesday, Juli would say, "Oh, no, unfortunately we're full on Wednesday," which wasn't true at all. Then perhaps Thursday? they'd say. "Let me look . . . ah, no, I'm afraid not. Full again." Well, what about Friday? "Um . . . yes, you have good luck, we have a nice table for you on Friday." So of course everyone would come on Friday, the restaurant would be full, and they'd all say, "It's been busy every night. This is the first time we could get in."

Sometimes, says Puig, "Juli also did things that make me think of Groucho Marx. He had an office with a glass window in the door, and when you'd call him, he'd stick his head out the window and he was all elegant with a shirt, tie, and jacket. When the door opened, though, we would realize that he wasn't wearing pants, and he'd go out into the restaurant like that." Puig tells me another story about a way Juli had of tormenting one of their longtime waiters—a story that involves one of the man's physical attributes—but he makes me swear not to repeat it.

■ ■ ■

"Juli is crazy," almost everybody says, usually with an understanding smile. ("Crazy like a fox" is sometimes the next phrase heard.) When I mention to one of Juli's friends that I've been talking with him, he says, in a tone that betrays his affection for the man, "In what language? Martian?" One day when Ferran is running down the structure of the dining room staff for me, I ask where, in the current incarnation of the place, Juli fits in, and he replies, "Oh, Juli . . . Paf!" with a gesture that seems to say, "I can't possibly explain." He pauses for a moment, then adds, "No one can understand my relationship with Juli. It's impossible."

One day I spent much of the afternoon and early evening in the kitchen at El Bulli, and then, when the dinner service was about to begin, I got ready to leave, to drive down the hill and pick up my wife for dinner in Girona, at El Celler de Can Roca. When I'd mentioned to Juli earlier that I wasn't quite sure how to find the place, he said, "Very easy." He tore a sheet of paper from a notebook and quickly filled it with lines and X's, circles and squares. "You'll get off the autoroute here," he said, pointing to an X. "Take the main road all the way"—his pen hovered over a squiggly line. "At the last roundabout before you enter the city limits, there's a big hospital"—a square with an X in the middle—"and you take *this* road"—another line. "There it is!" (a box). I thanked him profusely and headed out the back door of the kitchen to where I'd parked my rented Jetta, knowing that I wouldn't be back at El Bulli until after I'd finished writing this book— until the following season at the earliest.

Juli followed me out. His Voyager was parked near my car, behind the restaurant near the kitchen door. "Get in," he said. "My car's right here," I replied, thinking that he was offering to give me a ride to the regular parking lot. "Get in," he repeated. "No," I said, now imagining that he wanted to drive me someplace to show me something, "I've got to get going." "*Get in!*" Okay, I figured, I'd better get this over with. I got in and so did he. He turned on the ignition. The CD player came on. It was—what else?—the Stones. "Start Me Up." Loud as usual. He powered down the windows. He turned the sound up louder. In a kind of static echo of our drive back from lunch a few months earlier, he played the steering wheel like a conga drum and the whole car rocked as he pumped his body back and forth. He mimed driving fast, recklessly, jerking the wheel back and forth. He smiled maniacally, and a little conspiratorially; he seemed lit up from within. Then it was over. He stopped moving, turned off the CD, put up the windows, nodded to me, and got out. A few of the stagiares, who had been sitting on the kitchen step smoking, looked over, vaguely amused, as if nothing Juli did would surprise them anymore but they expected it to have surprised me. It didn't. I realized that this had just been Juli's way of saying good-bye. We shook hands and touched foreheads—an expression of greeting and leave-taking he favors—and I got into my own car and drove off thinking with a grin about "Jumpin' Jack," and wondering if any other kind of person would have had the imagination and the impetus to keep El Bulli together, or could have given Ferran the kind of support—at once practical and a little insane (*seny* and *rauxa*)—that has allowed him to flourish. I doubt it.

Juli's unconventional improvised map, incidentally, turned out to be eerily accurate, and we found the restaurant without a hitch.

7

Disco-Beach

"We knew that we had to be serious and professional, but we were very young and wanted to enjoy ourselves, too. To combine both interests wasn't easy."

—Ferran Adrià, in conversation with the author

Ferran completed his military service in mid-December of 1983. Because El Bulli wasn't set to reopen after its annual winter break until mid-March of 1984, he traveled south, to Seville, and worked for two months in the kitchen at a local institution called Restaurant San Marcos. Fermí Puig, having begun his own tour in the navy three months later than Ferran, finished his service just before the new El Bulli season started. He and Ferran met in Barcelona a few days before they were to report to work and set off for Cala Montjoi in Puig's old Citröen Deux Chevaux, a journey that would ordinarily take not much more than a couple of hours. It took them three days. They spent a day and a night visiting—and eating and drinking with—Puig's friends in Granollers, then drove up to Blanes, on the Costa Brava, to visit one of their former colleagues from the admiral's kitchen in Cartagena. The day after that, they stopped at a series of restaurants for more food and drink on the way to Roses, finally arriving at El Bulli the night before the reopening.

The next morning, Ferran was promptly assigned the post of chef de partie for meats, while Puig was given responsibility for seafood. Ferran must have been at least a little bit intimidated by the Gallic troika that ran the kitchen—he was only twenty-one when he arrived, and unlike Vinay, Janin, and Lutaud had no experience in serious French restaurants—but he kept his head down and worked hard. "Right from the first," Juli says, "he was very serious, very rigorous, and he paid attention to the details. He always knew if there were three sardines in the frigo or none. Marketta and I saw that he had extraordinary ability and willingness to work hard, a lot of heart."

When it was quitting time, though, Ferran knew how to have fun. The chefs and dining room staff were all friends, and drinking buddies. The first night he went to a disco with Juli, Ferran later admitted, he ended up crawling on the floor. Some weeks, when the restaurant closed for the evening on Sunday night, the whole staff would head for Barcelona for "party time," returning only Tuesday morning. They went out most nights during the week, too. "We'd work until midnight or so, assuming we had customers," says Puig, "and then everybody went to the discos in Roses to meet Swedish girls." (The liberalizing effects of the Swedish girls, or *suecas*—who might have been from Sweden, or from Denmark or Holland or anywhere else in northern Europe—who crowded Spain's beaches and bars in the latter Franco years, bringing along very little clothing and very few inhibitions, were legendary.) "People knew us everywhere," Puig continues, "so we got invited for our drinks, and didn't need very much money. We stayed out all night. We had to start work every morning at ten A.M., and often we wouldn't get back to the restaurant until nine. We hadn't slept. We'd all crowd into the walk-in refrigerator to try to sober up in the cold. We were a fantastic family. We were very young. . . ."

El Bulli's longtime jack-of-all-trades, José Lozano, was hardly young by that time, but he spent many nights in Roses, too—often in the company of the restaurant's dishwasher, a short, mustachioed, gap-toothed Moroccan named Ali (nobody remembers his last name), who was sometimes photographed in a T-shirt with a thin black bow tie knotted around his bare neck. "José and Ali were very close friends," says Puig, "and also friends of red wine. They both had very small motorbikes, and on their nights off, they'd ride downhill to town to drink and watch soccer matches. They'd always park in front of the Guardia Civil barracks. By three or four in the morning, if the bikes were still there, the Guardia would go out looking for them in the bars, then put them and their bikes in a police car and drive them back to El Bulli."

Everybody liked Ali—"He was an institution," Puig says—but he was often the butt of practical jokes around the kitchen. A waiter would dress up like Dracula and hide in the walk-in, and somebody would send Ali to get more onions there. Or someone would set fire to the rags Ali always had hanging from his waist, provoking yelps loud enough to be heard in the dining room. If this sounds cruel, says José Andrés, who knew Ali in the late eighties, it really wasn't. "I think Ali waited for those tricks," he says. "He was also very theatrical and his exaggerated reactions were deliberate." Andrés adds that, from the beginning, Ferran had a close relationship with both Ali and Lozano; "I always admired that," he says.

The chefs in this era may have been a family, but Daddy wasn't happy. "Things were very hard in the summer of eighty-four," says Puig. "Vinay had started a low-intensity war with Juli. It's hard to say what it was about. They were both just angry about the kinds of things that happen in a restaurant." When I press him for details, he adds, "It was lot of nonsense. Juli had hired some young waiters who were friends of his, good people, and this gave Jean-Paul the impression that the discipline in the dining room had relaxed a little. Then there were ridiculous rules like Juli prohibiting the kitchen staff from drinking Coca-Cola—things like that." In Ferran's view, it basically came down to a personality clash between the two men. "Vinay and Juli," he says, "were two men whose characters just didn't match. And Jean-Paul thought that he was a great chef while Juli was only the head of the dining room." Puig adds that Vinay and his wife had been thinking for some time about starting a place of their own, even to the point of having invested in a quantity of Villeroy & Boch china, which they stored in Lyon for the day when they'd need it. "The stress of living through an August at El Bulli, which was the busiest time, magnified the situation," Puig continues, "and by late August, Jean-Paul had already started telling people privately in the kitchen that he planned to leave at the end of the season." When I asked Vinay, twenty-five years later, why he departed, he replied that, like the chef Jean-Louis Neichel, he had simply wanted to have some equity. "I asked Dr. Schilling again and again if I could buy or lease El Bulli," he told me, "but he always said no."

An architect and restaurant owner from Madrid, who had earlier tried to lure Juli to the Spanish capital to run a restaurant there and who had bankrolled Jean-Louis Neichel's Barcelona place, offered backing to Vinay. "The deal was off and on," says Ferran, but an agreement was finally reached. Not only his pastry-chef wife but three key members of the dining room staff elected to go with him, as if they couldn't imagine El Bulli without Vinay. Fermí Puig decided that he would leave, too. "Jean-Paul was my head chef," Puig explains, "and I wanted to follow him." (Vinay's new place, La Ciboulette in Barcelona, lasted for about three years.)

Vinay's departure set off shock waves. "It was a disaster for El Bulli when I left," Vinay says today, not inaccurately. The Schillings felt betrayed by his decision and saw their dreams of gastronomic prominence dissipate. Ferran says that even Juli, for all his problems with Vinay, was "very sad" when he left. The kitchen and the dining room alike were demoralized; everyone's faith in the future of the restaurant was shaken. But if Vinay hadn't left, it turns out, there might have been significant changes at the restaurant anyway. Even before Vinay had made public his decision, Lutaud, Ferran, and a popular waiter named Toni Gerez were hatching a plan to defect. A woman who ran a little *chiringuito* on the beach below El Bulli had offered them the chance to take over a restaurant in Setcases, a pretty little stone village on the River Ter, high in the Pyrénées, a good two-hour drive inland from Cala Montjoi. Why were they thinking of leaving—especially Ferran, who had just barely arrived? "We were doing well at El Bulli," Lutaud explains, "but we were thirsty for new adventures. It's as simple as that."

Full of casual restaurants, bars, pensions, and two-star hotels, Setcases has a not unpleasant modest-level touristy feel to it (the ski resort Vallter 2000 is nearby), and while it's much farther from "civilization" than Cala Montjoi, it is also more easily accessible, being just a few miles off a main road crossing the Pyrénées. The three would-be refugees from El Bulli scraped together a deposit of 100,000 pesetas, then about seven hundred dollars, and put it down on the establishment they thought they could turn into something of their own. (Neither Ferran nor Lutaud has set foot in Setcases for decades, and neither had the least recollection of where their proposed restaurant was, but Gerez remembers clearly that it was in "the first small house on the left as you drive into town.") Today, it's difficult to imagine how Ferran would have evolved in the mountains, away from the sea, in a town full of tourists. "It is certain," he says when I ask him what kind of restaurant he would have had in Setcases, "that it wouldn't have been like El Bulli. I couldn't have done this level of gastronomy there."

Juli, meanwhile, valiantly tried to hold El Bulli together. Vinay was already out the door, and Lutaud and Ferran were preparing to follow, so he turned to Puig. The most popular of the local discos with the El Bulli crew—somebody even once called it "the El Bulli of discos"—was Chic, a sprawling, halfheartedly mock-Moorish struc-ture behind two mute black plywood towers that had opened in 1980 at the edge of Roses on the main road to Figueres. Juli, not only a habitué of Chic but a friend of the proprietor, had the run of the place. Confronting the impending mass exodus from El Bulli, says Puig, "Juli took me to Chic and borrowed the owner's office, and we sat there and had a drink. 'Look,' he said to me, 'stay with us and I'll send you around to all the best European restaurants for two or three years to learn, and then come back and I'll make you head chef.' But I had already decided that I wanted to go with Vinay, so I said, 'No. But I'll do something important for you: I'll tell you to forget about me, but that you must keep Ferran and Lutaud.'" Do you think they will stay? asked Juli. Puig said he'd try to convince them.

"Ferran and I had been living in a little room next to the kitchen," Puig continues, "with no furniture except for two beds and a Juve y Camps cava case as a table. We got the keys to the kitchen at two A.M. that night and went in and grabbed a bottle of wine and a very big dish of rabbit confit and took them back to our room. I told Ferran that he was wrong to leave, and that even if it meant forfeiting the deposit in Setcases, his future should be here at El Bulli. I kept working on him, and finally convinced him. The next day, we all went back to the of-fice at Chic—Ferran, Lutaud, Juli, and me—and I talked them into working out a deal between them." Everyone was happy except Vinay. "The truth is," Lutaud told me, "that Jean-Paul was angry at Ferran and me when we decided to stay."

According to Puig, "Lutaud was a fantastic chef, but, like me, he was a little lazy. We named him 'Slow-Hand,' like Eric Clapton. Fer-ran was different. He was a very hard worker. In that aspect of his life, he is just absolutely passionate. You can party with him but when he works, he works." Juli saw a creative streak in Ferran, too. "Ferran was Frank Zappa," says Juli. It was Juli's inspiration to ask Ferran and Lutaud to run the kitchen as a team, and for two and a half years after

Vinay's departure in November of 1984, El Bulli had two head chefs. "I thought they'd keep Vinay's menu, at least for a little while," says Puig, "but they immediately introduced a new menu of their own. The only thing they kept was the terrine of foie gras." (In fact, as an economic imperative, they also turned out some conventional dishes at lunchtime—grilled fish, entrecôte béarnaise—for the touristic clientele that climbed up from the beach.)

A trip the two chefs made to Madrid inspired an innovation that Ferran later described as one of the "iconic dishes" of his career. The ancient preservation technique of escabeche ("escabetx" in Catalan) involves cooking fish or poultry (and occasionally meat) in olive oil and then marinating it in oil, vinegar, and spices. Dining at a Madrid institution called Currito, Ferran and Lutaud ordered partridge en escabeche, with the bird still on the bone, a typical dish in informal settings, but not something usually seen in upscale restaurants. They decided on the spot to refine it for their own menu, and when they returned to Cala Montjoi, they produced a boned pigeon marinated escabeche-style—a dish soon being imitated in Barcelona and beyond.

Dr. Schilling continued to arrive at Cala Montjoi several times a year, his appearance anticipated as if he were Santa Claus—a not inappropriate comparison, because the trunk of his Mercedes was always full of presents for the restaurant: cutlery, glassware, and china from Germany, great wines and brandies from France. It sometimes took him a month to drive from Germany to Spain because he made so many stops along the way. He also continued to invite his staff to come with him in the other direction, to good restaurants in France and elsewhere, for inspiration and new ideas. There is a story that the doctor's staff had become so well-known for their research trips at some establishments that one day, when Juli ordered a certain dish at Alain Chapel, the waiter jokingly said, "No, don't take that one. It'll be too hard to copy."

When the restaurant closed for its annual winter vacation in early 1985, Dr. Schilling arranged for Ferran to do a two-week stage at Georges Blanc in Vonnas—Ferran's first hands-on experience in a real French kitchen. What impressed him most, says Ferran, was seeing twenty-five or thirty people working in one kitchen, when there weren't more than half a dozen at El Bulli. "It was like another world," he says. In 1986, the doctor sent Ferran to another French landmark, the legendary Pic in Valence; Lutaud did parallel stages at Troisgros in Roanne and Michel Chabran in Pont de l'Isère.

On March 28, 1985, almost exactly a year after Ferran had returned to El Bulli as a regular employee, his brother, Albert, joined the staff. Albert is seven and a half years Ferran's junior, so he was a mere fifteen at the time, but the two have always been extremely close. "Albert showed talent in school," the boys' mother, Pepi, told me, "but he had a problem with his studies. His teacher said, 'He's brilliant but he doesn't like to study.' I think he did study, but he didn't retain what he read. Ferran came home on a visit from El Bulli one day and Albert said, 'I don't want to go to school anymore,' so Ferran said, 'Okay, come with me.'"

Before Albert got to El Bulli, Ferran arranged for him to do a two-week stage with Jean-Paul Vinay and Fermí Puig at La Ciboulette—his first-ever kitchen job—so that he wasn't a *total* novice when he arrived in Cala Montjoi. When he did show up, on what he remembers as a "gray, unsettled day," he was promptly importuned by Juli, who wanted to establish from the beginning that he would get no special treatment just because his brother was co-chef. "He peppered me with questions which, to tell the truth, I did not begin to understand," Albert has said. As his baptism in the kitchen, Lutaud made him dress a duck—a creature, he claims, that he had never even seen before. It didn't take long for him to become acclimatized. "[A]s always," he has written, "first things first: very soon discothèques, parties and girls became my main concern."

A kitchen snapshot from the era shows Albert as a skinny young man with a mop of curly russet hair and a goofy grin—a schoolkid who looks a bit lost but game for anything. "It was really something for your first job to be at a two-star restaurant run by your brother, who was only twenty-three years old," he says, "and once I started, I found that I loved the métier." He began his culinary career with a two-year apprenticeship, rotating through the various stations in the kitchen, as was traditional. "I did the fish station," he says, "but I was allergic to shellfish, and in those days it was almost all shellfish. After that, I found the meat station to be flat, boring, always the same thing. Kristian Lutaud knew pastry very well, and he taught me the basics. I loved it. Each day it was something new." He went on to do stages at several top pastry shops, including Escribà in Barcelona (in later years he honed his skills at restaurants like Guy Savoy in Paris and Martín Berasategui near San Sebastián), and in 1987 he was officially put in charge of pastries and desserts. It became, he says, "my own little world."

Another newcomer in 1985 was Xavier Sagristà, a Barcelona native who as a culinary student had done a brief stage at El Bulli, under the newly arrived Vinay, four years earlier. Sagristà was a particularly imaginative chef, and he was to become a key figure in the development of the restaurant. In his introduction to Sagristà's book, *Entre mar i muntanya: Apunts de cuina a l'Empordà* (Between Sea and Mountain: Notes on Cuisine in the Empordà), Ferran writes, "Looking back over the years, I realize that without Xavi, the El Bulli of today would have been difficult to achieve. He is one of the creators. The personality of Xavi was decisive, because he counteracted all my flaws and that helped me. Our relationship in this period was exciting."

The bad news was that, also in 1985, in reaction to Vinay's departure, Michelin took the restaurant's second star away. And when the Spanish food magazine *Club des Gourmets* published its annual "Los

100 Mejores Restaurantes de España" that year, El Bulli was not included. Neither occurrence did much good for the restaurant, and business continued to be sporadic. "Apart from Easter week and summer," says Albert, "I think we averaged six customers every three days." The hotelier and chef Jaume Subirós remembers the restaurant well from this period. "There would be days, weeks, with no customers," he told me. "It was a big crisis. When guests arrived, the chefs would look in the frigo and see what they had. They were in solitude, almost abandoned." The restaurant was closed all day Mondays and at Tuesday lunch. On one occasion, Lutaud told me, they reopened on Tuesday night for dinner and nobody came. The next day, nobody. The day after that, nobody. Nobody on Friday either. "Finally," he continued, "somebody decided to go out to the road, and found that the front gate had been locked all that time. Juli had forgotten to open it. Fortunately, Marketta never found out." The pastry chef Paco Torreblanca, a good friend of the Adrià brothers, told me that, some years later, he'd asked Ferran why he stuck it out at El Bulli when there were sometimes no customers for days on end. "Because I have an idea," Ferran replied, "and it's a good idea."

Whether or not they had customers, the El Bulli staff seemed to be having fun. Photographs from the mid-eighties are full of funny hats, costumes, and clowning around. One shows Sagristà sitting in a huge stockpot with a string of nyora chiles around his neck, a green apple in his mouth, and a jester's cap on his head. He captioned it "Secondary effects of this job." The gang celebrating the birthday of a cook in a photograph from 1986 looks particularly festive, and the cook himself is holding a two-foot-high phallic-shaped rag doll and wearing an oversize toque labeled "Chef Caca." Artur Sagués, who came to work at the restaurant as a waiter around this time, told me, "I had worked for a while as a cook in a psychiatric hospital, making lunches for outpatients. When I came to El Bulli, I had had no restaurant experience. But I came to realize that the patients I'd cooked for and the team at El Bulli had a lot in common. . . ." When a young culinary student in Barcelona named Sergi Arola—now a well-known chef with restaurants of his own in Barcelona and Madrid—told his instructors that he wanted to do a stage at El Bulli, they discouraged him. "No," they said, "it's just a bunch of hippies there."

Lutaud assumed the role of unofficial greeter of newcomers to the restaurant staff: He'd fill them in on the rules of employment, help them get set up in their accommodations, and—most important— introduce them to the nightlife in Roses, at places like Chic and another disco called Si Us Plau (the Catalan phrase for "please," pronounced approximately "seese-plow"). The chefs were tireless, and when they weren't playing into the wee hours, they'd sometimes find more work to do. "The owner of Si Us Plau," Lutaud tells me, "was a friend of ours. They served some food, and we used to help out a little." Then, in 1985, he and Ferran set up an after-hours bistro at the evocatively named Passarel-la Disco-Beach in Empuriabrava. Was this just to make a little extra spending money? I asked Ferran one day. He laughed. "It was to make enough money to pay the staff at El Bulli!" he said. "It wasn't until 1996 or '97 that the restaurant brought in enough to let us pay regular salaries to people who worked there."

A few miles from Roses, Empuriabrava is a curious town—Florida on the Costa Brava, complete with oversize marina, artificial canals, and nouveau-Mediterranean-style houses and apartment blocks; all that's missing are the faux-adobe walls and guard shacks. Passarel-la— it's still going strong—is an immense, sprawling one-story structure, or rather a cluster of structures (today it houses several clubs, a pizzeria, and a yogurt shop), facing the beach and built around a large patio with a pool, beside which the bistro was situated. "It was funny," Lutaud continues. "We were doing a little El Bulli there, though of course the food was much simpler." When he told me that, I pictured burgers and pizza around the bar—maybe something like what Ferran and Puig had done for the admiral's head butler in their navy days.

Then I found some photos of the place and a menu: The Bistro del Bulli, as it was called, was a real little outdoor restaurant, with tables and chairs and a bill of fare that offered such things as terrine of foie gras, warm quail salad with lentils, tuna tartare with basil, rabbit with salted turnips, and warm apple tart with calvados cream—pretty sophisticated for a "disco-beach." The enterprise lasted for only a year; Ferran says that it turned out to be too much work for not enough money. In fact, he later said that it was through his experience at Passarel-la that he first realized how important it was to make a business out of a restaurant.

Becoming Ferran

"When I first knew him, he wasn't Ferran Adrià."

— Carmen Casas, in conversation with the author

Two things vital to Ferran's professional evolution occurred in 1987: The first was that in January of that year, Kristian Lutaud quit El Bulli, leaving Ferran—at the age of twenty-five, not quite seven years after he had first set foot in a professional kitchen—as the restaurant's sole head chef. Like other chefs at El Bulli before him, Lutaud had decided that he wanted to do something on his own, and he went off to open a restaurant in Javea, between Valencia and Alicante. By all accounts, Ferran accepted his own change in status calmly, and just kept his head down and went on cooking.

The second thing that happened was a chance encounter that was to push Ferran in a whole new direction. A few months after Lutaud's departure, Ferran was invited to join a group of other Spanish chefs on a visit to the great restaurants of the Côte d'Azur—among them Chantecler, the dining room at the Hôtel Negresco in Nice. Chantecler was the preserve of Jacques Maximin, a chef whom the *Guide Gault/ Millau* had variously called "impossible," "the hurricane," and "the Bonaparte of the ovens." Arguably the most original of what might be called nouvelle cuisine's second generation—he is twenty-six years younger than Paul Bocuse—Maximin was famously inventive, serving dishes like duck mousse inside turnip-petal ravioli and persillée (a kind of gelatin-bound terrine) of spiny lobster and sweetbreads. Though it never won more than two Michelin stars, his restaurant was considered by some connoisseurs to be the best in the region.

The Spanish chefs were lodged at the Negresco, and one morning they happened to meet Maximin in the hotel lobby. He spontaneously invited them to attend a demonstration he was doing later that day at the Hotel Martinez in Cannes for the Fondation Auguste Escoffier. They eagerly accepted. After the demonstration, there was a lunch featuring some of the dishes Maximin had just made. Óscar Caballero of *La Vanguardia* quotes Maximin as telling the group, "The dishes that are in front of you have been made by me and my team. It is up to you to create your own cuisine. All the recipes in the [cook]book written by me are exclusively mine. I have created them. It is my cuisine, not that of some other chef. . . ." Somebody—nobody remembers who—asked Maximin, "What *is* creativity?" and he responded either (depending on whose version you believe), "Creativity means not copying," or, "To create means not to copy." This simple formulation, Ferran says, changed his life, and certainly his professional direction—though not exactly in the way the myth-makers sometimes claim.

When Kristian Lutaud left El Bulli, Ferran had initially concentrated on holding the kitchen steady, keeping the "nouvelle" faith and continuing to cook in the great tradition of French cuisine, however modernized. To this end, he turned to the Robert Laffont cookbooks he'd first seen in the navy and other books by important French chefs—in order, he later wrote candidly, to "copy in whole or in part their recipes." Then he went to the Côte d'Azur and had, according to most accounts, a great epiphany. Upon his return from France, it is said, he immediately "threw out" his Gallic culinary bibles and began cooking food that was wholly his own.

That, of course, isn't quite the way it happened. Maximin did leave a strong impression on Ferran. "You have to remember," he says, "that in that era, 'creativity' was a word used for artists and musicians, but never for chefs. It was Maximin who made me realize that I had the right to create." But, he adds, "After Maximin, I decided nothing. I was a young cook. I didn't calculate. I didn't suddenly have a vision of the future. The evolution was something that happened year by year." His first three years at El Bulli had been, Ferran has said, a period of "apprenticeship and copying." Now he was beginning his "years of searching for a personal style." What that meant, as Juli once explained it to me, was that "he continued to work with all the techniques of the great French chefs and aside from that he developed many new recipes based on traditional dishes from all over Catalonia and other parts of Spain, with results that were just fantastic. It was later that he left behind the traditional inspirations and began creating new dishes with very sophisticated recipes." His first steps into the avant-garde, in other words, were in some senses steps backward—a seeming contradiction that Ferran considers key to his culinary maturation.

Jean-Louis Neichel and Jean-Paul Vinay had begun to incorporate local products and at least some Catalan culinary notions into their cooking at El Bulli, but Ferran made this a mission. He expanded on the mar i muntanya theme, started improvising on classic Catalan sauces like allioli (a mayonnaise-like but eggless emulsion of olive oil and garlic) and romesco (a Tarragonese condiment of dried chiles, tomatoes, almonds and hazelnuts, and garlic), and concocted a stripped-down version of suquet, the traditional Catalan fish and potato stew, using filtered seawater from the cove in place of fish fumet—a dish that occasioned much amazed comment among local

---

chefs. He also started employing ingredients that had never before been thought of as appropriate to haute cuisine, like crayfish roe, anchovies and sardines, green olives, and ibérico ham fat. One of his guiding principles, said Ferran, was that "all products have the same gastronomic value, regardless of their price." (One memorable example of this philosophy came some years later, when he decided to serve "chips" of deep-fried rabbit ears as a snack.)

It was also in 1987 that, for the first time, El Bulli's annual winter closing was extended from two months to five; it closed in mid-October, not reopening until mid-March the following year. This was Juli's idea, Marketta later said, and because it dramatically reduced annual expenses and avoided the doldrums of the slower months, "It was the salvation of El Bulli." It also encouraged another innovation: "Since we were now closed for such a long period," says Ferran, "we felt obliged to reopen with an entirely new menu. Beginning in March of 1988, then, we began to change the menu completely every season."

Taking advantage of the long winter breaks, Ferran began taking annual vacations in the Canary Islands, visiting his old friend and colleague Fermí Puig, who had ended up running a couple of popular restaurants there. "I would always come back with new perspectives," he says. This was the period when he started thinking seriously about new ways to transmute the textures of familiar foods into unfamiliar forms—a concept whose eventual extreme elaboration was to become his hallmark. His menus from the late eighties included light mousses of truffles and of corn that might be seen as precursors to the foams he later became renowned for. He also got interested in gelatins and molds, began experimenting with the caramelization of fruits and vegetables, created techniques for making sauces "à la minute," did away with traditional-style garniture on the side (instead integrating such accents into the dish itself), worked with his brother to expand the definition of what they called "the frozen world" (freezing savory purées, among other things), and invented a number of "personal carpaccios" using ingredients like scallops, foie gras, calf's brains, bone marrow, and ceps.

Around this time, Ferran started frequenting a tiny restaurant in Roses that became, in some senses, his platonic ideal. It's called Rafa's, and Ferran once joked that "it's the only place that's harder to get into than El Bulli." With only five small tables inside and a couple more on the pavement out front, it is built around a one-man open kitchen that turns out exquisite fish and shellfish perfectly cooked on a very hot stainless steel griddle with olive oil and salt. Period. Two women serve, while Rafa himself—Rafael Cantero—deftly turns the very best from the daily fish market into dinner. When he runs out of fish—no, when he runs out of fish that he thinks is fresh or good enough—he'll close, even if it's in the middle of the Saturday night dinner hour. The menu is verbal. When I went to Rafa's one night at Ferran's insistence (not that I needed much convincing), the choices included appetizers of shrimp, crayfish, clams, tiny squid, and espardenyes (sea slugs), and main courses of sole, lemon sole, John dory, sea bass, monkfish, scorpion fish, and three or four other fish. Everything is cooked exactly the same way, and there's no garnish, no sauce, no lemon wedges—and no side dishes. After a small plate of butterflied fresh anchovies glistening with olive oil and sprinkled with salt and minced garlic that was brought as a complimentary beginning, I ate a half-and-half order of shrimp and crayfish, big, salty, and perfectly (under)done, and then a lemon sole that couldn't have been better. It was, in a way, the most elegant meal I'd had in recent memory, and one of the best. "I think Rafa was an important influence on Ferran," says the filmmaker David Pujol. "Through this very simple cooking," he continues, "Ferran discovered that the essence of a product, the purity of the ingredients, is the most important thing. Many of his most famous dishes are created with the same attitude, the same personality."

The late eighties and early nineties were Ferran's first golden age:

Full of youthful energy and enthusiasm, gifted with real culinary skill and creative inspiration, surrounded by a top-notch (young) team headed by Xavier Sagristà, and given culinary carte blanche by Juli and the Schillings, Ferran absolutely blossomed; El Bulli sang. The Barcelona writer Xavier Agulló started dining at the restaurant shortly before Ferran encountered Maximin, and he went often enough to be able to track Ferran's progress. "Every time I ate there in the late eighties," he says, "it was for me a kind of illumination. Every time, Ferran went further. Even when he was copying nouvelle cuisine, they were very good copies. Then he started inserting Mediterranean products into his cooking, then Catalan recipes, then the next year there'd be dishes that had nothing to do with any cuisine."

Agulló admits that his visits to the restaurant sometimes had more than a strictly gastronomic intent: "We brought girls to El Bulli to seduce them," he says. "They were always so impressed. You'd say, 'I'm going to take you someplace you can't imagine.' There would be silence in the car when you started up that dark, winding road. It was like going to Lourdes. Then you'd get there and it was warm and comfortable, and the food was magic, like nothing else. A lot of them cried from sheer emotion when eating some of the dishes, they were so good. And then afterwards, at the Hotel Mar y Sol . . ."

Around this time, José Andrés, then an eighteen-year-old aspiring chef, found his way to El Bulli. Gravitating to Catalonia from his native Asturius, on the Atlantic side of Spain, he'd found a summer job at L'Antull, one of the best restaurants in Roses, "cooking paella for the tourists." One day, Ferran came in and sat at the bar and ordered garlic shrimp. Andrés was intrigued. "The owners of all the bars and restaurants in Roses talked about El Bulli as if it was something different," says Andrés, "a wild place, crazy, owned by Germans—so of course to me and the other young chefs around town, it had an air of mystery and romance." He got the chance to dine at El Bulli one day, invited by the mother of one of his friends, and he realized that it was not like any other restaurant he had imagined. One day he hitchhiked up the hill to Cala Montjoi, knocked on the kitchen door, and asked for a job. He got it. When an interviewer asked Ferran, twenty years later, why he'd hired Andrés, Ferran chuckled and replied, "Because there was nobody else. At that time, El Bulli was not as important as it is today."

"Ferran encouraged us to use our imaginations," says Andrés, who ended up working for Ferran on three different occasions in 1988 and 1989, and has since become one of his closest friends. "Whenever we learned some new technique, we were always thinking of different things we could do with it, things that never would have occurred to whomever had invented it." Experimentation was constant. "One day," remembers Andrés, "Ferran had a bowl of almond-milk gelatin in his hand, and he was just standing there and looking at a pot of boiling oil on the stove. And looking at it. And looking at it. Everybody knew what he was going to do, and we all said, 'No, Ferran, don't!' But he scooped up a spoonful of the gelatin. We all stepped back. He dropped it in the oil—and of course it exploded and spattered goop all over the kitchen. We all knew this was going to happen, and of course he knew it was going to happen, but he had to try it, he had to see it for himself." (He finally figured it out; in 1998, the first liquid croquettes appeared on the El Bulli menu.)

"Another time," Andrés continues, "he was thinking, well, in traditional cooking, we use the shells of lobsters or crayfish for bisque, so let's see what happens if we dry the shells of some sea crabs on top of the oven and then make a powder of them to flavor soup. We did, and the results were terrible, very fishy, with an unpleasant texture. But he had to discover that on his own. When there was a disaster like this, for Ferran it was as if he had rung the bell on a door that was locked. At least he had made the attempt. He couldn't get it now, but he would try again and again."

Some of the most revolutionary things Ferran ever did were

the simplest, adds Andrés—like that use of seawater in suquet. "Or the way he solved the problem of overcooked clams and mussels. Everybody cooked them by shaking them in a hot pan until they opened, and often they had turned to rubber by then from the heat. In 1988, Ferran had the idea to put them in a strainer and dip them in boiling water for three or maybe five seconds, that's all. They would be perfectly cooked, still glistening, just barely done. If the shells didn't open, okay. You could open them by hand—and the texture was perfect. *This* kind of thing is what's important, not the foams."

Like almost everyone who worked at the restaurant during these years, Andrés remembers the after-hours drinking and club-going. "We were party animals," he says. "You have to realize that we were younger than the chefs at most other restaurants. We were sixteen, seventeen, eighteen years old—and that's not the same as that age is today. We were *very* young, and we behaved like it. We'd stay out all night and at six or seven in the morning we'd be eating roast chicken somewhere before heading back to Cala Montjoi. We'd finish at the beach, watching the sunrise. I am amazed there was never a death on that road going back. We drove fast, and we were tired, drunk. I used to jump in the water sometimes just to wake up, or to sober up. Some of us had to work with sunglasses on in the morning." When did you sleep? I ask. Andrés laughs. "We had a break between five and seven every afternoon, and generally you could have a siesta. But we had a competition all the time for who could make the best family [i.e., staff] meal—there was real pressure—and if we had a big lunch crowd and then it was your turn to make the family meal, you had no break before starting dinner prep. If you were so stupid as to have gone out the night before, by the end of the day you wished you weren't alive." Was Ferran still partying with the gang? I ask. Andrés hesitates. "Ferran went out with us," he replies, "but he kept his distance. He wasn't there all the time. Already in 1987, 1988, he knew how to be the boss." Even during working hours, says Andrés, Ferran had begun to be a little apart from the others. "He'd come down from his 'studio'—a room upstairs—with his books and notebooks, with an aura about him. . . ."

At the same time, Andrés adds, "That bastard was a visionary. What we did was so pure. That kitchen was like a place out of Harry Potter. We were like kids. We had a childlike approach to everything. Ferran still does." Ferran's friend Vicente Todolí, director of the Tate Modern in London, makes the same analogy: "What Ferran does is like cuisine elaborated by a genius child," he says. "I'm from Valencia and there are oranges everywhere, so when I was a kid, we'd try to boil oranges, just to see what happened. We didn't know what would and wouldn't work, so we tried everything. That's basic to Ferran. It's like when people look at a Miró and say, 'Any child could do that.' That's the whole point. Children have complete freedom. Nothing is impossible, for them. They have a kind of innocence. They're always starting from a new world. That's what Ferran is like."

At about this point in the history of El Bulli, you might expect that word would start getting around about Ferran and what he was doing—that Spanish food writers and serious restaurant-goers would discover and exalt the place, that French gastronomes would start streaming across the border to see what this renegade Catalan was up to, that trend-spotters in England and America would make the pilgrimage and pen knowing little "secret restaurant" pieces full of superlatives about Ferran. That didn't happen. In the midst of Ferran's creative ferment, the French newsweekly *L'Express* ran an article about El Bulli in which there is no mention of him or any other chef; instead, says the article, at the restaurant "Juli Soler Lobo will serve you, among other things, warm oysters with caviar, spiny lobster with foie gras in saffron sauce, and fillets of red mullet with artichoke chips." Even more curiously, the conservative Madrid daily *ABC* profiled Marketta, again mentioning Juli but not Ferran—and stated that "the style of cuisine at El Bulli is the style of Marketta," concluding, "The future of the restaurant, [Marketta] says, will be in the hands of someone with ability, knowledge, and experience. When? Who knows? For now, she continues working at El Bulli day by day." I asked Ferran whether there was a reason that he was slighted, and he replied, "There was nothing personal against me. It was just that with Jean-Paul Vinay leaving, Juli and Marketta became very disillusioned and skeptical. It was difficult for them to fully believe in a twenty-six-year-old boy."

There was also some hesitation on the part of Spanish critics to take Ferran seriously. They "got it" when he was cooking nouvelle cuisine, but when he started reinterpreting Spanish classics, bringing grilled fish, gazpacho, and allioli into the realm of haute cuisine, working with "common" ingredients like rabbit, sea urchin, and sardines, his efforts were not well received. One important figure who did support what he was doing was the novelist Manuel Vázquez Montalbán, who became a frequent customer at El Bulli and a good friend of Ferran's. (At the time of Montalbán's sudden death in 2003, he and Ferran were reportedly talking about collaborating on a book that would be the modern equivalent of Brillat-Savarin's early-nineteenth-century classic *The Physiology of Taste*.) Another was Luis Bettónica, who began to write about him and told others (like myself) to go to El Bulli.

Still, business remained erratic. "Every year it was tough to get through the winter months," Ferran has written. "We were almost bankrupt. In September we'd go to the bank and ask for credit that we couldn't pay back until summer." Ferran never compromised his standards, though. Building on the legacy of Annick Janin's pastry carts, Albert continued to produce a large and varied repertoire of desserts every day. "One day when the weather was terrible and we knew nobody was coming to the restaurant," José Andrés tells me, "I said to Ferran, 'Why don't we just put out ten or twelve of the desserts on the pastry cart?' He said, 'How many do we have in the cooler?' 'About twenty-five,' I said. 'Then put out twenty-five,' he said." There would be no half measures at El Bulli.

Carles Abellán, who arrived in the kitchen in 1988, remembers the era vividly. A classmate of Andrés's at hotel and restaurant school, he talked himself into a stage at El Bulli when he met Ferran at a meeting of young chefs in Barcelona, and ended up staying with him for fifteen years, off and on, in various contexts before opening his own first restaurant, Comerç 24, in Barcelona in 2001. "There were only six of us in the kitchen," he recalls. "Maybe two or three culinary students from time to time. We got no salary. We were there for 'the cause.' We had to knock on Juli's door and ask for money. 'You ask every day,' he'd say. 'What do you need money for? You have a bed, you have food.' The truth is, he wasn't wrong. My little room at El Bulli was the best house of my life, because I'd get up in every morning and open the window and look out on Cala Montjoi, then we'd go down to the kitchen in our pajamas and slippers and make coffee, and later go down to the beach. . . . It was a crazy environment. We were crazy young guys. Ferran put very strong pressure on us all the time, but it was incredible. I loved it."

Isidre Soler, now chef-proprietor of Tram-Tram in Barcelona, worked at El Bulli for a year in 1988. "It was so different in those days than it is now," he says. "It was just a few guys improvising. The restaurant didn't make any money, so Ferran always had to buy the cheapest ingredients—very fresh and of the best quality, but cheap. He'd buy tiny fish for soup, and we had to bone them all, which took forever. I later worked for Santi Santamaria [who was to become Ferran's nemesis] for a few months, and the first time I saw a big, whole fish in his kitchen, I almost cried. Ferran couldn't afford lobster, so he'd buy little langoustines, and then explore all the possibilities of what you could do with little langoustines. I think this kind of privation helped Ferran develop his imagination. Maybe if he had had a big, thriving restaurant and not had to be so creative just to survive, he wouldn't have become what he did. Maybe he would have been just one of the great chefs of classic cuisine. Instead, he became completely revolutionary." Ferran says that Soler is romanticizing a bit. "There were many economic problems at the time," he says, "but our menus still had lobster, truffles, caviar—so we didn't stop buying expensive products. What is true is that we did begin to work with fish native to the area, like tiny monkfish. But we never considered cost. It was more a matter of developing the use of 'minor' products." In any case, says Soler, "Ferran changed the mentality. People said, 'We've done it this way all our lives, we can't change,' and he'd say, 'Yes, you can. You can make something the old way and then throw it out, or make it into something else.'"

Dr. Schilling continued to be a presence at the restaurant, occasional but significant. Besides bringing glassware and liqueurs and other restaurant accoutrements, he'd also bring menus from the places he'd visited along his route, and he'd always make it a point to sit down with Ferran and Juli and the rest of the team and explain what he'd eaten and what he'd observed about the various dining rooms he'd visited. Maybe even more important, says José Andrés, "He always brought us a sense of tranquility, as if everything was going to be all right." Marketta, on the other hand, was "an iron woman," says Andrés. "She was very active, always making Juli run." Carles Abellán says that she was *quejica*—peevish, a complainer.

Marketta had by this time become something of the grande dame of El Bulli. "With her," says Xavier Agulló, "there was a liturgy, a ceremony: She would sit in a comfortable chair on the terrace looking at the sea, and the first thing you did when you arrived was to salute her. Everyone would stop by to pay his or her respects. *Then* you could eat." Periodically, Marketta would marvel aloud at the high level the restaurant had attained.

A photograph from mid-1988, published in *Blanco Negro*, the weekly magazine from the newspaper *ABC*, shows Marketta in a dark blue dress with her head down and her eyes closed (she looks tired); Juli in a tie and jacket, also with his eyes closed, and looking a little confused; and "Fernando," in chef's whites, hair cropped shorter than usual, squinting but looking straight ahead, with a look of intense concentration on his face, almost as if he's trying to peer into the future.

■ ■ ■

By 1989, Ferran—like Jean-Louis Neichel, Jean-Paul Vinay, and Kristian Lutaud before him—had started thinking about his career path and wondering how long he wanted to continue working for somebody else. He and Juli were getting offers of financing to open a restaurant together, either in Barcelona or somewhere else in Catalonia, though Ferran says that they never took them seriously. It turned out that they didn't have to. In 1990, Marketta decided that she no longer wanted to take an active role at El Bulli ("She was becoming a bit of a hermit," says Ferran), and she and Dr. Schilling at last agreed to sell the business—though not, as yet, the land or the buildings—to Ferran and Juli, if they wanted it. After some discussion, the two made the decision to stay in Cala Montjoi. They formed a business partnership, a *sociedad civil*, and "bought" El Bulli by assuming a bank debt of twenty million pesetas, then just under $200,000.

Now that they were proprietors, Ferran and Juli ceded some of their duties to two of the restaurant's longtime employees: Xavier Sagristà took over as head chef and Toni Gerez became manager of the dining room. Ferran remained as active as ever in the creative process, though. In conceiving new dishes, he and Sagristà started working with what Ferran dubbed "the table of associations": He made one list of all the available products, another of viable cooking techniques, a third of vinaigrettes, a fourth of emulsions, a fifth of herbs and spices, and so on, and from them, the two would try every possible combination of elements. This process led to a flurry of charts and other lists, in which every element of cuisine was broken down and catalogued, as if there were a culinary genome, a DNA of cuisine.

It was also in 1990 that the restaurant got its second Michelin star back, and Juli was named by Spain's National Academy of Gastronomy as the country's best dining room director. (Ferran had to wait two more years to be named best chef de cuisine.) There still seemed to be some confusion abroad about Juli's exact role at the restaurant, though. Writing about the place after it had won its Michelin honor, the *Gault/ Millau* magazine hailed "Julio Soler . . . [who] has understood the principles of modern cuisine, and his succession of young chefs applies them with intelligence and precision to local recipes"—adding "Soler addresses a discreet homage to Maximin with a superb tian of lamb, and the monkfish with onions and ham deserves a thanksgiving." Again, there is no mention of Ferran.

The 1990 *Guide Gault/Millau*, the magazine's annual Baedeker to restaurants and hotels, opened Ferran's eyes to the work of the two chefs he calls "my last French references"—Pierre Gagnaire in St-Etienne and Michel Bras in Laguiole, both with three Michelin stars and neither remotely similar to the other or to any other chef. He and Juli traveled up into the center of France to visit both. Gagnaire's menu at the time was aggressively idiosyncratic, offering such dishes as lobster cream with melon juice, pigeon chutney, and crispy crêpes, and hyssop-flavored young rabbit and rabbit kidneys with tripe, sweetbreads cooked with garlic confit, and spicy pepper sauce. Ferran says that it was by sampling creations like these that he first realized just how far it was possible for a chef to go. From Bras, who plies his trade in a rural environment and uses obscure mountain herbs and forgotten farmhouse techniques in his cuisine, Ferran says that he learned a new respect for nature and was reminded of the importance of illuminating the purity of raw materials. These restaurant experiences, says Ferran, opened a new road for him and further stimulated his desire to create his own language of cuisine.

Albert had by this time begun designing plated desserts, to be incorporated into the tasting menus, as a way of weaning diners off the famous pastry carts (they disappeared forever in 1992), and with the intention of further expanding El Bulli's sweet repertoire, he and Ferran traveled south, before El Bulli reopened for the 1991 season, to Paco Torreblanca's pastry shop in Elda, near Alicante.

The pastry-maker's art has had a tremendous influence on the food at El Bulli. Annick Janin's daily array of desserts was, as noted, once one of the great attractions of the restaurant. Kristian Lutaud was an accomplished pastry chef, too, and an early inspiration to both Albert and Ferran. So was Yves Thuriès, the artisanal chocolatier and pastry chef from the southwest of France, whose first book of recipes Albert calls "the Bible." Another inspiration was the late Antoni Escribà, who ran the 1906-vintage Pasteleria Escribà on the Gran Via in Barcelona—a man Ferran once described as being "like a father to him."

"Ferran likes things very controlled, and patisserie is like that," says Antoni's son and successor and Ferran's friend, Christian Escribà. He points out that, until recent years, the only person in a professional kitchen likely to have had a scale—or rather a scale that was sensitive to minute weights—would have been the pastry chef, and that the kinds of stabilizers and emulsifiers that Ferran has become famous (and is often criticized) for using in his kitchen, materials classified scientifically as hydrocolloids, have been common in commercial pastry-making for years. It's no accident, then, that words relating to patisserie and confectionery show up frequently on the El Bulli menu, describing savory creations as well as sweet ones—galette, cookie, cracker, biscuit, sponge, brioche, waffle, turrón, bonbon, caramel, and so on.

When the Adriàs turned up at Torreblanca's door in 1991, the pastry chef remembers, "I was working, and my wife came back and said, 'There's somebody at the counter who wants to see you.' I told her that I was busy and didn't have time to see anyone just then. She said, 'You'd better see him, because Kristian Lutaud sent him.' I went out and there was Ferran, with Albert. I'd never met them, and I asked, 'What do you want?' 'To know you, and how you work,' said Ferran. 'Okay,' I said. 'When would you like to come?' 'We'll stay now,' he said. I had to go to Paris to work on a meal for the American ambassador, so I gave them the keys to my house and told them I'd be back in a few days." When he returned, he invited the brothers to follow him for a week or so. Ferran, he remembers, was particularly inquisitive, always looking for the "why." "He'd be at the shop at seven every morning and stay until eight at night," says Torreblanca, "and all the time he was asking, asking, asking." Ferran's willingness—or rather his strong desire—to learn from others has never diminished.

By this time, Ferran felt confident enough to take another step away from upscale-restaurant tradition: Years before other chefs around the world started offering "small plates" on their menus, he introduced tapas to El Bulli—tapas Ferran-style, that is. These weren't the usual croquetas and deep-fried seafood and tiny open-face sandwiches but things like sardines with saffron, cauliflower, and green onions; lamb's brains and crayfish with tomato gratin; squid stuffed with green asparagus, mushrooms, and peas; and coca (the Catalan flatbread) topped with roasted eggplant, bacon, and rabbit loin chops. "We did some 'tapitas,' little tapas, at the restaurant in 1988 or '89," Ferran explains, "but we considered these as apéritifs. It was only in 1991 that we brought the philosophy of tapas into our cuisine."

At the same time, Ferran also started drawing inspiration from the physical world—Gaudí tiles, beach stones, and a bird's nest were among the objects echoed visually in his cuisine—and he made his first tentative stabs at creating culinary foams, which were later to become his most famous innovation, though their successful execution was to elude him for several more years. In one of his more revolutionary innovations, he redefined the whole idea of *fonds*—literally, bases or essences—which are the building blocks of classical French cuisine: Instead of the traditional stocks, glazes, marinades, and the like, Ferran started using gelatins, juices, and various kinds of milk as the groundwork for sauces.

In 1991, Ferran and Juli also began making improvements to the restaurant itself, building a large parking area for customers and cleaning up and replanting the gardens. They did nothing to the dining rooms—which, other than having benefitted from some refreshing, have remained basically the same for the past quarter-century. "When we wanted to change the decor," says Ferran, "we couldn't afford it. When we could afford it, we no longer wanted to." One casualty of the era was the legendary caravan, still sitting outside the kitchen door but increasingly derelict with the years; Juli led a crew of chefs in demolishing it with sledgehammers, and the remains were carted away with the trash.

Late in the year, after El Bulli had closed for the season, Ferran took a working sabbatical and forged a link for the first time with the art world. A mutual friend had introduced him to the Catalan sculptor Xavier Medina-Campeny, and the two "connected immediately," as Medina-Campeny puts it. Ferran apparently thought that his creative processes might benefit from exposure to somebody else's, and he asked the sculptor—a ruggedly handsome man in his sixties who looks as if he could have been chiseled out of one of the blocks of marble he uses in his work—if he could spend a few weeks at his studio, cooking while Medina-Campeny worked.

Medina's studio was part of the Palo Alto complex, a renovated 1875-vintage textile factory on the Carrer Pellaires, with walls of stucco, old brick, weathered wood, and oxidized metal swathed in ivy, bougainvillea, and wisteria, housing workspaces for about twenty artists, photographers, architects, and other creative types—including the once-ubiquitous Barcelona designer and artist Mariscal. (Medina-Campeny has since moved to another studio within the same complex.) "I'd built a kitchen along one wall of the studio, under the front window, in 1988," Medina-Campeny tells me. "I'd lived in New York for a few years and the space reminded me of a loft in Hoboken or Staten Island, and that was the feeling I was trying to get. I gave Ferran the keys to the studio so he could come and go, but I was usually there. Every morning, he'd go to the market and buy things and then come and start cooking and experimenting while I worked. Some days, one or the other of us would say, 'I'm not inspired today,' and we'd just go out to eat. There was definitely some kind of fusion between us. We excited each other. He was always trying something different. I remember one day he opened up a squid with a scalpel and put herbs inside. . . ."

Ferran says that his days at the studio were like a working vacation for him, a chance to cook and think about cooking without having to worry about serving the results to paying customers. He and Medina-Campeny collaborated on a notebook recording the daily menus Ferran prepared, illustrated with sketches, by both men, and with recipes, scraps of poetry, lines of music, and Polaroid photos (some of the pages may be seen—though not very clearly—in the History section of the El Bulli Web site). Among the dishes Ferran created were a salad of raw celery and cilantro with fried celery leaves and macadamias; raw favas with mint jelly and goat brains roasted with lime; chestnut croquettes with dove meat and persimmon; tuna with salsify and veal marrow; soup of barnacles and potatoes with chervil and a poached egg; sea bream with anchovy salt; individual terrines of confit chicken and lobster . . . He called his experiments cooking purely for the sake of cooking, and he realized how valuable it would be to his creative process to be able to do something similar on a regular basis—though he later wrote that the dishes he made during this period "are not taken into account in the analysis of our evolution"; he meant that he never catalogued them as his creations, though some of them may have led to dishes that were served at El Bulli and entered into the canon.

The following year brought the Olympic Games to Barcelona. The event put Catalonia on the map for Americans and much of the rest of the world—but it didn't do much for El Bulli. In fact, says Ferran, 1992 was "the worst year of crisis in the history of El Bulli." One problem was that, in what could be called a bold leap of faith, considering that they didn't yet own the physical structure of the place, Ferran and Juli began major alterations: They closed the bar that had faced the terrace, put in a new entrance and again replanted the exterior gardens, and, most dramatically of all, began to construct an entirely new kitchen—the old one was badly ventilated and far too small for the kind of food being produced—spending money they didn't have. The other problem was the one the restaurant had been facing for years: a lack of steady business. The customers who did come were mostly visitors from France or Germany. The Spanish still largely ignored this inaccessible restaurant with its maverick chef—and those who did come, everyone remembers, were difficult and demanding.

"In the early nineties," the writer Xavier Agulló tells me, "there was a little circle of people who believed in Ferran. We were like monks. We went there in bad weather, with fog on the road, because every time you went, there was another surprise. It was really like a race to creativity with nobody saying 'stop.' When I started writing good things about El Bulli in the Barcelona newspapers, though, people insulted me. 'Oh, El Bulli,' they'd say. 'That crazy man, that *faggot*! I used to go to the beach there and wash myself off with a hose before going to eat. It's nothing special. . . .'" What Ferran was doing in the isolation of Cala Montjoi was simply so unusual, so far out of what was then the Spanish mainstream, that it was impossible for some people to digest.

One diner who did come to the restaurant during the Olympics was Joël Robuchon. In the late twentieth century, no chef, with the possible exception of the ascetic Swiss master Fredy Girardet, was more respected by his peers than Robuchon. He had never heard of Ferran or El Bulli, he later said, but he was in Catalonia anyway—he has long had a vacation house to the south in Calpe, near Alicante— and friends of his urged him to go. When he reserved a table, Ferran and Juli were both honored and apprehensive. To have this great culinary figure in their restaurant was, as Ferran says, "very important," and of course they had to make sure that he was pleased with what he ate. Unfortunately, when he arrived, with his wife and children, Robuchon announced that he could try only a few dishes, as they were due in Perpignan in a few hours to catch the TGV back to Paris. Ferran was disappointed, but began to send out food. "I was served the first apéritif," Robuchon later recalled, "a gelatin of almonds with tomato coulis, and I was very surprised, because I had known all the great Spanish chefs of the epoch but had never before seen this level of cuisine in Spain." Next came one of Ferran's early signature dishes, caviar with marrow—and Robuchon said, "Never mind the train. I want the whole meal."

In those days in Spain, restaurant critics wrote books, chefs didn't. But Ferran felt that he had things to say about cooking, and reasoned that a book would reach a wider audience than his small out-of-the-way restaurant would. In 1992, then, Ferran and his team began working on what was to become his first published volume: *El Bulli: El sabor del Mediterráneo* (The flavor of the mediterranean). Ferran surprised me one day at the Taller by pointing to a copy of *El sabor* and saying, "That book has had more influence on food in Spain than anything I'm doing now." My face must have betrayed a look of astonishment, because he looked straight at me and said, "No, *really*." The book is largely forgotten today, he added, "because if it isn't spherification, people don't consider it the food of El Bulli." A few weeks later, standing near a copy of *El sabor* sitting on the service bar in the El

Bulli kitchen, he brought it up again. "I was the first who made Catalan cuisine as modern cuisine," he told me earnestly, "and not just Catalan dishes but dishes from all over Spain. But that moment is finished for me now. I can't do it anymore." He demonstrated by walking past me and the book. Then he turned back and said, "This was the language that I spoke. Then I moved on to one that I didn't."

El sabor was published in 1993 by a small Barcelona house co-owned by one Miquel Horta i Almaraz, "an eccentric Marxist millionaire" (as he was once described) who would later play an important role in the story of El Bulli. It was not a book people generally understood. It looked like a cookbook at first, but turned out to be more a work of culinary philosophy. Of course, there *were* recipes, and beautiful color photographs of the food, most of which looks wonderful: the mixed grill of vegetables with truffles and ham, the marinated scallops with foie gras, the sweetbreads with shreds of calamari and white beans. (Looking at the images today, you almost wish that, no matter what wonderments he has since produced, Ferran *hadn't* left such food behind.) Nonetheless, when *Sabor* first came out, with editions in Spanish, Catalan, and German, it sold no more than a thousand copies.

Ferran takes justifiable pride in having introduced Mediterranean elements into haute cuisine, both through his cooking at the restaurant and through *El sabor*, which is a reflection of that cooking. It must be pointed out, though, that there were antecedents. As long ago as the late seventeenth or early eighteenth century, François Massialot, chef to the Duc d'Orléans, included olives and lemon rind in his recipe for truffled pullet with foie gras. Another seventeenth-century French chef, Pierre de Lune, flavored his pâté of turkey not only with beef marrow, prunes, bacon, and sugar, but also with such exotica as dates, pistachios, Corinth raisins, orange flower extract, and pomegranate seeds—all products that would have been imported from the eastern Mediterranean or North Africa. In Ferran's own era, Jo

Rostang at La Bonne Auberge in Antibes was serving monkfish terrine with ratatouille and rack of lamb with zucchini gratin as early as 1982; in 1984, Jacques Maximin's menu included zucchini stuffed with John dory, truffles, and basil, and mesclun salad with fresh anchovies and rouget fillets. A perusal of the Gault/Millau guidebooks from the early eighties will turn up a number of other examples. That in no way minimizes Ferran's enormous influence. Other people may have started working in the same direction, but he's the one who seized the Mediterranean idea and took it to the limit.

Ferran wasn't really the first person to start modernizing Catalan cuisine, either. I was eating things like canelones stuffed with fish mousse in blue cheese sauce, raw hake salad with caviar, and chicken liver mousse with raisins in crayfish sauce—all of them contemporary (for their time) and Catalan in inspiration—half a dozen years before *El sabor del Mediterráneo*. But Ferran brought a refinement and level of complexity to his own modernizations that had not previously been seen. From his red mullet fillets covered with a mosaic of tiny pieces of onion, red pepper, zucchini, tomato, and scallion, mimicking the *trencadís* or *pique-assiette* patterns used so effectively in the architecture of Gaudí and Josep Maria Jujol, to his inspired mar-i-muntanya combination of warm oysters and morsels of calf's foot, this is food of startling imagination and originality, often with recognizable links to rural tradition but presented with a precision that a Michel Guérard or an Alain Chapel would have envied. "*El sabor* was, if you will, the furthest expression of Escoffier," says the writer and food historian Toni Massanés. "After that, Ferran's food became something else. It left the planet."

It was also on the cover and in the pages of *El sabor* that Fernando Adrià, for the first time, became Ferran—taking the Catalan form of his first name. When I asked why he decided to make the change—or why he waited so long to do so—Ferran shrugged. "I knew that my first book would be published in both Spanish and Catalan," he explained, "and the custom would have been to call me Fernando for the Spanish edition, Ferran for the Catalan. I wanted just one name to be used, and I chose Ferran. It wasn't a question of nationalism. It was just that I was in Catalonia, so it seemed right." (He has never made the change legally, incidentally; like many Catalans, he has just never bothered.) Today, "Ferran"—no last name necessary—has become such a familiar and revered name in the world of cuisine that it's difficult to imagine the wizard of El Bulli going by any other moniker. Somehow "Fernando," much less "Nando," just wouldn't carry the same weight.

——

Two Thousand Years of El Bulli

"El Bulli in a way is a traditional restaurant, a restaurant with a direct connection to the Spanish or Catalan palate."

—Óscar Caballero, in conversation with the author

El Bulli, in its contemporary incarnation, is utterly, unequivocally original, a thing apart, a restaurant unlike any other in history. But it is essential to an understanding of the place—Ferran makes this point frequently—to acknowledge that it is also part of a continuum, with antecedents both philosophical and technical in the long history of European cuisine. It is a product of evolution as much as revolution.

Darwin called cooking—which was invented somewhere between ten thousand and two million years ago (anthropologists disagree wildly)—"probably the greatest [discovery], excepting language, ever made by man." But cooking, of course, is not cuisine. The job of the cook has always been to change food physically: first to separate it from its natural environment, either himself or through the agency of a forager or farmer or the like—to uproot it, cut it down, pluck it, catch it, slaughter it; then to shape it for further attention by peeling it, seeding it, gutting it, cutting it up, discarding its inedible or infe-licitous portions; then—and this is as good a definition of "cooking" as any—to alter its molecular structure, either through a process like drying, soaking, salting, smoking, or marinating (or through the ac-tions of induced fermentation), or, more commonly, especially in the modern age, through the application of heat; and finally to combine it with other, complimentary, foods and/or to add seasonings or flavor-ings to render it more palatable. It wasn't until sources of food supply became regularized, though, and we were able to exercise some con-trol over the growing of plants and animals, through agriculture and husbandry, that we had the luxury of actually thinking about how to make food taste better instead of just how to get our hands on it in the first place. And it almost certainly wasn't until certain societies, or segments of society, found that they had an abundance of food on a consistent basis that they began to philosophize about it—to appreci-ate it as something more than a mere (mere?) adjunct of survival; that gastronomy was born.

I think it can be argued that since that happened, whenever it was, there have been two main currents in what might be called elec-tive cooking, cooking whose goal is something other than simply ren-dering raw materials edible: the quest for purity of flavor, for the preservation and perhaps enhancement of a foodstuff's essence; and the desire to mislead (at least theoretically in a benevolent manner)—to divert and amuse the diner by turning a meal's ingredients into some-thing unexpected and perhaps not easily identifiable.

Chefs have long been—to quote Mick Jagger in quite another context—practiced at the art of deception. The Greek writer Euphron, in the third century B.C., describes a dish created by the chef Sotirides for King Nicomedes: On a military campaign in Scythia, far from the sea, the monarch craved sardines; "Sotirides carved pieces of turnip into the shape of small fish, boiled them, dressed them with oil and salt, and arranged exactly forty poppy seeds on top of each"—so, cooking as sleight-of-hand, more than two millennia ago. Roman cuisine indulged in what one writer has called "ironic transformations in order to fool the guests at the table." The famous ur-cookbook ascribed to Apicius recorded the formula for a dish (*pace* Sotirides) of salted fish made without fish. It noted of another recipe that "at table no one will recognize what he is eating."

On the other hand, there was a counter-current to these deceptions early on. In the fourth century B.C., according to the Greek comic playwright Anaxippus, two cooks named Sophon of Acarnania and Damoxenus of Rhodes called for stripping away spices ("the old trite seasonings") and cooking with just oil, a new pan, and a hot fire—shades of Rafa's. A chef in the Athenian poet Philemon's play *The Soldier* brags of having prepared a perfect fish, without cheese or herbs, that "when baked . . . looked exactly like what it was when alive."

Restaurants, in which food both deceptive and straightforward is available to anyone who can afford it, are a comparatively recent development. Some scholars date the birth of these institutions—as opposed to travelers' inns, which were primarily places to lodge, with a stewpot on the fire if you were lucky—to the ninth or tenth century A.D., when they apparently first appeared in China and the Islamic world. The latter included Moorish Spain, where as early as the 820s, the Persian polymath Abu al Hasan, known as Ziryab, decreed that meals should be served in three courses—soup, main dish, and dessert. (Ziryab is also credited with having introduced asparagus to Spain.) The word *restaurant*, from the French verb *restaurer*, to restore (in the sense of putting the color back in someone's cheeks), was first used in Paris in the mid-eighteenth century—and the first restaurant in the sense that we know the term today, with customers sitting at individual tables and ordering from a menu, was probably the Grand Taverne de Londres, opened in the French capital in 1782 by a well-known local gastronome named Antoine Beauvilliers.

El Bulli descends directly from Beauvilliers's establishment. For the Schillings, the founders of El Bulli, French restaurants—and the restaurants in Germany and elsewhere that emulated them—were the platonic ideal; when the doctor took the people who worked for him on educational jaunts, he took them not to Copenhagen for smørre-brød or Rome for fettuccine Alfredo but to places like Vanel in Tou-louse and Georges Blanc in Vonnas for the best French cooking, old and new. Chefs Jean-Louis Neichel and Jean-Paul Vinay, who won El Bulli its first Michelin stars, may have drawn on regional products and worked local accents into some of their dishes, but what they cooked was French food—classical at heart, if with the vocabulary of nouvelle cuisine. And until he left it so unequivocally behind, nouvelle cuisine was Ferran's religion.

What is nouvelle cuisine? Sophisticated medieval European cooking (as opposed to simple everyday sustenance), French and oth-erwise, tended to be complex and overwrought, employing whole spice racks full of flavorings and combining seemingly disparate ele-ments. In the mid-seventeenth century, a Burgundian chef named François Pierre La Varenne published the first great French cook-book, *Le cuisinier françois,* in which he sought to codify and simplify French cooking; he advocated the use of fresh herbs in place of spices, helped popularize "new" vegetables (peas, cucumbers, artichokes), championed the use of butter in place of rendered animal fats as a cooking medium, and formulated many of the stocks and sauces that were to become definitive of haute cuisine. The term *nouvelle cuisine* was first used to describe the recipes of several of La Varenne's succes-sors in the 1740s, and was applied again to the cooking and philoso-phy of Georges Auguste Escoffier (1846–1935), another great codifier of haute cuisine, who modernized and lightened French cooking further.

Nouvelle cuisine in the modern sense, however, was born in the late 1960s, and first publicized to a wide audience by the food writers and fledgling magazine and restaurant guide publishers Henri Gault and Christian Millau in the early 1970s. A convenient birth year for the movement—for it was nothing less than that, with something of an evangelical edge—is 1965: That's when Jean and Pierre Troisgros, at their eponymous restaurant in Roanne, invented what was to become one of the genre's definitive dishes, saumon à l'oseille—salmon with sorrel—the fish sliced very thin and seared rare in a Teflon pan, twenty-five seconds on one side, fifteen on the other. (Escoffier, by contrast, called for grilling salmon steaks for twenty-five minutes.) And 1965 was the year that a former pastry chef named Michel Guérard, who was to become one of the leaders of the movement, opened his first restaurant, Le Pot-au-Feu, in Asinières, a Parisian suburb.

The origins of this new style of cooking can be dated back to the late 1950s and early 1960s, when several prominent French chefs, including Alex Humbert of the historic Maxim's in Paris and Jean Delaveyne of Le Camélia in Bougival, just outside the city, along with the legendary restaurateur Fernand Point of Le Pyramide in Vienne, quietly started to foment a revolution in their kitchens: Responding to changing tastes and perhaps feeling creatively stifled by the weight of culinary tradition, they began to question portions of the Holy Writ— i.e., Escoffier's *Guide culinaire*—calling for the replacement of some of the heavy sauces that had for so long defined classical French cuisine with lighter ones that would allow the integrity of the raw materials to shine through. Though not a chef himself, Point turned out to be the most influential of the lot: Jean and Pierre Troisgros, Paul Bocuse, and Alain Chapel, among others, worked in his kitchen and absorbed his lessons. Returning to their families' restaurants—the Troisgros brothers to Roanne, Bocuse to Collonges-au-Mont-d'Or, and Chapel to Mionnay (all close to Lyon)—they started cooking in a different way, cutting down on flour and cream (if not usually on butter), shortening cooking times to leave ingredients in more recognizable form, and incorporating ingredients that Escoffier had never known, like the miniature vegetables that Point helped popularize.

Nouvelle cuisine developed more or less spontaneously out of their kitchens, and those of like-minded chefs like Guérard, Raymond Oliver, Jacques Manière, and Alain Senderens in Paris, Roger Vergé and Louis Outhier on the French Riviera (both of them also Point alumni), Paul and Jean-Pierre Haeberlin in Alsace, and, very slightly later, the Swiss chef Fredy Girardet outside Lausanne. In 1973, the *Gault/Millau* magazine—which, along with the same enterprise's annual guidebook, modernized restaurant criticism even as its heroes were modernizing cooking—turned a trend into an institution: Celebrating some of these new chefs, the publication ran an article with a headline reading "Vive la Nouvelle Cuisine Française!" and the name stuck—probably helped by the fact that the French had earlier identified such phenomena as *la nouvelle critique*, the new criticism, and *la nouvelle vague*, cinema's new wave. The first English-language publication to pick up the term was probably the British magazine *Harpers & Queen*, in 1975.

Gault and Millau, who began to differentiate between traditional and "nouvelle" restaurants in their annual guidebook (printing ratings for the traditional ones in black, the nouvelle ones in red), went on to establish what they identified as the basic principles of nouvelle cuisine. These included simplicity of preparation, reduced cooking times, the use of the freshest possible seasonal ingredients, the banishment of strong marinades and roux-thickened sauces, the incorporation of regional and traditional dishes into the world of haute cuisine, the introduction of previously unfamiliar ingredients and combinations, and the employment of new kitchen tools and equipment—like Teflon pans and even the microwave, which Paul Bocuse once bragged about using.

The movement was absolutely revolutionary. As Ferran put it in

The New York Times in 2008, exaggerating only slightly, "From the 1900s until nouvelle cuisine, nothing new appeared in the culinary sense. Until then, people took a recipe and reproduced exactly what it said. Since nouvelle cuisine, there have been so many things happening." Nouvelle cuisine gave chefs the liberty to interpret French cuisine in a new way—their own way, anchored to tradition but willing and able to reach far beyond it, too. In that sense, it presaged Ferran's own development. "Remember," he told me one day, "that like the cooking of El Bulli, nouvelle cuisine used little-known vegetables and seafood, worked with sweet and sour or sweet and salty tastes, brought in regional influences, and used new cooking tools." Some chefs even began playing with textures in what might be called a pre-Bullian way—like Marc Meneau at L'Espérance in Saint-Père-sous-Vézaley, who grafted nouvelle ideas onto traditional roots and created dishes, like oysters in seawater gelée and an astonishing foie gras cromesquis, liquid inside a crisp shell, that seemed to anticipate some of Ferran's creations.

Jean-Louis Neichel brought a taste of nouvelle cuisine to El Bulli in 1975—but it might be said to have officially reached Spain in 1976, when Paul Bocuse visited Madrid to speak at a culinary conference. Two young chefs from San Sebastián, in the Basque country, Juan Mari Arzak and Pedro Subijana, were among the attendees, and Bocuse's exposition of the new culinary philosophy that was taking over French kitchens impressed the two as dramatically as Maximin was to impress Ferran eleven years later. They became fervent converts, and when they returned to San Sebastián—where Arzak was cooking at his family's establishment and Subijana had recently opened his own restaurant—they began applying the ideas of nouvelle cuisine to the refined versions of traditional Basque dishes that they'd been preparing all along. The first steps were small but significant, like making salsa verde from just parsley and garlic, without the usual thickening of flour or cornstarch, or cooking the ingredients of a classic potaje, a soupy vegetable stew, individually so that each was done just to the perfect point. Arzak and Subijana also recruited a group of a dozen other chefs from San Sebastián and its vicinity, among them Karlos Arguiñano, Ramón Roteta, Tatus Fombellida, and José Juan Castillo, dubbing them the "new Basque chefs" and organizing regular meetings to create menus, trade recipes, and cook for a small number of modern-minded customers. Arzak's restaurant went on to earn three Michelin stars—at the time it was only the second place in the country to win that honor—and he himself became Spain's most famous chef until Ferran came along. (Subijana today also has three stars.)

There was another important culinary innovator in Spain in the 1970s, though, on the other side of the country—in Catalonia—and, though he had no direct contact with Paul Bocuse or any of the other chefs of the nouvelle cuisine, he too started working toward a contemporary cooking style. And he started before 1976. Josep Mercader i Brugues, born in Cadaqués in 1926, opened a roadside hotel and restaurant—originally called the Motel Ampurdán, today the Hotel Empordà—in Figueres, Salvador Dalí's birthplace, in 1961. Mercader was classically trained—he was a disciple of Pere Granollers, who had run the kitchen at the Hôtel de Paris in Monte Carlo for years before returning to Catalonia at the start of World War II—and his cooking was resolutely French, with a few Spanish accents. In the early seventies, though, he began adapting traditional Catalan dishes to a more modern style. This made perfect sense, since Catalan cuisine is genetically imbued with a bit of madness, and was already known, as we have seen, for unusual combinations of ingredients.

Favas a la catalana—which Manuel Vásquez Montalbán once described as among "the gastronomic pillars of the [Catalan] nation"—is a warm dish of big, long-cooked, pewter-hued fava beans with bacon and blood sausage. In 1972—when Ferran, remember, was ten years old—Mercader had the inspiration of reinterpreting (deconstructing?) this Catalan classic into a cool, summery salad of still-green baby favas with shreds of *jamón serrano*, translucent wisps of pig's foot, and plenty of mint. (Ferran referred to the same combination of flavors in 1995 with his cappuccino of baby favas with mint.) In 1973, Mercader translated allioli into a garlic mousseline that he gratinéed on top of salt cod, and had the idea—an expression of Catalan thriftiness if ever there was one—of saving the spines pulled out of salt-cured anchovies, soaking them in milk, dredging them in flour, then quickly frying them for an unusual and delicious snack. (Óscar Caballero of *La Vanguardia* calls this "the first modern tapa.") In 1974, he rethought escalivada, the Catalan combination of roasted eggplant, red peppers, and onions, into a mousse moistened with anchovy vinaigrette. Around this time he also invented what became perhaps his most widely copied dish, *gelat de crema catalana*—simply the crème brûlée–like Catalan burnt cream, complete with caramelized sugar topping, processed in an ice cream maker.

Curiously, perhaps out of his immense respect for his friend Juan Mari Arzak, Ferran doesn't seem to give Mercader, his fellow Catalan, much credit for his modernizations. When I mentioned this fact to the journalist Pau Arenós, he told me, "Ferran thinks that Mercader wasn't a chef of ingredients"—surely a misconception. It does occur to me, though, that Ferran would never have eaten food cooked by Mercader, who died suddenly of a heart attack in 1979, four years before Ferran first came to El Bulli. In fact, though he worked briefly at one of the greats of the era, Finisterre in Barcelona, Ferran is unlikely to have eaten as a customer in any of the top restaurants of the era around Catalonia in their prime. He would have been first too young, then too busy, to have had great meals at places like Reno in Barcelona (where Juli Soler had worked as a boy), famous for everything from its house-smoked salmon to its *canelones* (the Catalan version of cannelloni Rossini, introduced to Barcelona by Italian restaurateurs in the nineteenth century and now considered the definitive traditional dish of the city); or Agut d'Avinyó, also in Barcelona, run by the remarkable Ramón Cabau, who was said to be able to tell just by glancing at it whether a dish had been properly salted; or Lluís Cruanyas's original Eldorado Petit in Sant Feliu de Guixols, which brought Catalan fishermen's food to the level of haute cuisine. Maybe he simply didn't realize what was going on in other kitchens.

When I tried to convince Ferran one day that there really was contemporary Catalan cuisine being cooked by talented chefs in the region when he was just settling in at El Bulli, he grudgingly accepted the possibility. "But the question I have," he added earnestly, seeming slightly but genuinely bewildered, "is why didn't their cooking evolve more from their first steps?" It was a valid point. The first commandment of the creative person, as he is fond of saying, is to evolve. (The Irish chef Ross Lewis, who did a brief stage at El Bulli, told me that Ferran had a similar complaint about the famous restaurants of London, finding them quite orthodox, without artistry or unique style, simply mimicking the French.) On another occasion, Ferran pointed out to me that while there was an identifiable "Basque nouvelle cuisine," coalescing around Arzak and Subijana, the innovative Catalan chefs of the same period, for whatever reasons, never came together in collaboration, never launched a parallel unified movement. Nonetheless, Ferran stresses that while he doesn't consider them to have influenced him, he has great respect for Mercader, Cabau, Cruanyas, et al. And if they didn't evolve as he thought perhaps they should have, he says, he recognizes that *El sabor del Mediterráneo* is itself, in a sense, an evolution of the work they started.

In any case, ultimately, Ferran learned nouvelle cuisine not from Arzak and the other Basque pioneers, and certainly not from any other Catalan chef, but directly from France—first out of those Robert Laffont books Fermí Puig had introduced him to, and then through countless meals and a handful of stages at some of the leading restaurants of the genre. "I drank the waters from the source, from where nouvelle cuisine was born," he says.

But nouvelle cuisine, of course, was just the setup for Ferran. It got him ready for what was to come. He absorbed its lessons and moved on. And in so doing, he found a way to resolve that ancient conflict of intentions, to weave those two culinary currents—the quest for simplicity and purity of flavor and the desire to entertain or to benevolently mislead the diner—into a single stream.

10
"The Best Cook on the Planet"

*"[B]eing avant-garde means being before your time. Para-
doxically, only time will tell whether you were or weren't."*

—Ferran Adrià, *Los secretos de elBulli*

Ferran had come to rely increasingly on Xavier Sagristà as a creative
collaborator, and when Sagristà left the restaurant in 1993, Ferran
changed direction. (Sagristà departed, with Toni Gerez, to take over a
beautiful rural restaurant and hotel complex called Mas Pau, near
Figueres, with Ferran and Juli as partners; the latter are no longer involved, but Sagristà and Gerez are still in charge, and the dining room
is excellent.) Ferran's new idea was to shift focus away from the creation of new dishes, and instead attempt to develop new concepts,
techniques, and what he called "elaborations" that could be applied to
many different ingredients. He also began thinking about and writing
down the elements of his developing culinary philosophy. Some key
points: serve small portions; seek new products; work with the contrast
of textures and temperatures; assume that all foods have the same

potential value (sardines are worth as much as caviar); "the element of surprise is important."

These and other provisions appeared in print for the first time in the course notes for a series of three-day seminars-cum-cooking-classes "for professionals and aficionados," called "Tres Días en Cala Montjoi," that Ferran instituted in the restaurant when it closed for its 1993–94 winter hiatus. His friend Xavier Agulló, who attended the following season, reports that—hardly surprisingly—the events were unconventional. "We'd sit around a table with Ferran, fifteen or twenty of us," he tells me, "talking about his crazy ideas. He gave us ideas instead of recipes. And he'd make food for us and then say, 'Guess what's in this one, and tonight at dinner I'll make you two or three dishes that are made only for you, no one else.' I won the contest one night. He served us what was to become one of his most famous dishes, his menestra en texturas, and I guessed the ingredients." This was Ferran's play on a menestra de verduras, one of the staples of the cooking of the northern Spanish region of Navarre—a plateful of assorted cooked vegetables that might include such things as chard, artichokes, peas, asparagus, green beans, favas, carrots, even sometimes cardoons and/or the stems of borage plants, depending on availability and the season. Ferran has worked seasonal and inspirational variations on his version over the years, too, but the menestra that Agulló tasted was probably the original one, involving avocado, tomato purée, corn mousse, cauliflower mousse, basil gelée, a quenelle of fresh almond ice cream, peach granita, and a mousse of beets.

Everything was like a game to Ferran, Agulló says. At one of the sessions, he put fried corn on a piece of duck liver, and got so excited that he was almost jumping around the restaurant, saying, "What do ducks eat? What do ducks eat?" The sessions had practical value to Ferran and his team, too. Until he began the classes, Ferran says, none of them had ever sat down in the restaurant to have a meal, and the experience gave them a new perspective on the menu and the way it was served.

In 1994, Ferran and Juli found themselves confronting a crisis in Cala Montjoi: "We had spent all our money and gone into debt buying the business and building the new kitchen," says Ferran. "Dr. Schilling had always said that the land and buildings would be their gift to us when they completely retired." For whatever reasons, the doctor changed his mind. In 1991, he had learned that he was in the early stages of Parkinson's disease. As it progressed, he realized that he could not continue coming to Cala Montjoi for very much longer, and in 1994, he and Marketta decided to sell the property—everything but the house and the land it stood on. He announced this abruptly; if Ferran and Juli didn't want it, Dr. Schilling said, he'd find another buyer. "It was a very complicated situation," says Ferran, "because the Schillings had promised us special conditions that they consequently did not live up to—but after making such a large investment in the kitchen, we felt forced to buy the place anyway." They had no means to do so—but they had a friend who did: the publisher of *El sabor del Mediterráneo*, Miquel Horta. "We went to Miquel and made him a proposition," says Ferran, "that he participate in our project as a partner. He accepted right away. He was our 'Mr. Humane.' He helped us very much." Ferran and Juli were able to close the deal with the Schillings, and at last became the owners of El Bulli in every sense.

Unfortunately, Horta's involvement with El Bulli was to become the source of some controversy. "In 1994," says Ferran, "the company had a net worth of two hundred fifty million pesetas, and we offered Miquel a twenty percent interest for fifty million. By 2005, the net worth of the company had quadrupled to the equivalent of a billion pesetas, and we bought back his interest for twenty percent of that." As to why they wanted to end the partnership at this point, Ferran will say only, "It was a personal, not a professional, matter, and because of that I never speak of it." (Newspaper reports refer to Horta's mental problems.) In 2008, however, Horta's sons announced that they were filing suit against Ferran and Juli on their elderly father's behalf, claiming that the two had taken advantage of his deteriorating condition to dupe him, and that the shares had been worth as much as twenty times what the partners paid.

Xavier Agulló, who knows the situation well, told me, "I can assure you that, whatever the children say now, at the time of the sale, everything was done correctly, everything was right." In any case, Ferran told me in March of 2010, up to that point neither he nor Juli had been served with legal papers, beyond a request for financial records of the contested period. Horta is still alive but not well, and Ferran says, a little ruefully, that he has had no contact with him for years. "The whole situation is very complicated," he says. "You could do a whole book just about that." Jean-Claude Ribaut, who writes about gastronomy for *Le Monde*, has suggested that Ferran and Juli are closing El Bulli in its present form in 2012 as "a strategic position" in the sons' action against them—an accusation that Ferran dismisses with a shake of his head and a wave of his hand, as if it's too silly to even contemplate.

■ ■ ■

Though Ferran and Juli have for many years refused offers to open additional restaurants, they did begin, as early as 1987, to do outside catering—unusual for high-quality establishments in Spain in that era. The idea was partly to be able to bring a taste of the restaurant's cuisine to a broader audience—but it was also, admits Ferran candidly, simply "to earn money to survive." On one memorable occasion, the El Bulli team prepared a wedding banquet for Xavier Agulló in the cloister of the Convento del Carmen at the Castell de Peralada, at which all the food was suspended from trees in the garden. (I asked Agulló for some specifics, and he told me, "The only thing I can picture clearly is chicken wings marinated in soy sauce. I tell you, the party was so wild I can't remember anything else.") In 1995, Ferran and Juli set up an official branch of the business, dubbed elBullicatering, with a Barcelona restaurateur named Eduard Roigé in charge. It happened that Ferran knew Esteban Terradas Muntañola, architect of the newly opened Barcelona aquarium, and through him he learned that there was unused space in the new structure. He'd decided that the catering operation should be fully separated from the restaurant and his other business interests, and arranged to take over a portion of the aquarium's second floor, including a kitchen, as catering headquarters. The enterprise—which, Ferran has said, "required further refinement of the precision and 'assembly line' knowledge of El Bulli"—went on to cater four or five banquets a year, one for as many as 3,200 guests, until Ferran and Juli made the decision to stop accepting almost all outside catering work in 2009. "There weren't many banquets," Ferran says, "but they were very important ones." Clients included the Canal+ TV station and SEAT, the Spanish car-maker—whose 600 model, remember, had been the very symbol of the Desarrollo.

Ferran tells a funny story about one banquet in a book called *Don't Try This at Home: Culinary Catastrophes from the World's Greatest Chefs*. One of the dishes on the menu was cep carpaccio with lobster, and he and his staff had cleaned, cooked, shelled, and cut up a thousand of the pricey crustaceans for the purpose. Because of the volume of work involved, it was executed the night before the event, and the cut-up lobster pieces were wrapped and stored in white polystyrene containers—which were then placed inside a refrigerated walk-in. What hadn't occurred to anybody was that the polystyrene would insulate the lobster—from the cold—so the lobsters sat overnight at what was essentially room temperature and were spoiled by morning. Discovering the mishap, Ferran and company spent half the day calling around Barcelona buying every lobster they could find, eventually replacing about half of them; they processed them at record speed, and by increasing the quantity of ceps and decreasing the amount of lobster in each serving, they were able to present the dish more or less as planned.

Ferran and his team took on a major project in late 1995, consulting for a new restaurant called Talaia Mar, at the Port Olímpic on the Barcelona waterfront—a marina that had been built for the 1992 Olympic Games. Ferran brought in Carles Abellán from the El Bulli kitchen as head chef, and filled out the Talaia crew with five other young men: Sergi Arola, Oriol Balaguer, Rafa Morales, Marc Puig-Pey, and Marc Singla. (All six chefs have gone on to have illustrious careers of their own.) "Talaia was very important," he says. "It was the first cosmopolitan Mediterranean restaurant, the first place to serve modern tapas." In overseeing the project, it also occurred to Ferran that the Talaia kitchen, in the quiet hours between the lunch and dinner service, would be a good place for him to work on new ideas, away from the demands of El Bulli. He started spending afternoons there, from about four to seven P.M. every day. "We did experiments," he says, "but we didn't consider this a workshop."

Pau Arenós, a reporter for *El Periódico*, heard rumors about a chef from the Costa Brava, not very well known, who was supervising the food at this Port Olímpic restaurant and using it for some sort of off-hours experimentation, and he talked himself into an assignment to spend three days there for a story. "You have to remember that Ferran was basically unknown outside gastronomic circles at the time," says Arenós, "and I wasn't a specialist in food, just a general-interest reporter. He wasn't even cooking when I got there, but just from talking to him that first time, I was absolutely sure that he was unique. He was talking about food as if he were talking about literature. I had been a journalist for twenty-five years at that point and had never before, *never*, known with such clarity that I was in the presence of a genius. I left the restaurant and called a friend and said, 'I've just met Picasso.'" Arenós remembers eating two of the dishes for which Talaia

Mar became famous, bacon ice cream and the celebrated decon-structed potato omelette. "One of the things that struck me most strongly about Ferran in the days I was at Talaia," Arenós says, "was how very intuitive he was. When he worked, he didn't really have a plan, but it always seemed as if he did."

By the mid-nineties, the kitchen staff at El Bulli had grown, and was much more disciplined and organized than it had been a decade earlier. More dishes were added to the menu and the service became more complex, but the food itself showed tendencies toward minimal-ism. Savory vegetable sorbets, caramelized herbs, and fruit carpaccios were among the innovations. This is also the period, says Ferran, when the evolution of the cuisine "became not a question of a single chef, but of a philosophy of work." The new dishes and new way of working paid off.

For several years in the 1990s, the *Guide Gault/Millau*, which listed the top restaurants and hotels in France, Belgium, and Switzer-land, included a handful of restaurants near the French border in Catalonia and the Basque country. In 1995, it awarded El Bulli a score of 19/20. To Ferran, this was a landmark, and indeed it was a signifi-cant honor, coming from this francocentric—French—guidebook. El Bulli was the only Spanish restaurant on this level. It should be pointed out, though, that twenty other establishments in France, Belgium, and Switzerland shared the same score—and that eighteen were rated even higher, at 19.5/20. More significant, perhaps, was the fact that in the same listing, the San Sebastián restaurant of Juan Mari Arzak—justly considered the father of contemporary Spanish cooking—only got 18/20.

The same year's edition of the influential Spanish restaurant critic Rafael García Santos's guide, *Lo mejor de la gastronomía*, which had been rating El Bulli among its top restaurants for several years, awarded Ferran its highest score, 9.75 points out of 10—while Arzak got only 9.50. "That two important guidebooks had rated us above

Arzak," says Ferran, "caused problems between Juan Mari and me for a while. Then, two or three years later, Arzak called me and said, 'I was an idiot. I want to move in the direction of the vanguard.'" Fermí Puig thinks that "for Arzak, that was the luckiest day of his life. If he hadn't done that, he could have become an icon like Bocuse, no longer relevant, with cooking that hasn't changed for forty years."

I ask Arzak for his side of the story, sitting at the bar at his restaurant one afternoon. "I was a bit the guru of Spanish food," he begins, "and people told me that Ferran did bizarre things. But I went anyway. The first time, I didn't understand a lot of what he was doing, and there were things I didn't like. But there were also things I did like, and those dishes that I understood were just extraordinary. If something is better I can always learn. I look at everything, ask about everything. I make my own cuisine. I have many inspirations, but I am certainly inspired by Ferran. I spend time in his kitchen every year, and I always learn. The cuisine of Ferran is very contagious." Today, says Arzak, he and Ferran are like brothers. "We even spend our vacations together," he says. "We go someplace tranquil: the Bahamas, the Canary Islands, Marrakesh. These are not gastronomic tours, though of course if there is something interesting to eat, we will eat it. If we can eat well, so much the better. But that's not the main purpose. It's to relax." Maybe so, but José Andrés came along on one trip, to Zahara de los Atunes, in Andalusia, and he remembers the two chefs challenging themselves every day with new projects—"Let's make the ultimate bouillabaisse!" and so on.

High scores in the guidebooks were important to Ferran and El Bulli, but even more important was the endorsement of Joël Robuchon. He had returned to the restaurant several times after his first visit in 1992, and in an interview on the French television station TF1 in 1996, the year he officially retired, he identified Ferran as his "heir," calling him "the best cook on the planet." This caused an unimaginable scandal in French culinary circles. Robuchon realized that he

---

had made a lot of his French colleagues disappointed and angry—how could a Spaniard could be the world's best chef?—"But I said it," he added, "because I sincerely believed it." There remains some controversy about Robuchon's remarks. The Paris-based German writer Jörg Zipprick, a vocal critic of Ferran, is convinced that Robuchon praised Ferran so highly just to tweak his own rival, Alain Ducasse, who Robuchon thought had been getting too big for his britches. But Robuchon was unequivocal in an interview with *L'Express* in 2009, saying, "I was retired and they asked me who, in my opinion, had replaced me as the No. 1 in gastronomy. When I said 'Ferran Adrià,' I was accused of wanting to cut the grass out from under the feet of the French contenders. Today, surprisingly, everyone agrees with me: Ferran Adrià is undoubtedly the most brilliant creator in the world." Michel Guérard has since noted that, if he had been asked, he would have said the same thing.

In late 1996, with the publication of the 1997 *Guide Michelin*, El Bulli finally got its long-overdue third star—an event that went all but unremarked in the international food community. Pau Arenós told me that when the Michelin news was announced, he wanted to report it on the front page of *El Periódico*, but his boss said, "No, this Adrià is unknown." It was as if El Bulli, shrouded by the Mediterranean mists in its little Catalan cove, were all but invisible. In any case, says Ferran, by that time the honor was almost beside the point. "The third star was important for us, of course," he tells me, "but it was only one of the important things. We had no party to celebrate. Everything remained the same. We had been doing things that were more radical every year, and we just kept on doing them."

After Joël Robuchon had praised him publically, Ferran flew to Paris to thank him in person. "When we spoke there," he tells me, "Robuchon said, 'I'll give you some advice. From now on, it won't be easy to deal with everything that will happen to you. The repercussions will be large and you'll have to dedicate a lot of time to interviews and promoting the restaurant. A moment will come when you won't have time to create.'" Ferran took this to heart. By the time he severed El Bulli's relationship with Talaia Mar not long afterward, thereby losing his part-time laboratory, he was utterly convinced that setting up an independent workshop was essential to his creative process. He just wasn't sure how to go about it. "I thought that we should do some research and see how other chefs handled their workshops," says Ferran, "but when we started to ask around, we found to our surprise that nobody had ever heard of this kind of thing. We were on our own."

Ferran leapt right in: In October of 1997, he brought his brother, Albert, and one of the chefs, Oriol Castro, into the El Bulli catering operation at the aquarium, marking out a small office for theoretical work and turning them loose in the catering kitchen, when it wasn't busy, to test out dishes and ideas. "Our room in the aquarium had beautiful views," Albert remembers, "but it was pretty bare—just one table, one chair for me and one for Oriol, a few books, and a few note-books." This, says Ferran, was what he considers the birth of the restaurant's Taller, or workshop. He also notes that, while Albert is best-known for his contributions to the "sweet world" at El Bulli, and is often still described (erroneously) as the restaurant's pastry chef, his contributions to El Bulli over the years have gone far beyond that: Ferran has always considered Albert to be an essential collaborator, and has said, "One comment from Albert is worth more to me than three months' worth of pastries." Albert remained in charge of the Taller, at the aquarium and then in the dedicated space it now occupies, until 2008, when he retired from any day-to-day role at El Bulli to spend more time with his family.

The American chef Ken Oringer, now owner of two restaurants in Boston, did an informal weeklong stage at the aquarium workshop after it had been running for a couple of years. Though it had filled up considerably from the "one table, one chair" days—a photograph from the period shows at least two of the former, three of the latter, and walls lined with bookshelves, at least some of them full—Oringer remembers that it was still "like the pantry of a home-ec kitchen, a side pantry. The team would do three or four experiments a day," he says, "and I still can't get over how completely open they were, sharing everything. They were breaking all the rules, writing new ones, and they'd share it all with anybody. Some three-star chefs in France wouldn't even give you a copy of their menu. I saw that Ferran was a meticulous cook, but he threw himself at food with reckless abandon. He respects tradition so much, but at the same time he's not afraid to take risks. You could see the intensity, sort of a madman look in his eye. He was like a kid running around the kitchen showing you stuff."

For a time, the centerpiece of the workshop was the Pacojet, a Swiss-made appliance that mixes and purées frozen ingredients without thawing them. An accidental by-product of the sorbets the team produced with it was a kind of ice powder, which had a texture nobody had ever seen before. They figured out how to achieve the effect intentionally, and it became part of the repertoire. During this period, Ferran, Albert, and Oriol would make regular tours of Barcelona's food and equipment purveyors, including the baking and kitchen supply store Solé Graells, the specialty food merchants Guzman and Gurmalia in the Mercabarna wholesale market, and the stalls in the Boqueria—Barcelona's legendary main covered market. They'd bring everything back to the aquarium and list everything on white boards tacked to the walls, then consider each one and figure out what they could do with it.

Instead of taking his third Michelin star as evidence that he had reached some kind of professional or creative summit—instead of breathing a sigh of relief and coasting on his reputation for at least a year or two—Ferran seemed to go on the offensive after receiving the honor, pushing farther and farther into unknown territory. He calls 1997 "the year of provocation." This was the year he introduced his first hot, sweet soup, basically a diluted chocolate ganache (chocolate cream icing), and his first "pasta-gelée" (paper-thin sheets of milk curds standing in for pasta). It was the year that saw, as Ferran put it, "the explosion of the world of our raviolis," like a pasta-less liquid coconut version and ravioli made of assorted vegetables preserved in syrup, and the year of preparations simultaneously savory and sweet (for instance, salted madeleines and ice creams).

No provocation of 1997 was more provocative, however, than Ferran's smoke foam—which was just that, a lightly gelatinized froth of nothing but water flavored with woodsmoke, served in a glass with a few drops of olive oil and some strips of toast. "The idea," Ferran explained, "was to make you recall eating grilled bread with olive oil. It is an iconic dish, used to arouse a reaction." Even Ferran's supporters didn't always like it. "Smoke foam was *terrible*," the critic Carmen Casas told me with an emphatic smile one morning, "like what you get when you cross a busy street. But it was very interesting." Pau Arenós agrees: "Smoke foam was the dish I have liked least at El Bulli," he says, "but it was the most important dish, because it made a gas into a solid. It was a clear expression of Ferran's message: 'Everything is possible.'"

Ferran has often said that he doesn't like explaining the techniques he uses to his customers, because he wants them to be able to react to his food on a purely visceral and emotional level. "You don't want a magician to reveal what's behind his tricks," he points out. On the other hand, he is not proprietary about his innovations and is happy to explain everything he does to his fellow chefs, one magician to another. And the general public did get a chance to peek behind the screen when Ferran published a new book, in 1998, called *Los secretos de El Bulli: Recetas, técnicas y reflexiones* (The Secrets of El Bulli: Recipes, Techniques and Reflections). Though it contains some eighty-seven recipes—including those for such definitive El Bulli dishes as gazpacho with lobster, deconstructed arroz a la cubana and chicken curry, and, yes, smoke foam—it also offers almost a hundred pages of philosophy and aperçu. Among other things, Ferran provides an expanded version of the list of guidelines he first formulated for his "Tres Días" sessions at El Bulli (among the additions, "not much interest in meat dishes"; "dishes that are seldom easy to define by means of the vocabulary of classic cuisine"; and "flavor is the most important thing").

He also writes that "creativity . . . forms part of my work, and I enjoy it as a gift, which is why I try not to give it more significance than it really has." In Ferran's view, there is nothing spontaneous about this creativity. The process is extremely organized. He gives his readers this example, considering one of his many variations on mar i muntanya, the definitively Catalan genre of dishes that combines fish or shellfish with poultry, meat, snails, and/or game:

Problem: mar i muntanya

Idea: caviar and marrow

Definition of the dish: marrow with caviar

Gathering of information: Is there something like it already? Has someone already done it?

Analysis of information: How can we make it?

Creativity: How can we combine the elements in the right form?

Materials and technology: What caviar should we use? How and where do we cook the marrow?

Experimentation: testing, trying things out

Final test: Tasting until it gets to the right point

Making it at the restaurant: Finding ways to reproduce what we've created

Ferran and his team were very busy in 1998. The publication of *Los secretos* was followed quickly by that of three more books from El

Bulli: One was Albert's maiden effort as an author, *Los postres de El Bulli* (The Desserts of El Bulli), a book full of stunning photographs, technical advice, culinary philosophy, and highly original recipes whose minimalist names—Cherries Vanilla Vinegar Gingerbread, or Lichis Apple Fennel—don't begin to hint at their complexity or beauty. Almost immediately, this volume, now out of print, became an inspiration for pastry chefs all over Spain and beyond. (Published in 2008, his second book, *Natura*, with its stunning edible landscapes, was possibly even more influential.) The others were *Cocinar en 10 minutos con Ferran Adrià*, written for the Corte Inglés department store chain, and *Las 50 nuevas tapas de Ferran Adrià*, done in conjunction with the Spanish magazine *Woman*, for which Ferran had been writing a series of columns featuring accessible recipes. "Nobody speaks of these books," says Ferran in what sounds like real disappointment; he is genuinely proud of them. In fact, the Corte Inglés book is impossible to find these days, and the tapas book isn't much easier—but the latter, particularly, did have real influence, far more than Ferran's introduction of tapas onto the El Bulli menu had had seven years earlier.

Tapas aren't Catalan. They were born in Andalusia—*tapa* literally means "cover" or "top," and one theory is that the original tapas were little slices of bread garnished with a bit of ham or salted fish, to be placed atop one's glass of sherry to keep the flies out—and subsequently found wide acceptance and elaboration elsewhere in Spain, especially in Madrid and San Sebastián. But not in Catalonia: When I first started spending time in Barcelona in the early eighties, it dawned on me after three or four weeks that not one of my new food-loving local friends had yet taken me to a tapas bar, or even mentioned one. I finally asked somebody about this and he said, "Oh, it's mostly the Andalusians who've moved here to work who eat tapas. We might stop in for a glass and a snack now and then, but we Catalans like to have our dinner sitting down."

In his book, Ferran defined tapas as "little dishes of various tastes and textures, pleasures to stimulate the curiosity as well as the appetite"—which gave him considerable leeway. Some of his recipes were straightforward (rabbit chops with allioli, brochettes of mozzarella and cherry tomatoes marinated in basil oil), while others expanded the possibilities of tapas into new territory, as he had earlier started doing at the restaurant—for instance tomato polos (like Popsicles) "painted" with rosewater and guindilla chile oil, brochettes of cauliflower and raspberries and of crayfish in romesco breadcrumbs, baby clams in gelatin with passion fruit juice, and caramelized quail eggs. To what extent *Las nuevas tapas* was responsible may be debated, but it wasn't until after the book was published that Barcelonans started taking tapas seriously—and that the very concept of the contemporary tapas bar, serving modern as well as traditional "little dishes," took hold all over Spain.

In 1998, elBulli S.L. also signed two major contracts: a long-term deal to run La Terraza, the dining room at the elite Casino de Madrid in the Spanish capital, and an agreement to manage—and provide food for—a forty-four-room luxury hotel called Hacienda Benazuza, in Sanlúcar la Mayor, near Seville. The idea at Benazuza, says Ferran, was to somehow translate the quality and uniqueness of a three- or four-hour meal at El Bulli into a twenty-four-hour-a-day hotel experience. The main dining room, La Alquería, which has earned two Michelin stars (Ferran thinks it has the possibility to earn three eventually), has been described as the next best thing to El Bulli itself—and in fact the menu offers a retrospective selection of dishes from Cala Montjoi. Two casual restaurants offer more traditional food. (At one point, Ferran was full of plans to expand the Benazuza concept to other Mediterranean locations, including Mallorca and Croatia, but he changed his mind. "I looked at hotels carefully," he says, "and it's a very difficult business.")

By the late nineties, the basic philosophy and working structure of

El Bulli as we know the restaurant today were pretty well established. His cuisine, Ferran has explained, was by then already based on "three pillars" that have defined it ever since: "technical and conceptual research, the role of the senses in creating and eating, and the sixth sense, i.e., the role of reason and reflection on the act of eating." Since that time, he continued, his influences have expanded its horizons to encompass "other creative fields such as industrial design, science, art, [and the] food industry" and "not so much . . . the aesthetics but . . . the whole philosophy of Asian cooking, especially from Japan." Another development: In the last few years of the twentieth century, one technique or family of techniques typically monopolized the menu each season—I remember the French chef Jean-Pierre Silva telling me once, with a look of delighted amazement on his face, that he'd had dinner at El Bulli "and every single course was a foam!"—but by the early twenty-first century, the kitchen had what Ferran calls a "heritage" of techniques and ideas to utilize, so menus could be varied and offer diners a far greater range of experiences than had previously been possible.

■ ■ ■

The tomfoolery of the early eighties had lasted well into the nineties at El Bulli. By all accounts, the kitchen team of this period was a bunch of good-looking, energetic, fun-loving young men (and an occasional woman, like Montse Núñez, known as "the aunt," who cooked at the restaurant from 1991 to 2000), not making much money but doing good work and having a great time. Photographs from the era—there are a number of them on the El Bulli Web site—tell the tale: In 1991, Xavier Sagristà and another El Bulli chef, Marc Cuspinera, were shot in the kitchen holding bloody pigs' ears up to their heads. The year after that, the whole crew posed sporting copper cloches as hats; the caption reads, in the English translation on the El Bulli Web site, "Although it seems the opposite, we were not all the day joking." Obviously they weren't, or they wouldn't have been able to put such good food out on the tables—but, at least judging from a progression of photographs from year to year, there was a spirit of camaraderie and fun that slowly faded as the staff grew and the stakes got higher.

At some point as he evolved from merely an extremely talented Spanish-influenced French-style chef into the most original culinary innovator of our time, Ferran must have begun to feel a little like a Prince Hal with a kitchen full of Falstaffs. He had partied as hard as anyone—he got into this whole cooking thing in the first place, remember, so that he could spend a decadent summer in Ibiza—and at the height of what I like to think of as the disco-beach era, he was as well-known in the bars and clubs of Roses and vicinity as any of his cooks, staying up as late, drinking as much, and chasing as many girls as anyone. But things changed, and so did he.

Jeff Cerciello, who was a stagiare at El Bulli in 1993 (and later became culinary director of Thomas Keller's Bouchon, Bouchon Bakery, and ad hoc restaurants), remembers that even back then, when Albert and the rest of the kitchen crew would arrive at the restaurant at sunup, having come straight from the delights of Roses, "Ferran would always be there waiting, and sometimes he'd flip out when we'd come in all disheveled, wearing jeans and our jackets from the night before." But, adds Cerciello, "When it came time to cook, everybody was suddenly very focused. Everybody was just *so into* what we were doing. I've never experienced anything like that since." El Bulli in this era was, Ferran has said, a mixture of Bohemia and military discipline.

In the mid-nineties, in any case, photographs of the kitchen staff start getting more serious, less colorful, eventually becoming positively sober. Chef's whites and blue aprons replace T-shirts and jeans. Eccentric haircuts disappear. A shot from 2001 of the stagiares throwing their kitchen towels up into the air—a closing-night ritual at the restaurant—shows a neatly dressed group standing evenly spaced around their work tables, with expressions that suggest all the spontaneity of North Korean schoolchildren offering a birthday salute to Kim Jong-il.

By the late nineties, Ferran had stopped going out with the other chefs, and had begun curtailing the excesses of his team. (In all the time I spent with him in 2008 and 2009, much of it away from the restaurant, I never saw Ferran drink more than a beer or two, if that, and occasionally a small digéstif.) He stresses that "the 'party' didn't stop dead. It changed and evolved in a natural way, without my having to convince anyone. As the years went by, we became more responsible, and by the time the third Michelin star arrived, we were really involved in the work and we lived only for that."

Albert Raurich, who started at the restaurant in 1997, told me this tale: "In those days," he says, "we were open seven months a year instead of six and stuck there all the time, and sometimes we just had to get away, so we'd go to Roses after the service and stay out all night. There was definitely still some partying going on. Then one day I was down on the beach with Lalo [Eduard Bosch, who had become head chef in 1996] having a beer, and he said, 'Ferran has asked me to put together the best possible team, the best that there has ever been at El Bulli, and if you want to be part of it, you have to stop the party.' I thought that was ironic, because we were sitting on the beach drinking at the time, but he was serious. I went out a few more times, and I then stopped."

11

First, the Concept

"Gastronomic imagination . . . precedes experience itself, accompanies it, and in part substitutes for it."

—Jean-François Revel, *Culture and Cuisine*

Ferran had become determined to set up a full-time workshop that would function symbiotically with, but independent from, the restaurant, and with this in mind, in late 1998, elBulli S.L. purchased an entire floor of an eighteenth-century town house on the Carrer de la Portaferrissa, a clamorous pedestrian shopping street linking Barcelona's medieval Gothic Quarter with its famous Ramblas in the city's heart. The process of designing, renovating, and equipping it took slightly more than a year, and the elBulli Taller opened in January of 2000. (The word, pronounced "tal-YEH," is Catalan for "studio" or "workshop," like *atelier* in French.)

It's an attractive space, warm and light. The reception area looks like the living room in some hip downtown Manhattan apartment, with a high ceiling, matte-finish gray marble floors, and clean-lined furnishings—a white couch, a couple of black chairs, and two orange floor pillows around a low wood table piled with magazines. Framed magazine covers (from America, Italy, France, Holland, Germany, Russia, Portugal, Greece, Japan—the world) crowd the walls of the entryway, and there are low shelves packed with stacks of books and a scattering of miscellaneous objects, including examples of what Ferran likes to call "carriers"—vessels designed especially to hold some of his creations. Portraits of Ferran and Juli by Matt Groening are on display (the creator of *The Simpsons* has never been to El Bulli, but the show's producer, James Brooks, has, and Groening did the likenesses at his request), as is a three-dimensional *Simpsons*-inspired mock cover of *Life* magazine by sculptor Miguel Herrera, on which an obviously dumbfounded Homer points to something unidentifiable on a plate while Ferran looks on. An open staircase leads up to a loft level holding offices and a narrow gallery lined with bookshelves. "Upstairs is business," says Ferran, "downstairs is creativity. You can't have them both in the same place." Off to one side is "the chapel," a narrow vaulted room that actually used to *be* a chapel, and is now a conference room filled almost wall to wall by one long table and its chairs; Ferran sometimes shuts himself in here, he tells me, when he wants to think and work without distractions.

The kitchen, which is the whole point of the place, is a large rectangular room, open on both ends (though one end can be closed off with a red floor-to-ceiling sliding door), amply sunlit through large windows giving onto a terrace. Along the edge of the long aluminum work table that runs the full length of the wall on one end of the room is a cryptic verse in Catalan by Ferran's sculptor friend Xavier Medina-Campeny: *"L'amant de cap Norfeu digué: pèsol, ploma, barca. La veu respongué:* tongue, tongue, tongue. *L'amant afegí: nap, gerd, trufa. Finalment la papil·la s'obrí."* ("The lover of Cap Norfeu [a cape just north of Cala Montjoi] says: pea, pen, boat. The voice responds: tongue, tongue, tongue. The lover adds: turnip, raspberry, truffle. At last the taste buds open.") On the other end of the kitchen, away from the worktable and the induction cooking hobs, is a two-sided rack honeycombed with small compartments. On the left side, each nook contains a small bottle filled with something, clearly labeled—spices, seeds, oils, alcohols, grains, legumes, strains of yeast; one holds something that looks like coarse-ground talc, but turns out to be powdered milk. The rack on the right has the same number of nooks, but only one of them holds a bottle, labeled "sal"—salt. In the Taller's early days, says Ferran, the rack was a storage space, and the elements placed there were actually used. "Later," he says, "it became an aesthetic element. There is only salt on one side because salt is the most important product in the kitchen."

A lot of the knee-jerk criticism of El Bulli is based on the fact that Ferran and his chefs don't cook like everybody else has always cooked, standing over a hot stove, shaking a skillet and flipping the food with that little chefs' gesture that mere mortals can rarely duplicate without lofting onions onto the floor, standing back a bit when the grease flares up, stirring sauces with a wooden spoon, adding just a dash more this or that. Instead, he and his team prepare food on flameless induction cooktops and, worse, sometimes with *cold*, in tubs of liquid nitrogen; they use machines that don't look familiar, or implements that don't seem to belong in the chef's tool kit, like electric screwdrivers and oversize syringes. The Taller, in particular, is rumored to be some kind of high-tech laboratory full of science-fictional paraphernalia—as if you'd have to pass through an airlock instead of an old wood-framed portal to get in, and then dodge laser-wielding robots and errant neutron beams somehow pressed into far-out culinary service.

Of course, ever since there have been kitchens, chefs and tinkers and, yes, scientists have been trying to improve them with new technology. In ancient Greece, slaves tending wood fires in the *opta-*

neion, or roasting room, went blind or died of lung congestion until efficient chimneys were added to the structures. The freestanding European-style stove, made from brick and tile and ventilated with a flue, was a life-changing innovation when it first appeared in Alsace in the late fifteenth century. The pressure cooker, the double boiler, the first oven with closed doors, the gas stove, the electric stove, the microwave oven, the food processor, sous-vide technology—each of these innovations, in turn, won acceptance and became old hat. So what's the big deal with some new contraptions for the kitchen? Anyway, the truth is that some of the appliances used by the chefs at the Taller are commonplace stuff, even in home kitchens—the Kenwood stand mixer, the juicer, the microwave. (Ferran once said that he hates any machine that can break down.) A small red-and-chrome Lavazza Modo Mio espresso machine occupies one corner, not for any futuristic purposes but simply to keep the staff happily caffeinated. Even the less familiar items are reasonably straightforward: The Thermomix is a sort of super–food processor that can weigh and cook ingredients as well as chop, grate, and knead them. The Roner is basically a bain-marie, except that it's a smart bain-marie, capable of holding more than twenty quarts of liquid at constant temperatures, from 41 to 212 degrees Fahrenheit. The Pacojet, as noted, is just a space-age ice-cream maker. The Vac-Star is merely a sous-vide device. The Hydraflow EziDri dehydrator is nothing more than a larger and more efficient version of a device that campers and survivalists have been using for decades.

■ ■ ■

Throughout 2009, I spent a number of mornings and afternoons at the Taller, both with and without Ferran, asking questions, watching the chefs work, snooping around (with Ferran's permission). On my second or third visit, it suddenly dawned on me that, for certain kinds of people, working at the Taller has got to be a dream job: The chefs basically come in every day and get to play with their food—not just get to, but are encouraged to. Everything is fair game, every culture, every ingredient, every conceivable way of dealing with it.

Of course, they are required to keep extensive and detailed records of everything they do, the failures as well as the successes—on paper, but also with digital cameras. The chefs also take careful notes, and photographs, when they're out and about, traveling abroad or just roaming around Barcelona or the Catalan countryside. Back at the Taller, all the notes are transferred to a large master notebook and used as a non-digital database of ideas. Another notebook catalogues the results of extensive testing for dishes that are being seriously considered. Each one gets its own page, with name and principal product, date of testing, *valoración* (positive or negative), description/ elaboration, field (new product, technique, technique applied to product), and ideas for usage (as dessert, as cocktail, integrated into a dish). The Taller functions whenever El Bulli is closed, with a team of about a dozen chefs working in morning and afternoon shifts; Ferran once estimated that about five thousand experiments might be conducted here annually. Out of that, perhaps a hundred or so new dishes would eventually make it into the restaurant. In the mid-2000s, an independent marketing study estimated that this process—that running the Taller—cost about 250,000 euros (about $375,000) a year. More recently, Ferran has said that running the Taller and the restaurant together costs 500,000 euros annually—adding that "without the Taller, El Bulli as it is today would not be possible." He adds, "What's important is that we do this every day, every day."

One afternoon at the Taller, after Ferran has left me free to poke around at will, I start leafing through some of the other notebooks that are stacked and scattered on a high table beneath the shelf of ingredients. One contains a list of new products—or products that the kitchen had thus far used very little—for possible future use. These include (parenthetical notes are mine):

Olluco (a potato-like Andean tuber, *Ullucos tuberosus Caldas*, sometimes used instead of potatoes for *chuño*, the ancient freeze-dried staple of Peru and Bolivia)

Mini vegetables

Crosnes (also called Chinese artichokes)

Boniato (sweet potato)

Carambola (aka star fruit)

Cider apples

Carissa (a tart berry, *Carissa macrocarpa*, sometimes called Natal plum)

Toasted soy flour

Japanese fruit and rice vinegar

Oregano flowers

Ham shoulder fat

Veal throat

Chicken cartilage

Fresh hare from the Vall d'Aran

Thrushes

Espardenya (sea slug) skin, whole espardenyes

Giant razor clams

Bottarga Trikalinos (Trikalinos is a company producing gray mullet; bottarga are dried, cured roe sacs)

Umeboshi (Japanese pickled plums)

Katsubuchi (Japanese dried fish flakes)

Nori fried with sesame

From another notebook, this one from the eight days Ferran spent in Japan in 2009, participating in the Tokyo Taste gastronomic confer-

ence (those eight days yielded eight pages of ideas, of which these are
only a few):

> False stew of vegetables—crudités in thick sauce, looks like stew but
> vegetables are raw
>
> Panceta or kobe with egg yolk
>
> Enoki with egg yolk sauce
>
> Black garlic with mirin with xanthan and rice vinegar
>
> Wasabi and yuzu
>
> Cocktail citrico with peels of many different citruses
>
> Butter with soy as sauce
>
> Chinese tea with boiled rice
>
> Combination of parmesan and mentaiko (marinated Japanese pol-
> lack roe)
>
> Sweet yuzu spuma with xanthan as dessert
>
> Airbag con moshi (mochi)

Maybe the most interesting thing I find, though, is a list, in still
another notebook, of "Sources of inspiration"—an indication of how
broadly Ferran casts his net:

> Art and design exhibitions, modern and classical
>
> Science texts
>
> Books of culinary history
>
> Gourmet shops
>
> Walks
>
> Furniture fairs
>
> The Spanish Aerosol Center

Later that day, after Ferran returns, I notice that on the big calendar pinned to a bulletin board at one end of the kitchen, he has blocked out certain days for (his favorite word) "creativity." "How can you plan to be creatively inspired on a certain day?" I ask. "Don't ideas come when they want to come?" He shakes his head. "No, no, no, no," he says. "You have to actively look for inspiration. On this level, you don't just sit and wait for the bulb to go off. The work of creativity is very, very difficult. It's very complicated. Ideas aren't creativity. You look for them and you make notes. After the ideas, with the notes you start to make cuisine. I'm interested in speaking of the *synthesis* of creativity. It's a very animal thing, the capacity for synthesis. During the creative process, I think only of creative cuisine. It's like hibernation, as if I'm in a monastery."

Most of the time when I'm at the Taller, if I'm not walking around poking my nose into things, I'm sitting on a wide, low-back red leather chair at the glass-top metal table, actually two of them pushed together, at the terrace end of the kitchen, just observing and making notes of my own. Ferran comes and goes, one minute talking intensely on his cell phone on the other side of the kitchen wall, the next minute sitting down across from me puzzling over something in his notebook, the minute after that heading out the door for half an hour. Oriol Castro, Ferran's right hand, is there most days, as is Mateu Casañas, present-day head of the "sweet world," and two other key members of the El Bulli creative team, Eduard Xatruch and Eugeni de Diego. Now and then, one of the crew disappears to walk a block to the Boqueria, Barcelona's extraordinary main covered market—which is in effect the Taller's walk-in refrigerator and storeroom, stocking most of the foodstuffs the chefs need.

One day, when Ferran is not around, somebody brings in a burlap bag full of snarled, dirty roots of some kind—asparagus roots, it turns out. Castro peels a piece, cuts it into bits, and passes them around. I try one. It has a faint licorice flavor but makes the back of my throat tighten. Will the roots end up on the El Bulli menu in some form? I ask. "We don't know yet," says Castro. This is the religion of the Taller: Approach every ingredient, every combination, every technique with an open mind and discover the possibilities, go where it leads you— which is sometimes not at all where you were expecting to be led.

Later, Castro sits down with me and tells me that he has been working with a concept that fascinates him, the concept of the "twist"—as in the twist of lime or lemon garnishing a cocktail. "The aroma of a twist of orange . . . ," he begins. "If you put the twist with something like sautéed shrimp, you wouldn't remember the orange because the shrimp flavor would predominate. But if you did it with a bite of simply cooked potato, you would have the 'flavor' in your nose instead of in your mouth." He likes the idea of foods "tasted" by aroma. "You must respond emotionally to food," he says. "When I smell mushrooms, I smell the country, the cellar of my grandparents. It's memory-emotion."

Another day, Castro is stirring different thickeners into iced consommé to see which one yields the best texture—traditional sheet gelatin, agar-agar, two kinds of carrageen . . . "We started with the idea of something Ferran saw in Japan," he explains. "It was a sheet of nori with toro inside, but it evolved into a kind of wonton. We had the idea to put cream whipped with curry powder inside a wonton wrapper made with transparent gelatin." Later he and one of the other chefs are pouring gelatin into indentations made in white silicone blocks by different foods—mussels, shrimp, mushrooms, even rabbit brains, one of Ferran's favorite ingredients (though how the brains were coaxed into making an impression in the silicone I can't imagine). Ferran walks by. "You're working with gelatins today," I say. "No," he replies, "we're working with molds. First the concept, then the flavor." The most important job of the Taller, he says, isn't to create new dishes, but to develop new ways of making dishes.

Later, Castro shows me a new version of cabell d'àngel, literally angel's hair, a traditional Catalan confection of candied winter squash, used to fill pastries. This one is made not with squash but with gelatin and agar-agar flavored with honey. Later still, he brings over a bowl of broth with what appear to be the short Catalan noodles called *fideus*; they're actually made out of cheese, he tells me, through a process similar to spherification.

The next day, work continues with the silicone molds, this time with the forms of peanuts, hazelnuts, almonds, and chestnuts. "First comes the concept," says Castro, echoing Ferran, "like the chassis on a car. Then we build on it." Ferran comes into the kitchen. "The chefs here are an independent team," he tells me. "This year I'm not here very much. I just come in and taste. Albert was in charge of the Taller, but he has pulled away. He has said before that he is leaving to spend more time with his family [he and his live-in girlfriend of eighteen years have a three-year-old son], but he has absolutely quit this time. . . ." He pauses. "But little by little he is coming back."

Later in the morning, indeed, Albert comes in. There had been rumors that he'd had some kind of rift with his brother, which I found hard to believe. Every time I'd seen them together, they were engaged—physically close to each other, talking with passion, throwing out ideas, gesturing, smiling. Today, though, he and Ferran start arguing heatedly, their voices rising. Then I realize that what they're arguing about is soccer. There's more to life than El Bulli, even at the Taller.

12

Molecular Gastronomy and the Foam Guy

"Ferran Adrià [is] the Holy Father of molecular gastronomy, inventor of food served as foam. . . . Molecular gastronomy . . . has become a religion to chefs like Ferran. . . ."

—Kristen Matthew,
The New York Post Page Six Magazine

Ferran Adrià invented something called "molecular gastronomy," which brings science into the kitchen, using a lot of chemicals and laboratory instruments to produce weird food. His greatest contribution to contemporary cuisine is turning all kinds of ingredients into foam.

That's more or less the popular conception of Ferran, expressed frequently in articles about him and confirmed in almost any casual conversation in which his name happens to come up. "Oh, the molecular guy." "Oh, the guy with the foams." Beyond the more sophisticated epicurean magazines, newspaper food sections, and foodie blogs, in fact, it is rare to find a mention of Ferran in print in which the term "molecular gastronomy" doesn't also appear. Those two words have become (pick your metaphor) his heraldic motto, his indelible gang tattoo, the albatross around his neck. The link between his name and that phrase has been seared into our associative networks. The words "molecular gastronomy" will figure in the headlines of most of the obituaries that will one day be written about Ferran.

Of course, all cooking is molecular, by definition, in the sense that it involves altering the molecular structure of various substances, usually through the application of heat. And there is indeed a recently defined field of study called molecular gastronomy—but unfortunately for the common wisdom, it has very little to do with Ferran. Those who think of Ferran as a "scientific" chef probably don't realize that most of the culinary innovations for which El Bulli has become famous, including warm gelatins, hot foams, ice powders, and spherification, were developed through inspired tinkering, with no hint of scientific assistance or corroboration. Like Vicente Todolí and his friends trying to boil oranges as kids in Valencia, Ferran and his creative team—even at the Taller—basically tried everything, however unlikely, not knowing what would work and what wouldn't, or why some things did or didn't. Using intuition and imagination, they discovered new techniques by trial and error, and occasionally sheer luck. "[W]e have never ascribed any scientific origin to our creations," he once said, "which have come about from a purely culinary quest. . . ."

Ferran was smart enough to realize that there were consistent scientific principles behind his successes (and failures), however, and in 2003, he contacted the food-loving organic chemist Pere Castells and asked if he'd be interested in collaborating. Castells said yes, so Ferran invited him to the Taller. "In 1998," recalls Ferran, "we had used agar to make warm jelly. A scientist would have known that agar could withstand high temperatures without melting, but we didn't. When we figured that out, I started thinking that there might be some other products that would have properties we could exploit." He adds with a wry smile that "the first time a guest at El Bulli was served a warm jelly—the dish was Roquefort sorbet with hot apple and lemon jelly—he didn't even notice that it was anything unusual!"

When Castells arrived at the Taller, Ferran continues, "One of the first things he mentioned was sodium alginate. It was like he was speaking Martian."

At first, says Ferran, the relationship with Castells was informal, but it gradually took on a more professional nature, leading to the implementation of a science department at the Taller. Assisted by Ingrid Farré, a food technologist, Castells began offering scientific explanations for processes already established, developing systems for organizing kitchen experiments, and helping to refine the Taller's working structure in general; the two also began gathering information from outside sources and establishing contacts with the manufacturers of new equipment and food products.

His interest in science aside, Ferran basically wants nothing to do with the whole idea of molecular gastronomy. The way he once explained it, "The [avant-garde culinary] movement that began in Spain in the early nineties went unnamed. People kept saying, 'We need a name.' So 'molecular gastronomy' comes along and the media says, 'Let's use this.' But this is a lie, the biggest lie in the history of cooking. We keep on thinking about it, and still no one understands why they call what we do 'molecular gastronomy.'" Pau Arenós, writing in *El Periódico*, coined a new term for avant-garde cooking: "techno-emotional cuisine." He defined its practitioners as "all those who believe that what matters are feelings, and who accept any technique or technology to stimulate them." Ferran prefers to sidestep any and all labels for what he does. "The name for our cooking," he says, "is 'El Bulli.'"

■ ■ ■

Cooking and the physical sciences have had a long, erratic relationship, sometimes flirtatious, sometimes antipathetic. The French chemist Hervé This (pronounced *teece*), one of the co-founders of the molecular gastronomy movement, dates science in the kitchen at least back to the ancient Egyptians, citing the so-called London Papyrus, which mentions the use of a scale to determine whether fermented meat was lighter than fresh meat. (He is presumably a better chemist than historian: Though the papyrus fragments he refers to were discovered in Egypt, they are Greek, dating from the late fifth and early fourth centuries B.C.). A number of scientists over the past several hundred years have invented devices that made cooking easier or more efficient, but have also addressed foodstuffs themselves: The chemist Antoine Baumé (1728–1804) devised the first "stock tablets," early versions of today's bouillon cubes; the great Louis Pasteur (1822–1895), among his many other accomplishments, influenced food and wine production tremendously through his studies of bacterial contamination and fermentation and his development of the process that came to be known as pasteurization; the physicist and chemist Louis Camille Maillard (1878–1936) first identified the phenomenon by which food browns and intensifies in flavor—known now as the Maillard reaction.

For centuries, too, non-scientists have recognized the importance of science in the kitchen. The French gastronome Alexandre Grimod de La Reynière (1758–1837)—who was arguably the world's first restaurant critic—thought it self-evident that "one cannot be a decent cook without being at the same time a chemist, a botanist, a physician, a draughtsman and a geometer." To Mrs. Beeton, the famous nineteenth-century English cookbook writer, the kitchen was "the great laboratory of every household." Filippo Marinetti, in his 1932-vintage *Futurist Cookbook*—admittedly more satirical polemic than cookery manual—actually called for the installation of a battery of scientific instruments in the kitchen, including "*ozonizers, . . . ultra-violet ray lamps, . . . electrolyzers, . . . colloidal mills, . . . atmospheric and vacuum stills, centrifugal autoclaves, dialyzers.*"

What's astonishing, ultimately, isn't that Ferran and other contemporary chefs should be taking science seriously today but that chefs haven't always done so. Cooking is done in almost every household in the world almost every day, whether we define it as the skilled concoction of multi-course feasts or just the sticking of frozen waffles into the pop-up toaster; no room in the house sees more chemical reactions or physical transformations of matter than the kitchen. Isn't it curious, then, that most of us have paid the underpinnings of the processes we use so little mind? That we prepare food for eating by rote, without asking ourselves how and why the culinary processes work?

A book published as long ago as 1893, called *Science in the Kitchen*, by Ella Eaton Kellogg, wife of the celebrated physician and nutritionist (and breakfast cereal pioneer) John Harvey Kellogg, decried this situation eloquently: "It is a singular and Lamentable fact . . . ," reads the preface, "that the preparation of food, although involving both chemical and physical processes, has been less advanced by the results of modern researches and discoveries in chemistry and physics, than any other department of human industry. . . . The mistress of the kitchen is still groping her way amid the uncertainties of mediæval methods, and daily bemoaning the sad results of the 'rule of thumb.' . . . [T]he attempt to make wholesome, palatable, and nourishing food by the methods commonly employed, is rarely more successful than that of those misguided alchemists in transmitting lead and copper into silver and gold."

Rather than misguided alchemy, I think there's a sense in which cooking—not just home cooking but also the elevated idiom of haute cuisine—has until recently been a bit like folk medicine: Practitioners of both occupations did things in a certain way because they had always been done that way, and seemed to work pretty well most of the time. In the case of medicine, while old remedies are still sometimes employed (more so in some parts of the world than others) and occasionally still surprise us with their efficacy, we have long since subjected traditional curative practices to scientific scrutiny and developed a sophisticated system of research-verified remedies and procedures that in many cases owe nothing to tradition. The idea of "food science," meanwhile, was until recently applied mostly to commercial food production and to nutrition and food safety issues. Professional chefs and home cooks alike, for the most part, went on blithely doing things a certain way because Escoffier—or grandma—had told them to. Sometimes this worked out just fine, and sometimes it didn't, but nobody stopped to ask (or seemed to care) why in either case.

One of the first modern-day scientists to betray a serious interest in culinary processes was a Hungarian-born British physicist and avid amateur cook named Nicholas Kurti, who in 1969 gave a presentation called "The Physicist in the Kitchen" to fellow members of the Royal Society in London. In the course of his lecture, he used a microwave oven, still something of a novelty at the time, to produce what he called a "frozen Florida"—that is, a reverse baked Alaska, warm on the inside and cold without. Later in the evening, Kurti produced an eight-egg soufflé and inserted thermocouples to record its internal temperature at various depths. At this point he made a remark—often misquoted—that was to become famous: "Is it not quite amazing that today we know more about the temperature distribution in the atmosphere of the planet Venus than that in the center of our soufflé?"

There's a soufflé in the French chemist Hervé This's story, too. As a young man in 1980, while working for *Pour la Science*, more or less the French equivalent of *Scientific American*, he decided to make a Roquefort soufflé, using a recipe that had appeared in the popular women's magazine *Elle*. The recipe called for adding the eggs two by two. Out of curiosity, he disregarded this advice and added them all at once. The soufflé flopped. He made it again, this time adding them one by one. The soufflé was better, but not perfect. Finally he tried following the recipe—success! He wanted to know why this should be the case, and resolved to begin applying the principles of scientific observation to recipes and food lore. "I realized," he later wrote, "that old wives' tales [about cooking] should be collected and tested experimentally."

How did scientific investigation into culinary phenomena become "molecular gastronomy"? It all started in 1988, when a British-born, Berkeley-based cooking teacher named Elizabeth Cawdry Thomas happened to accompany her physicist husband to a conference at the Ettore Majorana Foundation and Center for Scientific Culture in Erice, in Sicily. At dinner one evening, she found herself talking about the science of cooking with a physicist from the University of Bologna, who encouraged her to organize a workshop on the subject for the center. She invited her friend Nicholas Kurti as the workshop's official director, and also brought in Harold McGee, a onetime literature teacher with a Ph.D. from Yale who approached cooking with intellectual curiosity and rigor and had written an enormously influential book, published in 1984, called *On Food and Cooking: The Science and Lore of the Kitchen.* Kurti in turn invited Hervé This.

Asked to come up with an academic-sounding name for the subject of the workshop, Kurti suggested "Molecular and Physical Gastronomy." The first program was held in 1992, and there were five more over the next twelve years. The French chef Pierre Gagnaire and the highly original British chef Heston Blumenthal of the Fat Duck in Bray both attended a few of them, and Blumenthal has said that the 2001 meeting was the first time there had been discussion of using scientific observation to develop new culinary techniques, as opposed to simply better understanding old ones. Ferran never came near Erice.

Following Kurti's death in 1998, This dropped the word "physical" from the event's name, and "molecular gastronomy" became both the titular subject of the event and an international catchphrase.

The Collège de France established the first molecular gastronomy laboratory in 1995. Since the start of the twenty-first century, culinary schools around the world have begun to set up molecular gastronomy programs, or at the very least to add classes addressing the subject. Subsequently, molecular gastronomy associations and enterprises began appearing, seemingly everywhere—the Experimental Cuisine Cooperative in New York City, Gastronomy Lab in Brazil, Asociación de Gastronomía Molecular in Argentina, Cook & Chemist in the Netherlands. . . . In 2006, a center for the study of molecular gastronomy was even chartered in Cuba.

A term often used alongside "molecular gastronomy," or even as a synonym for it, is "molecular cuisine." While the former has come to describe a field of study, the latter sounds like a culinary genre—and this idea vexes Ferran a lot. "The public should not be tricked into believing that molecular cuisine is a cooking style," he says. "Everybody says it comes from Spain and that I created it," Ferran complains, "but no one here has ever used the term." The first person to mention it in print, he adds, was probably the Italian physicist Davide Cassi.

Indeed the relationship of El Bulli to the sciences has been greatly misunderstood. To cook well, Ferran once wrote, it is essential to learn "history, techniques, products, tradition and innovation, culinary processes, etc. . . . and then think, discuss, try out, reflect, choose. . . ." This, and not some more conventionally rigorous system, is El Bulli's version of the scientific method—and Ferran and his chefs were approaching food this way for more than a decade before he first regularized his association with members of the scientific community. The development of spherification—a technique for enclosing flavored liquid in a skin of, as it were, itself—is a good example: One day in 2001, Albert Adrià and the El Bulli chef Oriol Castro were visiting a friend's food packaging plant in Tarragona, and they saw a "Mexican" sauce being canned, in which floated pearl-like globes of alginate. Albert was already familiar with a soft drink full of tapioca pearls, called Orbit, which he'd seen in Japan. The tapioca (a starch extracted from cassava roots), though, was flavorless—the point was simply to add texture—while the alginate version was imbued with artificial essences. Albert and Castro were fascinated by the idea, and began to wonder if it might have some application in the kitchen at El Bulli. Albert went out to a pharmacy, bought some calcium alginate, and brought it to the Taller. He and Oriol and Ferran and other members of the team then proceeded to attempt to reproduce the globe effect with various substances—and the next thing anybody knew (but after a couple of years of informal research and trial and error), the food world was oohing and aahing over spherified olives. So much for the popular image of batteries of scientists creating Frankenfood in some sterile laboratory.

I first saw the process demonstrated on my initial visit to the Taller, back in 2003. The restaurant was open, so the workshop was not, but Albert conjured up a deep plastic container filled with clear liquid, a shallower tray with something else clear, and a bowl of a watery electric-green purée. With a small spoon, he carefully let drops of the purée fall into the liquid in the deep container. He didn't wave his hand and exclaim "Shazaam!" but he might as well have: The drops almost instantly formed themselves into plump green pearls. He spooned one out and rinsed it quickly in the shallow tray, then offered it to me. I popped it into my mouth; it was the very essence of peas, as vivid a flavor as I've ever tasted—a pea raviolo in which both the filling and the "pasta" were nothing but peas.

Some of Ferran's critics say that Ferran hasn't invented anything, and there are indeed a number of pre-1991 patents for the use of spherification techniques in food products. (The earliest I could find was granted to an English food scientist in 1973, for the purpose of making artificial fruit.) But Ferran has always said that he does not invent—he just recognizes opportunities. Seeing what other people don't see, he has said, is the definition of creativity. In the case of spherification, what Ferran and his team worked out was a refinement of earlier procedures. Originally, the technique involved dissolving calcium alginate (formed from calcium chloride and sodium alginate—a kelp derivative that Ferran likes to call "seaweed flour") in a liquid of some kind (for instance, a thin purée of melon or peas), then feeding droplets of the mixture into a solution of calcium carbonate. A chemical reaction would form the liquid into perfect little orbs. Unfortunately, once the reaction started, it didn't stop immediately, and the liquid inside the orbs would solidify into gel.

The El Bulli inspiration was to reverse the process—Ferran dubbed this "inverse spherification"—adding calcium carbonate to the liquid in question and adding the drops to a bath of alginate solution instead of the other way around. The initial results seemed virtually the same, but simply rinsing the spheres in water stopped the reaction while their interiors remained liquid. This made possible a whole new sensory experience for the diner—a literal flood of flavor, of essence, when the sphere exploded between the teeth. A further refinement of the process, which Ferran dubbed "moldable spherification," used liquid nitrogen to freeze the calcium carbonate mixture in molds of various kinds before bathing it in the alginate solution, so that the results can take many shapes (like little knots of gelatin), not just spherical ones. "When people watch spherification," Ferran says, "they think 'Wow, it's like something from NASA, something from Mars!' But really, if they turned around in our kitchen and looked at the induction cooktops we use, that would be much more a space-age technique, much more complicated. Even the microwave in your kitchen is more 'Martian' than spherification." He adds, "No one has ever explained to me why it's okay to use sheets of gelatin in food but not agar or alginate. These things have been used by the best pastry chefs and ice-cream makers of the world forever."

It is illustrative of Ferran's legendary generosity that as quickly as the El Bulli team developed spherification and other new techniques, they sought to share them. "Ferran would come and do demonstrations," says Juan Solé, proprietor of the prominent Barcelona baking and kitchen supply store called Solé Graells, "and he'd explain what he'd been up to—and then people would call me up, because they know that we have all the latest materials, and ask if I could get them the products he uses. After a while, I talked to Ferran and said, 'Explain all this to me, and if it's possible we'll organize a way to commercialize what you use.' He did, and we started working to find the best examples of every substance. Ferran and Albert tried more than seventy kinds of lecithin, for instance. In 2004 we started Texturas, with four products for spherification and four gelatins. The next year, we added xanthan and products for inverse spherification. We now have seventeen products in all, and we distribute them all over the world."

More recently, Solé Graells has developed new lines with Albert, including Ingenios, which are "gadgets," and Lyo-Sabores, which are freeze-dried fruits, tomatoes, and substances like honey and yogurt in powder form. These had an interesting provenance: In 2002, visiting a supermarket with José Andrés in Washington, D.C., on his first trip to America, Albert noticed the "Just" line of freeze-dried fruits and vegetables—Just Corn, Just Tomatoes, Just Raspberries, etc.—and brought the idea home to El Bulli.

Joël Robuchon has said he thinks it was a mistake for Ferran and Albert to make their materials so readily available. While he had complete faith in Ferran's use of "additives" (i.e., xanthan, calcium chloride, and the like), he explained, "they can be dangerous" in the hands of lesser chefs. The French seemed to have been particularly taken with Texturas, in fact, and for a couple of years in the mid 2000s, France saw what one critic called the "flowering of an incalculable number of gelified raviolis of every kind"—most of them badly made "gelified membranes that are too thick, no more agreeable in the mouth than they are digestible."

Sometimes the innovations that have come out of El Bulli involve not ingredients but ways of treating them. One whole section of the restaurant kitchen, for instance, is a kind of cold station—not in the traditional sense of a garde-manger or pantry, but in the sense that food is "cooked" there with extreme cold rather than heat, primarily through the agency of liquid nitrogen, which boils at -361 degrees Fahrenheit. Ferran first saw liquid nitrogen being used, he says, when he watched Hervé This use it to freeze sorbet on television in 1996. "We paid no attention to him," he admits. (In fact, the first liquid-nitrogen-frozen ice cream, remarkably enough, was made not in the latter twentieth century, but by the Victorian-era cooking teacher Agnes B. Marshall, known as "the queen of ice cream"—she invented the ice cream cone—who demonstrated the technique at the Royal Institution in London in 1901.) One of the showpiece dishes served today by Heston Blumenthal at the Fat Duck (he is a serious student of historical English cooking, and incorporates many of its conceits into his avant-garde menu) is "nitro-scrambled egg and bacon ice cream," a tableside preparation in which a bacony custard concealed in an eggshell is turned into the most delicious frozen dessert in a matter of seconds. Blumenthal did a demonstration of the dish at Madrid Fusión in 2004, and, he says, "As far as I know, that was the first time anyone—at least anyone in a restaurant context—had used liquid nitrogen with a siphon. Ferran was sitting up front that day."

Ferran came to recognize the possibilities inherent in liquid nitrogen—he and Albert and Castro began experimenting with it in 2002—and today the chefs at El Bulli know their way around liquid nitrogen very well, and use it almost casually. It can be dangerous, however, and not just for its freezing abilities: In July of 2009, *Berliner*

Morgenpost reported that a twenty-four-year-old aspiring chef in Germany lost both hands when—according to his girlfriend—he attempted to empty a canister of liquid nitrogen in the course of an experiment in "molecular gastronomy" and it exploded.

■ ■ ■

There is a perception in some quarters that Ferran somehow cooks with chemicals instead of natural ingredients. In fact, most of the "chemicals" he works with—agar carageenan, xanthan gum, and so on—are what is known as hydrocolloids, and these are old news in the kitchen. A colloid is a mixture of substances in which one is dispersed evenly throughout another; a hydrocolloid is one in which the colloid particles are dispersed in water. As the food scientist Belle Lowe wrote back in 1932, in her *Experimental Cookery from the Chemical and Physical Standpoint*, "So many of the ingredients used in food preparation are colloidal in nature that food preparation may be classed as one field of applied colloid chemistry." Indeed, any time a chef wants to change the physical properties of a liquid—thickening it, for instance, or stopping it from moving (as if it had suddenly but temporarily turned into a solid)—hydrocolloids will probably do the trick. Jell-O—or, rather, the gelatin it includes—is a hydrocolloid. In any case, as the Harvard University physicist Otger Campàs once told me, Ferran's innovations don't really involve "chemistry" at all. "Texture is *not* chemistry," he explained. "It's a purely physical consideration involving the geometry of structure, having to do with mechanical properties."

Are hydrocolloids and other substances that change the way matter behaves "natural," though? Looking for a definitive answer to that question, I visited CP Kelco in San Diego, a major international manufacturer and distributor of culinary hydrocolloids and related products. Though Kelco works primarily with major commercial food companies, one of the staff scientists, Ted Russin, also acts as a liaison with noted chefs, among them Thomas Keller. I met with him and two of his associates, and basically learned that naturalness is a highly subjective concept. "We have a joke," says Rick Jones, Kelco's public relations officer, "that if you really want your food natural, you should eat corn with the husk on."

"The term 'organic' is legally defined by the American Food and Drug Administration and the equivalent body in the European Union," notes Henri Monty, Kelco's director of business development, "but there is no universally agreed-upon standard for 'natural.' The term really doesn't mean anything. But what we are selling are products based on plant extracts and bacterial fermentation extracts, which come from nature." Xanthan gum, for instance, is the result of the bacterial fermentation of a substance found on cabbage leaves. A more recently discovered material, gellan, is a polysaccharide taken from a bacterial excretion on lily pond leaves. Carageenan (which Kelco sells) and agar (which it doesn't) are of course derived from seaweed.

At times, Ferran seems not so much annoyed as befuddled by the negative reaction so many people seem to have to the culinary use of "chemicals." "If I tell people that I'm going to cook a fish in a crust of sodium chloride," he likes to say, "at least some of them will object, 'Oh, no, that's chemical cooking!' But if I say that I am using an old traditional method of baking fish in salt, which of course *is* sodium chloride, that's fine." During an onstage *New York Times* "Times Talk" conversation with Anthony Bourdain and Eric Asimov in October of 2008, Ferran made a similar point another way: "People see smoke coming from liquid nitrogen, and they say, [he demonstrates with an exaggerated gesture—Ferran the physical comedian] 'OH!' But if they see steam coming from a pot of boiling water, no 'Oh!'" Later in the program, held in the auditorium of the then-new New York Times Building, he swept his hand in the air and said, "Renzo Piano used science in fifty thousand different ways to make this building, but nobody calls it 'scientific architecture.'" He makes the same point over and over again in interviews, using different creative fields—design, filmmaking, and on and on. "When you see a cartoon on TV," he said one day, "you don't think of the science behind it."

Taking part in a panel discussion called "¿Existe le Cocina Molecular?"—Does Molecular Cuisine Exist?—at Madrid Fusión in 2009, Ferran abruptly jumped up from his chair and went to the back of the stage where foods for a later event had been put out. He grabbed a small round loaf of bread and a bar of chocolate and held them up to the audience. "Scientists study both of these," he says, "and these are products we eat every day. What is strange about this? Science has been in the kitchen forever. What's new is the dialogue between scientists and chefs." As for molecular gastronomy, says Ferran, "The best way to digest it once and for all is to never talk about it again."

■ ■ ■

No "scientific" creation of Ferran's has been more widely remarked, imitated, misunderstood, and for that matter scorned and parodied than his *espumas* and *aires*, his foams and airs.

Foam is a curious substance, fragile but persistent, formed when gas bubbles are trapped in and distributed throughout a liquid or a viscous solid. We're used to foam, and tend to like it, when it is attached to certain beverages: the crema on the top of a well-made espresso, the mountain of schlag on a cup of Viennese hot chocolate, the glorious faintly amber head on a pint of slowly pulled draught Guinness, or the ebullience of bubbles spilling over from a quickly filled flute of champagne. Foam has never been something we've looked for in our food, though. Our ancestors, in fact, would very likely have refused to eat anything that bubbled; foam would have been taken—often with good reason—as a sign that food was spoiled or noxious ("Like a hell-broth boil and bubble . . ."). "We used to take a blowtorch to foam if we got it in a sauce," Thomas Keller told me one day, "because it was considered a flaw, and you didn't want it in anything that left the kitchen."

I first saw foam of a sort in a culinary context (not counting the Reddi-Whip that Mom applied so generously to her instant chocolate pudding when I was a boy) at a restaurant called Tristán in Porto Portals, a luxury marina on the island of Majorca, in the autumn of 1986. Tristán had opened earlier that year under the Italian-Tyrolean chef Heinz Winkler, a disciple of Paul Bocuse, who had won three Michelin stars cooking at the anagrammatic Tantris in Munich. I ate at Tristán several times while Winkler was in charge—he left after two years to open his own place back in Germany—and found the food superb in general. What surprised me, though, was that several dishes were cloaked in sauces that were noticeably frothy, something I'd never seen before. When I asked the maître d'hôtel to explain these unusual sauces, he said, "The chef reduces meat and vegetable essences and then aerates them with a Turmix [a professional immersion blender]. That way he can give them body without adding cream or a roux." I wrote to Winkler recently to ask for details about his technique. "Unfortunately," replied his assistant, while Winkler would confirm that my recollections were basically correct, "he wants not to tell you something about the materials and the development of the techniques." I thought this was pretty funny: Ferran Adrià, the most innovative chef in the world, freely shares his recipes and tells anyone who's interested how he does it all, while Winkler still jealously guards his long-outmoded twenty-five-year-old secrets.

Four years after my first meal at Tristán, roughly two hundred miles north of Majorca, Ferran started thinking about mousses. Mousses are basically purées of various substances, both savory and sweet, simultaneously lightened and enriched with eggs and sometimes cream; they vary greatly in density, but are rarely what you'd call "light." Was there a way to make them more delicate, wondered Fer-

ran, and to more purely convey the flavors of their principal raw materials? Was there a way to make mousses without eggs or cream?

Ferran says that the idea of creating a mousse with air as the only
lightening agent came to him originally in 1991 when he happened
to notice the residual foam in the glasses of fresh-squeezed fruit juice
served at a popular juice bar in Barcelona. Tasting it, he realized that
while it was very light in consistency, it had all the flavor of the fruit.
I can't help wondering whether Ferran might also have been inspired
on a subconscious level—he denies the possibility—by one of the
staples of traditional Catalan cooking: the sauce of garlic and olive oil
called allioli. Its Provençal counterpart, aïoli, is made with eggs; allioli
is made without them, but attains an emulsified texture nonetheless,
thanks to the smooth and gentle motions of a practiced hand. At the
very least, Ferran would certainly have understood, through allioli,
that eggs were not essential for the thickening of a liquid.

Ferran's first attempts to harness the foam effect for culinary purposes came not at El Bulli but during his sabbatical in the studio of
the sculptor Xavier Medina-Campeny. Several accounts to the con-
trary, these attempts did not involve a bicycle pump. "Ferran saw that
I was using an oxyacetylene torch for my metalwork," says Medina-
Campeny, "and it has two tanks, one for fuel and one for oxygen. He
asked if he could borrow the oxygen tank, and then tried just pump-
ing oxygen directly into some tomatoes. He did this two or three
times, but all that happened was that at a certain point the tomatoes
exploded." Ferran has referred to "some amusing domestic disasters"—
and to having temporarily redecorated the walls of the studio.

There's an interesting version of the story—and an unexpectedly
acute appreciation of what Ferran is about—in, of all places, *Up Till
Now*, William "Captain Kirk" Shatner's autobiography. Judging an
early iteration of the American version of *Iron Chef*, he encounters a
young chef who makes crab sorbet, "fishy and crabby," and is elimi-
nated right away. "A few weeks later . . ." writes Shatner, "I was reading

an article about the great chefs of the world. One of them has a small restaurant outside Barcelona. At this restaurant he gives his customers what amounts to basically one spoonful of a dish so they can truly understand its taste, and then they go on to the next dish. Apparently he bought a carload of tomatoes and an air machine that aerated the tomatoes and allowed him to get to the essence of the taste of a tomato. It was the pure taste of the tomato. And as I read that I realized that the young chef had done exactly that, with his sorbet. He had given us the absolute essence of the taste of crab. I understood that this young chef and the master chef in Barcelona were tied together by their desire to bring their artistry to the consumer." (The first crab ice cream, incidentally, was probably that made by Heston Blumenthal in 1997 to accompany his crab risotto.)

The main lesson Ferran learned from his oxygen-tank experiments at his friend's studio was that gas of some kind would be essential to the foam-making process. In 1993, the pastry chef Antoni Escribà, knowing of his experiments, brought Ferran a CO_2-fueled siphon from Switzerland to try out. Ferran took to calling this the "phantom siphon," because it tended to get misplaced between experiments, but in any case the foams it produced were disappointing; "They seemed fermented to us," he has said. A short time later, Ferran and Albert were consulting at a Barcelona restaurant called Bel-Air. One day, they happened to see a customer order a dessert with whipped cream. "To our surprise," Ferran later wrote, "the cream was served in the kitchen with a gadget they took out of the fridge, from which whipped cream emerged by pressing a lever at the top. Suddenly we saw the light, and we reckoned that this kind of siphon might solve the foam problem." They borrowed the device—which had to be charged from a large cylinder of nitrous oxide, the size of an overgrown fire extinguisher—and with it successfully produced a foam of consommé. The gelatin in the consommé, they realized, had given the foam its body, and they decided to add gelatin to future foams.

Using this device, on March nineteenth of 1994, they made what they considered a perfect foam of white beans. The following month, on April twenty-third, they first served a white-bean foam at El Bulli, garnished with sea urchin. Other savory foams, based on beets, almonds, and cilantro, came next, and then sweet foams, starting with one of coconut.

Enter Marc Calabuig. Calabuig was working in his father's international food product business when a customer in Croatia introduced him to the Austrian-made iSi siphon, a sleek, easy-to-use affair utilizing small nitrous oxide capsules as propellant. The iSi was standard equipment in Austrian coffeehouses to produce whipped cream and milk for coffee and hot chocolate, and Calabuig, who thought some of his Spanish customers would be interested in the device, began importing it. One of those customers suggested that he show one to Ferran. "At this point," says Calabuig, "I was just interested in selling to people who needed a good, fast way to make whipped cream, and I kept Ferran's name on my desk for three months. Finally I went to see him, and he took me into the kitchen and showed me that he was already using a siphon. He was very interested in trying the iSi, though, and it turned out to be just what he wanted." Soon, the El Bulli kitchen was turning dozens of ingredients into light-as-air foams—which, said Ferran, "can be substituted for the classic mousses which have always been made in our kitchens . . . without the addition of cream, eggs, or other fats that might diminish the flavor." Calabuig called the company that makes the iSi, he told me, and said, "Your bicycle is an airplane." In 1998, when Calabuig's father retired, he set up a company of his own, International Cooking Concepts, which today sells the iSi and other cutting-edge cooking equipment to restaurants all over the world.

For a few years in the early part of this century, foams seem to have found their way onto restaurant menus in every corner of the globe. Their popularity has since ebbed, but the basic idea has become commonplace, and will probably never disappear completely. Some foams are made incorrectly, of course, or out of things that shouldn't be foamed (I remember one of calf's liver at some silly place in Colorado, circa 2002). But as Ferran says, "There are good foams and bad foams, just as in classical cooking there were good mousses and bad ones." He has largely moved on, anyway, to an even purer expression of the idea: In 2003, the El Bulli kitchen produced their first "airs," made by a completely different process than foams. "We create them," Ferran explained to me, "by emulsifying the foam that is on top of a foodstuff we liquefy with a Turmix"—shades of Tristán—"injecting the maximum amount of air and consequently producing a foam that, due to its volatility, we call 'air.' They're the same texture as bath foam." And they're even more elemental than the original foams, because they contain no gelatin; they're just the ingredient, oxygenated almost to the point of abstraction—pure essence of flavor.

A New World

"Even I, sometimes, get tired by this Ferran Adrià we see everywhere."

—Ferran Adrià, *Le Figaro*, 2009

On July fourteenth, 2002, Ferran married his longtime girlfriend, Isabel Pérez Barceló. The ceremony took place at Can Magí, a beautiful nineteenth-century *mas*, or Catalan country house, in Sant Cugat del Vallès, on the other side of Tibidabo Mountain from Barcelona. Isabel described the occasion to me: "The wedding lasted one whole day. We had two parties. One, at lunchtime, was with our families and included the wedding ceremony. The second, in the evening, was for friends. Christian Escribà [the Barcelona pastry chef and Ferran's best friend] and the El Bulli catering team organized the whole event. Escribà also made two wedding cakes, one for lunchtime and the other for the evening. Best of all, he took it upon himself to organize the sweetest evening show that any of us had ever seen. This was the wedding gift from the Escribà family, which they called 'The magical evening of Ferran and Isabel.' The centerpiece of the evening was the presentation of the wedding cake called 'Reina de Cora-zones' (the Queen of Hearts)."

Ferran and Isabel had a long courtship: They first met in the sum-mer of 1989. "I have a friend who spends her holidays in Roses," Isabel tells me over dinner one warm September evening on the terrace at (where else?) El Bulli. "My friend was going out with a boy who worked here and one night after work he came to meet us at a café and he came with Ferran. Right away, we had a special connection. I knew nothing about El Bulli. I had never heard of it. But he was very nice, and we started as good friends. Our relationship grew over the winter when the restaurant was closed. We went to exhibitions, restaurants, the theatre, and six or eight months later we were in love. Even then we lived apart. There wasn't a lightning bolt. It happened slowly."

I ask her the obvious question: Who cooks at home? "I cook sim-ple food," says Isabel, who is petite and animated, with sparkling eyes and dark red hair—it's easy to see how a young chef would have no-ticed her across a crowded bar—"and when we first got married, I started to make dinner in the evenings. But Ferran would stand next to me and say, 'Put a little of this in' or 'Do it that way,' and finally I said, 'You cook.' He doesn't like to experiment at home, though. It's a place for him to relax. He makes tomato and mozzarella salads, grilled fish, sautéed vegetables." She adds that when he cooks, he always dirt-ies too many pots and pans, and she has to do the washing up.

Isabel has made Ferran a new man, say his friends. "Getting mar-ried gave him an element that had been missing from his life," says Heston Blumenthal. "He now looks at things differently." The Barce-lona restaurant critic Carmen Casas tells me that she has always liked Ferran—"He is adorable, droll"—but that she thinks he has become even better since meeting Isabel. "He talks about her all the time," she says. "You can see in his eyes how much he loves her. There's a light in his eyes when she's in the room. Perhaps he has a dimension we didn't know about: tenderness."

Ferran and Isabel have no children. El Bulli has taken the place of offspring for Ferran, as it did for Dr. Schilling. "My work has been everything to me," he says. He claims to possess no particular paternal instincts, and has said that he has seen couples end badly when they try to "have it all."

Ferran and Isabel now live in Marketta's house, across the road from the restaurant, during the months when El Bulli is open. After they got married, elBulli S.L. bought the place, with a contract that allowed Marketta to live out her years there. The negotiations were complex. Dr. Schilling, whose vision (and financial support) had created El Bulli in the first place, grew sicker with Parkinson's disease in the latter nineties, and, no longer able to drive, he finally stopped coming to Spain. He died in Germany in 1999, having realized his dream of seeing a three-star restaurant in Cala Montjoi. (Surprisingly—or perhaps not, considering the extent to which the Spanish press had always marginalized El Bulli—his death went all but unreported in Spain.)

El Bulli's jack-of-all-trades, José Lozano, the Cordoban who had been at Cala Montjoi "since forever" (as Ferran later said), was living in a small apartment at the house, and he helped with the chores and watched out for the increasingly reclusive Marketta. "He and Marketta had a very special relationship," says Ferran. "They had great affection for each other but there were also some problems. It was a love-hate relationship. He had problems with alcohol, but he was a good man." Upon Dr. Schilling's death, however, Erna—the woman the doctor had spent his life with in Germany—inherited half the house. Remarkably, considering that she had never been to Cala Montjoi with the doctor, she moved in. Even more remarkably—"The story is like something from a film," says Ferran—Lozano moved in with her. Isabel tells me that she always thought José was "a little in love with Marketta"—but that now he and Erna conspired to make Marketta's life difficult. Erna lived there for about a year before finally agreeing to sell her interest in the property and returning to Germany.

The restaurant staff looked after Marketta in her declining years, and, says Xavier Agulló, "Ferran and Juli spent a lot of money on Marketta's retirement. Some people will say that they treated her badly, but that is absolutely not true. Both always had great respect for her, and they paid and paid to give her a very good end to her life." Marketta died on October thirty-first, 2007, in a clinic in Figueres. Ferran told me one day, "Marketta was not my mother," but nonetheless he called her demise the cutting of an umbilical cord. Lozano went to live in a retirement home in Roses, with El Bulli paying half of his expenses— the rest were covered by his pension—and he died there on Christmas Day of 2008.

After Marketta's death, her old friend Thomas Spieker, who owned the Chic discotheque, wrote that "Marketta was discretion personified, always close to everything that was done at El Bulli, but hardly ever seen. . . . She was the soul of the restaurant, without a doubt; even when it had no star and was a very simple place, Marketta left her mark. . . . I'm sure that if Ferran Adrià never wanted to leave El Bulli despite the great offers that were made to him, it was because Marketta had turned that place into a something special, into something much more than a restaurant." Juli told me one day that "Marketta will always be the founder and the spirit of El Bulli. That's why we've left the dining room with the rustic decoration she gave it. I dedicate all our work to Marketta."

■ ■ ■

In 1998, to generate income beyond what their catering brought in, Ferran and Juli had launched a consulting business, with two major Catalan food companies as their first clients, the chocolate maker Chocovic and the Borges group, whose main business was in olive oil. Initially, they handled the business out of the upstairs offices at the

Taller, but Ferran wanted to, as he put it, "centralize all the activities that had no direct link with creativity." He found a 2,800-square-foot second-story space above a music school on the Carrer del Carme—the Calle del Carmen in Spanish—just off the Ramblas, and in early 2001, opened elBullicarmen there. The financial aspects of all the El Bulli operations are managed from "Carmen," as everybody calls it. The office is casual-looking, with gray concrete floors, coved ceilings of old brick, exposed ducts and track lighting, and regiments of gray steel bookcases jammed with folders holding press clippings, menus, and various documentary material from the past half century. The year that Ferran opened "Carmen," he also began collaborating with a Barcelona-based Swiss industrial designer named Luki Huber on the design of serving vessels for some of his dishes, as well as implements for use in the kitchen, among them a rejiggered electric screwdriver used to make El Bulli's virgin olive oil caramel springs and the "caviarera," a battery of syringes that release numerous drops of liquids into their spherification baths simultaneously to form various "caviars."

There was another milestone for Ferran and company in 2001: For the first time in its existence, the restaurant closed for lunch, and began serving just one meal on each of the five days a week it was open. This in effect halved the restaurant's income, but it was an essential move. "By this time," says Ferran, "we were so tired that I said, either we close for lunch or we close altogether." (It isn't strictly true that there is no lunch service at El Bulli, incidentally. About fifteen or twenty times a season, the restaurant offers lunch but not dinner.)

To make up for the income lost by the midday close, Ferran and Juli stepped up their consulting business. In 2002, for instance, Ferran signed a deal to develop new products for Lavazza, the big Italian espresso company. The results thus far include "the world's first solid coffee," called Èspesso; a beverage of espresso and passion fruit juice flavored with mint called Passion>me (*sic*); and Coffeesphere, an "egg" of spherified coffee that melts in the mouth. Around the same time, Ferran also began a short-lived consulting project with Lay's, the snack food brand, coming up with flavors for their new Mediterráneas Artesanas (Mediterranean Artisans) potato chips, sold in Spain under the Matutano label. Ferran raised eyebrows a few years later when he used another Lay's product, the cone-shaped snacks called 3Ds, for a dish he called "3Ds with ras el hanout [the classic Moroccan herb and spice mixture] and lemon basil shoots." "Is this," blogged Tony Naylor on the *Guardian* Web site out of England, "a bold demonstration of the modern theory that there should be no hierarchy of ingredients, or is Adrià just being a bit of a lazy bastard?" I'd suggest a third possibility: that it's simply an expression of Ferran's sense of humor, his way of having fun.

In 2008, Ferran shed most outside business ventures, to concentrate on "those things that spiritually nourish El Bulli." He closed down the catering operation, retaining only the contract for the Casino de Madrid, and stopped taking on new consulting clients. He made an exception in 2009, to "design" a new beer, with input from Juli and from Ferran Centelles and David Seijas, El Bulli's sommeliers. Developed for Estrella Damm of Barcelona, Spain's oldest brewery (founded in 1876), the beer is called Inedit—Catalan for "previously unpublished" or "unseen." Ferran's food is notoriously tough to match wines with, because the flavors are so diverse and change so quickly and dramatically in the course of a meal. Servers often recommend champagne for the whole evening—specifically Gosset, with which Ferran has had a long relationship—but Inedit was designed for the same purpose, and it works very nicely. It's an unusual, aromatic beer, a blend of lager (made with malted barley) and German-style Weissbier (made with wheat), flavored with orange peel, licorice, and coriander seed, bottled unfiltered in 750-milliliter wine bottles.

Along with everything else, a steady progression of books has come out of El Bulli, the most ambitious of which, by far, is the series of massive, pricey tomes known collectively as the "General Cata-logue." The idea of exhaustively recording the development of El Bulli's food—of producing an illustrated list of every dish that Ferran and his team has ever created, from the days of his first stage at the restaurant in 1983 onwards, surrounded by pertinent historical infor-mation and philosophy—grew out of the menu planning process for La Alquería, the main dining room at the Hacienda Benazuza, the El Bulli hotel project near Seville. Since dishes are not repeated from year to year at El Bulli, at least in principle—some of the "classics," like the virgin olive oil caramel spring and the spherified green olives, do still show up regularly (and the 2002 season was devoted entirely to a one-time-only retrospective of past creations)—Ferran had the inspiration of using La Alquería as a kind of museum of his earlier creations. In order to choose these dishes in the most organized pos-sible fashion, Ferran decided that it was necessary to arrange them by year and to number them. An early menu, for instance, included "Carpaccio of Ceps with Pinenut Vinaigrette ('87)," "Corn Mousse with Truffle Juice ('93)," "Chop Suey of Clams ('96)," and so on. This ordering, in turn, made it possible to draw up a chart or "evolutionary map" (his phrase), tracing the development of Ferran's cuisine. And *this*, eventually, led to what is unquestionably the most meticulous documentation of a restaurant's creative history that has ever been imagined.

The first volume of the General Catalogue appeared in 2002, cov-ering what were then the restaurant's most recent creations, from 1998 through the year of publication. The next two volumes, published in 2003 and 2004, respectively, worked backward all the way to 1983; two more followed, one a year, covering 2003–2004 and 2005; the period of 2006–2010 will be the subject of a book scheduled for pub-lication in 2011. The books, accompanied by separate indexes of dishes and CD-ROMs, are available in a number of different languages (the 1998–2002 edition comes in Spanish, Catalan, English, French, Ger-

man, and Japanese, the others in fewer tongues), and by all accounts
sell surprisingly briskly, in specialty bookshops, online, and at El Bulli
itself. Anthony Bourdain has called them "the most talked-about,
sought-after, wildly impressive and imposingly intimidating collectible
in the world of professional chefs and cookbook wonks."

Ferran has explained that the General Catalogue has a practical
purpose—that it is "the only way we have to combat plagiarism. . . .
[W]e set out our recipes, how each dish is made, etc. Basically, it is
like patenting our recipes." I've also heard him say more than once,
though, that he's interested in leaving behind accurate, incontrovert-
ible evidence of his and the restaurant's progress through the years;
"We know how to make all the dishes of traditional French cuisine
and nouvelle cuisine," he told me one day, "but with very few exceptions, we don't know who created them, or when, or how."

Unexpectedly for a chef who is so often described as an alchemist
or a magician, and whose cuisine at El Bulli is surely some of the most
sophisticated in the world, Ferran also seems to have an almost evangelical desire to demystify everyday cooking. This is extremely important to him; he has great respect for traditional dishes of all kinds, and
seems to take great pleasure in passing along little tricks—what the
French call *trucs*, devices—that anyone can use.

With this in mind, Ferran tackled another home-cooking project
in 2003—his first, remember, had been *Cocinar en 10 minutos con
Ferran Adrià*, published in 1998—this time in conjunction with the
Caprabo supermarket chain, one of the largest in Spain. This was
Cuinar a casa amb Caprabo i Ferran Adrià, with Juli and Albert listed
as co-authors. The title literally means "Cook at Home with Caprabo
and Ferran Adrià," and the ingredients are all things you can buy at a
Caprabo or similar store (at least in Spain). On the cover, Ferran—
looking a bit tired—seems to trudge along, laden down with heavy-
looking grocery bags ("Rough day at the Taller, honey?"). The spirit
of the book, though, is lively and light. Among the basic rules he of-

fers to readers are (I paraphrase): Take advantage of commercial products, but always the high-quality ones. Let the pros clean your fish, cut
up your meat, etc., giving you more time for other things. Don't try
complicated dishes unless you have the time and the materials. Avoid
things that take too long to cook. It's better to buy a good sardine than
a mediocre crayfish. Organize yourself. Remember that you have to
put the water on to boil or preheat the oven a little while before you
actually start cooking. . . .

No special kitchen implements are required, though he does suggest adding sauces with a dropper, a paintbrush, or a squeeze bottle.
Though there are a few more complex recipes—including the famous
deconstructed potato omelette and a scorpion fish carpaccio with a
"suquet" of potato balls—most of the prescriptions are things like:
deep-fry raw wild rice in good olive oil as a snack; dress up store-
bought mayonnaise with a little ketchup, or with chopped basil and
roasted pine nuts, or with anchovies, capers, and tarragon; serve fresh
orange juice foamed up through a soda siphon; enhance takeout pizza
with your own mozzarella, basil, and cherry tomatoes; make a potato
omelette in seven minutes with crushed potato chips. . . . Instructions
for making the same omelette and other quick-and-easy dishes, including a takeout rotisserie chicken spruced up with pine nuts and
dried fruit, appear in a series of eleven DVDs jointly titled "La cocina
fácil de Ferran Adrià" (The easy cuisine of Ferran Adrià), produced
by Ferran and company in 2005 and distributed with the Sunday edition of *El Periódico*. "There are many different ways of cooking and of
being a chef," he says, "and I have great respect for all of them."

■ ■ ■

The first mention of Ferran in *The New York Times* came in 1999,
when Amanda Hesser wrote a couple of thousand words about him,
complete with his recipe for parmesan ice cream sandwiches, under
the headline "In Spain, a Chef to Rival Dalí." The story that changed

Ferran's life and the history of El Bulli, though, was "A Laboratory of Taste" by Arthur Lubow, which appeared on August tenth, 2003, in the paper's Sunday magazine. "[W]hile there are many exciting chefs throughout Spain," wrote Lubow, "the name on everyone's lips, the man who is redefining haute cuisine into alta cocina, is a prodigiously talented, self-taught Catalan." He went on to propose that "standing in Ferran Adrià's kitchen at El Bulli, it is easy to believe that you have slipped down the rabbit hole. Adrià, who would have been the caterer of choice for the Mad Hatter, invents food that provokes all the senses, including the sense of disbelief." The article not only praises and parses Ferran and his creations but also attempts to put him into a broader context as a representative of Spanish cultural ferment. "Spain rising, France resting," Lubow wrote. "The more attention I paid, the more I noticed everywhere this invidious comparison, between smug, stagnant France and innovative, daring Spain." The French, of course, hated the piece.

The Paris-based German food writer Jörg Zipprick, author of a book criticizing Ferran and "molecular gastronomy," has suggested that the *Times*—that well-known mouthpiece of American government policy—commissioned Lubow to write his piece because the French had refused to support the American invasion of Iraq, while Spain had willingly sent in some troops. (Strangely enough, I heard the same theory from Ferran's sculptor friend Xavier Medina-Campeny.) Lubow found the idea rather funny when I mentioned it to him. "I never sensed anything in that direction from any of my editors," he said. "And of course, I was on the other side of that political issue anyway."

Ten years earlier, Ferran had been all but unknown outside a comparatively small circle of sophisticated diners in Spain and France. By late 2003, he was an international superstar. Recognition by America's great newspaper of record validated Ferran and his accomplishments for much of the world. Clearly he mattered. Articles about him proliferated, and Ferran was hailed as something more than just a chef—more even than just "the best chef": He was a veritable cultural phenomenon, who was obviously so intensely creative that no mere kitchen, even that at El Bulli, could contain him.

With his new fame, Ferran began to receive invitations to conferences and other events all over the world, and he started traveling widely in the months that the restaurant was closed. In February of 2002, he made his first trip to Japan, to give a demonstration of his cooking techniques; the following year, he visited China and Australia, among other places, and went back to Japan. "We have a very, *very* special relationship with Japan," he says. He fell in love with the place. He was dazzled by the unfamiliar foodstuffs he encountered, among them yuzu, wasabi, and miso paste, which became staples of his own cuisine. He was also seduced by the kaiseki dinners he enjoyed, especially in Kyoto—as well he might have been: Like what he serves to diners at El Bulli, these are ritualized multi-course meals built from deliberately contrasting flavors and textures. And he seemed very taken by the seriousness of the chefs he met and the purity of their culinary vision, sometimes literally religious in its intensity and its respect for cuisine as an expression of the natural world. "Every time I go to Japan," he says, "I find more things, more new foods—but what is most interesting to me is the philosophy, the approach to life." No one impressed him more in this regard than Hiroyoshi Ishida, a Buddhist monk who is also the venerated chef-owner of Mibu, an *ichigensan okotowari* ("invitation only") restaurant in Tokyo.

Mibu may be the one restaurant in the world that is harder to get into than El Bulli. The phone number is unlisted; there are only eight seats; to dine at Mibu, you need to be invited by a regular customer, and even the regulars are allowed to dine there no more than once a month. If you're Ferran Adrià, of course, you can get in anywhere: On his first visit to Tokyo, he was invited to Mibu by Yukio Hattori, one of Japan's most famous food personalities as president of Tokyo's largest cooking school and the on-screen commentator for the original *Iron Chef.*

Ishida, like Ferran, is continually inventing new dishes and working with textures as well as flavors, and Ferran immediately felt a strong culinary kinship with him. After he'd finished his meal at Mibu, Ferran declared that it had been one of the most memorable of his life. Hattori claims that Ferran was so moved by what he ate that tears came to his eyes.

The feeling turned out to be mutual. The summer after Ferran's dinner at Mibu, Ishida returned the favor, coming to eat at El Bulli with his wife (who runs the Mibu dining room). Whether or not Ishida's eyes welled up in the course of the dinner is unrecorded, but after he'd consumed the last morsel, he told Ferran that the meal had changed his life. He had felt himself closing down inside as he grew older, said Ishida, but dinner at El Bulli had let the light in, rejuvenating him. In gratitude, he offered to come back to the restaurant and cook for Ferran and his friends, as his gift to a fellow master.

The following March, before the restaurant opened for the season, Ishida and his wife arrived for a four-day stay, bringing with them Hattori and his colleague Setsuko Yuki, two cooks, and not just a cornucopia of Japanese raw materials but cooking utensils, table settings, even cooking water. One dining room was stripped of its furnishings and appointed with borrowed Japanese antiques and ikebana floral pieces. As at Mibu, only eight diners at a time were served (there were both lunch and dinner sessions)—all of them invited personally by Ferran and Juli. Ishida found Cala Montjoi to be a comfortingly spiritual place, he said, and he meditated daily on the beach. He was not amused, however, when he came back to the kitchen following an afternoon nap and saw Ferran replacing a pair of chopsticks he'd borrowed; "He just completely lost it," says José Andrés, who had been invited to one of the meals. Ishida was even more upset when he noticed Juan Mari Arzak poking around the kitchen one evening and sticking his finger in his sauces. "He said he wanted Arzak out of the kitchen that instant!" says Andrés. "I had to explain who Arzak was. But Ishida didn't care. This part of the kitchen was his, period." Ishida later calmed down, and everybody became friends again. The dinners were, in any case, a big success, and the whole episode was later immortalized in a Japanese comic book, a manga, called "Mibu—El Bulli," published in Tokyo in a small edition in Japanese and Spanish.

■ ■ ■

Despite everything else that was going on in 2003, Ferran somehow found the time and energy to go off in a new direction entirely, becoming involved with a project that may ultimately prove to be the most important, and lasting, thing he has ever done—but that remains surprisingly little known, and is seldom written about in the popular press: the Fundació Alícia, or Alícia Foundation.

Alícia is a food-related research and educational institution jointly sponsored by the Catalan regional government and the Caixa Manresa, a large regional savings bank serving the *comarca* (county) of El Bages, where the foundation is located. (The name *Alícia* is a concatenation of *alimentació* and *ciència*, the Catalan words for "food" and "science," respectively, but also a reference to *Alice in Wonderland*, said to be the non-scientific book most often cited in works by scientists.) The mission of Alícia, as its director, a respected food scholar and former chef named Toni Massanés, explained it to me, is "to organize and 'exploit,' in the best sense of the word, the application of science and innovation to cooking, but also to improve the quality of life for people with special dietary needs, to analyze school and hospital food, and to educate children in good nutrition and also gastronomy."

Spanish savings banks are required to spend a portion of their annual profits on cultural enterprises, so in 2003, to fulfill this requirement while simultaneously aiding in the economic revival of the region, the Caixa began planning to turn a property they own near the city of Manresa—on which stood a shuttered textile factory and the abandoned monastery of Món Sant Benet—into a cultural center with conference facilities and a hotel and restaurant attached. As a part of the development, they wanted to add a gastronomic educational component, and contacted Massanés, who had been writing a weekly food column for *Regió 7*, the largest newspaper in the region, asking him to assess the property and make some proposals. Meanwhile, Ferran's name had come up—as it usually does when people talk seriously about gastronomy in Catalonia—and he was invited to become an advisor to the foundation. Ferran thought about the possibilities and said, "I already have a laboratory for myself, now we should make one for everybody else." He wrote a six-page proposal of his own for the foundation, proposing that its purview should include not just gastronomy and gastronomic history but diet, nutrition, and preventative health.

Ferran asked Massanés to stay on as director, but he realized that it was also important to have the medical community involved, and he immediately thought of a man he'd never met but who was well-known in Spain—a Barcelona-born cardiologist named Valentín Fuster, who had been president of both the American Heart Association and the World Heart Federation and was now director of Mount Sinai Heart in New York. "Ferran called me out of nowhere," Fuster told me. "I didn't know him or know what it was about, but he told me about this new idea of Alícia, and said, 'Let's work together, you from the side of science and prevention, me from the kitchen.'" Fuster agreed, and the foundation began functioning officially in January of 2004.

Fuster and Ferran are also collaborating on a book, integrating concerns about the quality of food with scientifically sound dietary information. "The idea is to teach children and parents simple recipes, how to cook quickly things that are healthy," according to Fuster.

"I think Ferran's great contribution is to show that high-quality food is not a challenge to prevention, but an asset."

This is only a small part of what Alícia does, however.

When I first heard about the foundation, I imagined it to exist mostly on paper, perhaps with an office somewhere but with most of the work carried out in scattered kitchens and laboratories. I couldn't have been more mistaken. It may have started that way, but in 2007, the foundation moved into a purpose-built 21,000-square-foot contemporary-style building in the middle of the Món Sant Benet property. The test kitchens and research areas are glassed in and visible to the curious visitors who stream in and out all day—literal transparency. There are two main departments, Scientific Gastronomy and Alimentary Health, each with its own space—beautifully equipped facilities, spacious and flooded with natural light. The organic chemist Pere Castells is in charge of the former, working with his longtime colleague Ingrid Farré—there have been no scientists at the Taller since the beginnings of the foundation in 2004–with the culinary aspects handled by five-year El Bulli veteran Jaume Biarnés. The latter is the preserve of nutritionist and food technologist Elena Roura, with Marc Puig-Pey, who worked at El Bulli for seventeen years, as chef de cuisine.

When I visited the foundation, Puig-Pey and another chef were busy developing new dishes for the Manresa Hospital for the Elderly, playing with textures, paying attention to foods that would be easy to chew, and looking at ways to increase the nutritional value of dishes, since the patients tend to eat small amounts. They have also worked with diabetic and celiac diets, Puig-Pey told me—a celiac former Proctor & Gamble chemist from Cincinatti did a stage at Alícia working on gluten-free bread and puff pastry—and have developed two hundred dishes for people who can't digest protein, including an eggless tortilla española that a stagiare at Alícia assured me tasted very authentic. At the same time, I also met a chemical engineer from Belgium working with two Catalan pastry chefs on a basic guide to pastry science ("The 'why' of all the processes, scientifically laid out," Massenés explained), and two chemists, one Catalan, one Valencian, involved in a low-temperature sous-vide cooking project. That health is not Alícia's only concern became even clearer when I met a young Korean chef-nutritionist working on deep-frying techniques in an effort to come up with the ultimate french fry. "When we find it," Massanés told me, "we'll freeze it and send it off to the national food center in Navarra for analysis. They have a bigger lab there. If we can change the french fry to make it healthier in some way, we will, but in this case, the flavor and texture are the most important things."

About the last person you might expect to be a fan of Alícia, this meeting ground of food and science, is Carlo Petrini, the founder of Slow Food. Petrini, though, *loves* the idea of the work the foundation is doing, he told me one day when I talked to him by telephone in Turin. "If you're a diabetic or a celiac or have other alimentary disfunctions," he exclaimed, "or you're just old and can't eat everything, you still have the right to pleasure! And to have a great chef working with other chefs and scientists to make things that will give you pleasure—to me, that is the most important thing that Ferran does!"

How much is Ferran really involved in Alícia? I asked Massanés. "He really is the leader," he assured me. "He's in constant communication with us. He calls almost every day, even if it's just to say, 'Is everything okay?' and he comes at least once a month." Ferran says that, in his subconscious, "Alícia is like my retirement."

■ ■ ■

Given Ferran's interplay with scientists and doctors, it was probably inevitable that before long academia would come calling. In 2005, Camilo José Cela University in Villanueva de la Cañada, just outside

Madrid, endowed the Ferran Adrià Chair in Gastronomic Culture and Food Sciences. In 2007, the Department of Chemical Engineering at the University of Barcelona conferred an honorary university degree on Ferran—who, remember, had never finished high school—naming him Doctor Honoris Causa. In honoring Ferran, Claudi Mans, dean of the department, proposed that a number of other departments of the university could just as legitimately have offered the honor to Ferran: "Matters of food science and technology, essential in cooking," he said, "could be covered by the School of Pharmacy; matters of nutrition by the School of Medicine, or, on another level, by CESNID [the school's Center of Higher Education for Nutrition and Diet]; many organoleptic aspects, in the interrelation and emotion of perceptions, by the School of Psychology; aspects of physical transformation and chemical reaction involved in the preparation of food by the School of Chemistry, and also that of Physics; the artistic, esthetic, and design elements in cooking by the School of Fine Arts; matters relating more to the anthropology of food and the sense of food as culture, by the School of Geography and History, and issues related to the economic activity implicit in the development of [Ferran's] business by the School of Economic and Business Sciences and the College of Business Studies."

Ferran takes this degree very seriously, incidentally. One afternoon, we were talking about "natural" versus "artificial" foodstuffs, and he pointed out, quite rightly, that sugar and flour, among other commonplace substances, were processed, and therefore could be said to be "unnatural." But when he mentioned wine as another example, I said, No, distillation is processing but fermenting isn't. It can happen without human intervention. If you leave ripe grapes in a bowl on the table in a warm room long enough, I said—I used to use this example when I was teaching beginning wine classes—eventually the grape skins will crack and the juice will leak out; when airborne wild yeasts settle on the juice they will begin converting its sugar content to alcohol and CO_2; the results may be disgusting, but they will technically be wine. "No," said Ferran, "that's not wine. Believe me, I know what I'm talking about. I have a degree in chemistry from the University of Barcelona!"

Another Doctor Honoris Causa was granted to Ferran in 2008, this one from the University of Aberdeen in Scotland, under the auspices of its Centre for Modern Thought, which is dedicated to fostering "dynamic and theoretically informed cross-disciplinary research." Ferran's most prestigious academic association, though, developed when the Harvard University Materials Research Science and Engineering Center invited him to give a lecture on science and cooking in December of the same year, and he subsequently signed a "memorandum of understanding" with Harvard's School of Engineering and Applied Sciences, establishing a program of cooperation between students and professors on one hand and El Bulli and the Alícia Foundation on the other.

The Harvard connection was made initially through Otger Campàs, a Barcelona-born physicist now doing post-doctoral research in biophysics as part of the university's School of Engineering and Applied Science's Applied Mathematics group. A lover of good food, Campàs says that he taught himself to cook with Ferran's books (an accomplishment probably only a scientist could boast of). "Once a year, the Materials Research Science and Engineering Center hosts a lecture by someone who isn't a specialist in our field but who does related work, and I wanted to invite Ferran," Campàs explains when I visit him in his Harvard office one summer afternoon. "I'm studying what is called soft matter here [the term encompasses hydrocolloids, foams, gels, liquids, and polymers, among other materials], and that's a lot of what Ferran works with, too—except that he's cooking and I'm using emulsions to measure physical forces in living embryos." Campàs needed to get approval for the invitation from Professor

David Weitz, director of the center. Weitz admitted to me that he's not particularly interested in cooking, and had never heard of Ferran. When he explained to Weitz who Ferran was, says Campàs, "He laughed and said I'd never get him to come, but if I did, he'd find money for expenses. I sent Ferran an e-mail in Catalan asking him to come, and he said yes. David was very surprised."

When Ferran stood at a podium in a large Harvard lecture hall in early December of 2008, there were campus policemen at the doors to keep out the overflow; two adjacent rooms into which his presentation was being simulcast were also packed. He spoke for almost three hours, about the development of new textures in food, about the historical relationship between food and science, about "molecular gastronomy" and why it had nothing to do with his cooking, and about the concept of cuisine as language, a means of communication between creator and consumer. He illustrated his points with clips from DVDs revealing some of his techniques and displaying many of his finished creations, sometimes to oohs and aahs from the audience.

Then Ferran, with Isabel, repaired to Clio, Ken Oringer's elegant Back Bay restaurant, for a thirty-course dinner with a group of Harvard scientists and a handful of journalists. "I tried to give him ingredients he may not have seen before," Oringer later told me. "And I wanted to have fun like he does." The fun that evening (and into the early morning) was an array of dishes that suggests some imaginative satirist's fantasy of an El Bulli menu—things like geoduck and crispy duck tacos with sudahsi lime, shiso flowers, and sushi rice sorbet; yuzu gelée with black olive dust, mint, olive oil ice cream, and tomato jam; and venison cooked in espresso with cocoa crumble, uchiki kuri squash, and yogurt. *Time* magazine's man at the table, Howard Chua-Eoan, reported that "Adrià was happily relaxed but still peppering the scientists at the table with questions about the qualities of certain foods. Why, he asked, did red beets emulsify so much more easily than anything else he's used in the kitchen. None of the scientists had an answer but someone suggested putting the root crop through a molecular spectroscope to break down its chemical composition."

Touring research labs earlier in the day, Ferran had managed to learn a few other things, though. According to Elizabeth Gudrais in *Harvard Magazine*, postdoctoral fellow Jiandi Wan told him about double emulsions, "tiny bubbles, each inside another thin bubble, dispersed in a fluid." Another doctoral student showed Ferran "how she combines glucose syrup and sucrose ester molecules in a Kitchen-Aid mixer to produce a foam made of 'nanopatterned cells' that hold their shape and preserve a foamy texture in the absence of fat. . . ." Ferran, it was said, practically salivated as he listened to descriptions of some of the equipment used by Harvard researchers.

While he was at Harvard, Ferran talked to Campàs and Weitz about the possibility of regularizing a collaboration between the School of Engineering and Applied Science on one hand and El Bulli, the Taller, and Alícia on the other. Both sides thought it was a good idea. "Our first goal," explains Weitz, "is to have a course called 'Science and Cooking' or 'Cooking and Science.' I'm an educator, and have spent many years teaching introductory physics to people who don't particularly want to study it, and I'm always looking for an edge. The idea here would be to use people's interest in cooking to teach them good serious science. Why does food cook faster in a copper frying pan? Why does a meringue solidify? If we discuss issues like this, we're talking about basic scientific principles."

Weitz points out, though, that "chefs and scientists work differently, at a different pace. Chefs have enormous empirical knowledge, and to be honest there are things we can learn from therm. But there's a slight disconnect: Chefs tend to try something, and if it doesn't work, they move on to something else. We keep at it, we try to understand *why* it doesn't work and figure out a way to *make* it work. Our whole belief is that if we can understand something, we can make it better. Chefs just want to know how to get results."

"We're starting to send students over to Alícia," Campàs tells me, "and David and I are doing research for Ferran. We take a look at what they're doing in the workshop, and maybe they say, we have a problem, we're losing stability or temperature or texture, purely physical questions, and we make suggestions." Ferran is also organizing lecture programs for Weitz's department—the first took place in September 2010—in which chefs and scientists collaborate in dialogues on food and science. Participants in the first series included Ferran himself, Joan Roca, Carme Ruscalleda, José Andrés, Grant Achatz, and Wylie Dufresne, and the topics ranged from sous-vide cooking and "olive oil and viscosity" to "surfactants and micelles, crystals, colloids and polymer melts."

Campàs, too, stresses the differences between chefs and scientists: "Ferran goes much faster than we do," he says. "A Harvard graduate student here will take four years to study the stability of foam. Ferran wants to take advantage of the knowledge of physics to do what he wants *now.*" He wants to use science in his work as a chef, in other words, not be a scientist himself. Campàs has great hopes for the collaboration between Ferran and Harvard, he adds. "Ferran is just scratching the surface," he says. "This kind of research could make creativity grow exponentially. You don't need all these little bits of separate knowledge. You could develop a theory and abstract it. This could open whole new worlds in cooking. Ferran is just the tip of the iceberg."

■ ■ ■

In addition to inspiring scientific collaboration, Ferran has played an unwitting role as a kind of culinary Euterpe. In 2007, a prominent young French composer named Bruno Mantovani dined at El Bulli, and was so impressed by the lengthy tasting menu (thirty-five courses, in his case) that he went home to Paris and composed a twenty-nine-minute work for orchestra and electronic ensemble that followed and interpreted the meal dish by dish. The piece, entitled "Le livre des illusions (hommage à Ferran Adrià)," had its world premiere in the French capital, at the Salle Pleyel, in June of 2009. When Ferran first heard about the work, he told me, he thought, "That's nice"—but made no plans to attend the performance, mostly because it came less than a week before the year's seasonal opening of El Bulli, and he knew he would be phenomenally busy. Then he heard that it was to be performed by the Orchestre de Paris, and, as he said enthusiastically, "This is very important!"

"I wrote this work for a thousand reasons," Mantovani explained to me before the performance. "I'm absolutely mad for gastronomy, to begin with. And the worlds of music and food seem to me intimately connected, in the immediacy with which both are experienced and the way they can challenge the senses. And remember that musicians often use food metaphors when they speak of their own work—'spicy' harmony, 'acid' orchestration, and so on. When I ate at El Bulli, I thought of my meal at once in musical terms and made notes about everything I ate. I had written a piece earlier inspired by a wine tasting, but this was the first time I had used food."

Before Mantovani's work was played, he and the conductor and Ferran took the stage to explain a bit about the music and its sources— Ferran quickly described the origins and structure of several dishes— with illustrations by the musicians. In evoking the first dish, Ferran's famous spherified olives, Mantovani said, "The olive explodes when you bite it. Thus the orchestra begins with an explosion." (Cue a richly textured orchestral detonation trailing off with an electronic rattle.) "But then the olive oil floods your mouth." (Cue a dissonant audible skein of slushing and flowing.) "Then we put the two together." (Detonation, rattle, slushing, flowing.) Similar demonstrations were given for two other items, risotto of grapefruit (a dish in which grains of grapefruit pulp substitute for rice) and sesame sponge—which Ferran described, in his heavily accented French, as "a *biscuit* without flour, cooked in a microwave, a dish very typical of the cuisine at El Bulli." "I have to thank Ferran for having constructed so long a menu," said Mantovani after the demonstrations. "There aren't many chefs whose menus I could write an entire composition about."

Mantovani's music had about as much to do with that of his namesake—the Venetian-born light-orchestra conductor known only as Mantovani, who had countless schmaltzy hit records in the mid-twentieth century—as Ferran's food does with old-fashioned blanquette de veau. It was, for those not used to listening to contemporary orchestral music—with or without electronic garnish—probably pretty tough going. Some listeners, even the more sophisticated ones, later noted that they would have enjoyed it more if the thirty-five sections had been separated slightly instead of connected to one another. What did Ferran make of it all? I looked over at him about halfway through the piece. He had his head down and his eyes closed, but there was a firmness in his face that suggested concentration rather than slumber. The next day, he said that he had liked the piece a lot, sounding a little bit surprised at himself.

After the concert, Ferran invited me to have dinner with him at Joël Robuchon's L'Atelier. We ate gazpacho—"the same recipe as at El Bulli," said Ferran—with mild mustard ice cream, king crab sandwiched between very thin slices of daikon, squid cooked with chorizo and artichokes, duck foie gras with cherries and rhubarb, a tomato salad, textbook sole meunière (half a fish each), and miniature lamb chops with Robuchon's famous potato purée, made with nearly as much butter as potatoes. L'Atelier has something of a Spanish flavor to it—there is excellent jamón Ibérico available, and, besides that gazpacho and those squid with chorizo, there are stuffed piquillo peppers and refinements of other Spanish dishes on the menu—and Ferran told me that it was certainly inspired by the tapas bars Robuchon frequents when he's at his vacation home in the south of Spain. Robuchon himself wasn't at the restaurant, but at one point another diner came over to say hello. "That's the head of Michelin," Ferran informed me when he'd left.

The meal was very pleasant, very relaxed. Ferran's only concern, he told me, was that if certain critics didn't like Mantovani's composition, they'd blame him. Surely not, I said. "No, no, no, no," he replied. "Believe me. They will." (Though it received some news coverage in both France and Spain, as far as I can tell, nobody in either country ever actually reviewed the music.)

As we finished our lamb chops, Ferran said, "This is a restaurant for people who are tired of restaurants." So, in a different way, is El Bulli, I replied. "Yes, you're right," he agreed. Then we had a light dessert, strawberry sorbet with basil. It was delicious. "The combination of strawberries with basil would have never occurred to me," I said to Ferran. He looked me in the eye and a faint smile crept up. "1990," he said.

14

Anti-Ferran, Santi-Ferran

"He who sticks his head above the crowd will receive the rotten fruit."

—Chinese proverb

Ferran has his critics. How could he not? But as late as 2003, when somebody called Ferran's attention to the fact that an American chef had said of him, "That foam guy is bogus," he says that he thought with genuine surprise, "Oh, there's somebody who doesn't like what I'm doing." It had apparently never occurred to him that what he and his team were cooking might actually offend some people. "Ferran lived in a very naïve and happy world until the attacks started," Pau Arenós told me one day.

As with probably every chef, there are people who simply don't like the way Ferran cooks. They have eaten at El Bulli and found the experience unsatisfying, the dishes weird or affected or just not to their taste. That's normal. There are also people, apparently quite a lot of them, who object not to Ferran's food—because they've never actually tasted it—but to the whole *idea* of it. They read or hear about his creations and think somebody is trying to put something over on them—and they're too smart to be fooled. The British restaurant critic A. A. Gill, who became an unlikely champion of the restaurant after his first meal there (unlikely because he is not an easy man to please, and regularly skewers pretentious cooking in his pieces), noted in *The Sunday Times* that before his first visit, three different friends warned him that he'd find Ferran's creations ghastly. It turned out that not one of them had eaten there. "Why would we?" they asked. "It's so awful."

Then there's the "Emperor's New Clothes" school of criticism, vividly illustrated by one "Joe Schmoe," in a comment on the *Sunday Times* Web site: "Wow a business that is only open for 6 months a year! And he has people begging him to let them patronize his business. Haha, what a scam! Sure it's the 'Best Restaurant in the World' (rolling eyes) It's called 'marketing' folks. You make your product rare, jack up the price and tell everyone how exclusive it is, and all the knuckleheads with more money than sense will kill each other to be seen buying your wares. All you need is a friendly newspaper or two to promote your stuff. Piece of cake!" (In fact, El Bulli has no marketing or public relations operation: Juli Soler and the dining room manager, David López, handle almost all press relations on an informal basis.)

Antonio Burgos thinks that Ferran insults his very culture. A well-known and controversial author and journalist—he has been accused of racism and homophobia for his remarks, and offended José Luis Rodríguez Zapatero, the Spanish prime minister, by describing his young daughters as "horrendous tripe" and "eyesores in boots"— Burgos is a native of Seville and a passionate defender of Andalusian traditions. When Ferran took part in Andalucía Sabor, an international gastronomical event in Seville in the fall of 2007, Burgos made it clear that he didn't think much of Ferran's deconstruction of gazpacho (Andalusia's emblematic specialty) or his new technique for frying fish—this in a region where that means of cooking is so refined that an Andalusian housewife is said to be able to deep-fry the sea-spray. "Don Fernando [sic] . . . ," Burgos wrote scornfully, in a column in the conservative Madrid daily *ABC*, "recalled that in 1989, he came up with a unique gazpacho with lobster. . . . He recalled how he began to question the limits of gazpacho. . . . [He] said that we must consider what constitutes a soup, and whether it could also be a sauce or a sorbet. But wait, there's more. . . . Don Fernando Adrian [sic] also has to explain to Andalusians how to fry fish. In the fry-shops of Seville, the deep-fryers of Cadiz, and the cooking pots of Huelva, they have no idea. The Catalan chef presented in Seville a new way of frying fish, thanks to wheat fiber, which lets one fry liquid products such as spherified Pedro Ximénez grapes (drops of this sweet wine covered by a thin layer of gelatin . . .). You don't need the good oil from the mill of Ginés or chickpea flour, or anything. The one who knows how to fry fish well is he. Thank you very much, Don Fernando, for being so generous and for teaching the Andalusians." He concluded with a suggestion that now, perhaps, a noted Andalusian chef could head north to show the Catalans how to cook their favorite botifarra sausage with white beans.

What's off-key about Burgos's remarks, of course, is that Ferran has immense respect for traditional Spanish food. In fact, when Ferran gives the recipe for his non-soup gazpacho with lobster in *El sabor del Mediterráneo*, he precedes it with one for old-style gazpacho that is very likely more authentic than anything Burgos has had for years. As far as the Andalusian talent for frying goes, I once overheard a conversation between Ferran and Anthony Bourdain in which the two globe-trotting chefs were comparing notes on their favorite tempura bar in Tokyo, and Ferran said, "Do you know why I think the best Andalusian fried fish is better than the best tempura?" Bourdain said no. "Because of the flavor of the olive oil," he replied. Quite possibly from the mill of Ginés.

Criticism by those who *have* dined at El Bulli tends to appear not in magazines and newspapers as much as in blogs or on food-based discussion Web sites. "[C]an't they give us something we can chew with our teeth instead of messing our minds and palate?" asked one blogger. "Adrià clearly doesn't give a toss about serving delicious food," proposed another. At least one diner at El Bulli appeared for a time to have expressed his opinion of the place with his feet: Shortly after midnight on June 12, 2008, a food-loving self-employed courier from Geneva named Pascal Henry, who had saved his money for years and undertaken what was to be a round-the-world tour of Michelin three-star restaurants, got up from his table at El Bulli with several courses still to come, went outside, and vanished, leaving behind his hat and his notebook. When no trace of Henry could be found at local hotels over the next few days, the police were called and search parties were sent out. One newspaper declared his vanishing *"El misterio del gourmet desaparecido."* Theories abounded. Had Henry simply run out on the check? Had he fallen down the hillside? Was his dematerialization the ultimate critique of El Bulli?

None of the above, as it turned out. About two months later, Interpol found him back home in Geneva. After his reappearance, the Swiss wine and food writer Jacques Perrin interviewed Henry for his blog, Milles Plateaux. Henry explained that he had had a kind of existential crisis. After a Spanish journalist at the next table that night had asked him for his business card, he said, he went to his car to retrieve one. "I sat at the wheel. I stayed three minutes to wait . . . I turned the key and I went into the night. It was like a big black hole. . . ." For days, he drove aimlessly through France, contacting no one. He considered retiring to a Cistercian monastery. He questioned the meaning of life, and deduced that it was "not taking refuge in restaurants in order to feel well for a few hours." When Perrin asked if the food at El Bulli had disappointed him, Henry replied, "It was good but . . . when restaurants are put at the pinnacle, you expect an explosion of flavors, of tastes; without being at all pejorative, El Bulli wasn't all that astonishing . . . it was not . . . the ultimate dream of gastronomy."

The most extraordinary criticism of El Bulli that I've encountered came from the *Washington Post* art critic Blake Gopnik, who complained after his visit that Ferran's creations were too tame. "In fine-art terms," he wrote, "you could say that a lot of it is still stuck in abstract-land, riffing on the same old palette (or palate) of sensations. . . . If Goya's been allowed into these kitchens, he's been kept on salad duty. A dinner at elBulli . . . is definitely one of the most stunning, most daring meals you'll ever eat. . . . Yet for an art critic, it still feels like a bare start." Ferran, in other words, isn't avant-garde *enough*!

■ ■ ■

Ferran says that one of the most significant honors he has ever been accorded was an invitation to participate in Documenta 12—the 2007 edition of the major international art show held every five years in and around the Fridericianum Museum in the German city of Kassel, northeast of Frankfurt. Ferran's artistic imagination had already been acknowledged outside the culinary sphere. In 2006, for instance, he was awarded the Raymond Loewy Foundation's Lucky Strike Design Prize—which had previously gone to such luminaries of the design world as Philippe Starck, Karl Lagerfeld, and Bruno Sacco of Daimler-Benz. ("Our dialogue with the world of design," Ferran once told me, "is more powerful than with any other discipline." Take *that*, science.) He had also been asked to take part in exhibitions at the Tate Modern in London and at MACBA, Barcelona's Museum of Contemporary Art, among other institutions—though he had always declined.

Documenta was something different. When representatives of the show first approached Ferran, he says, he'd frankly never heard of it. He mentioned it to some friends in the art world, though—among them Marta Arzak, daughter of his colleague Juan Mari Arzak and head of the education department at the Guggenheim Museum in Bilbao—and learned that it was one of the most prestigious of all international art events. He decided to say yes.

The fact that he had been invited as an artist and not as a cook—that his work would appear in some context alongside that of "real artists" like John McCracken, Agnes Martin, and some of the more exciting younger figures from Africa, Asia, and the Middle East—was a vital distinction to Ferran, but it also outraged or at least annoyed professional and lay commentators alike. Manuel Borja-Villel, then director of MACBA, was indirectly responsible for Ferran's going to Documenta—it was he who introduced Ferran to the show's 2007 artistic director—but he was quoted as saying that Ferran's participation was an example of the "narcissism and self-satisfaction" inherent in this mounting of the show. He later told an interviewer for El País that "with all due respect to Ferran Adrià, whom I consider an absolutely exceptional chef, I think that this speaks to a certain dilettantish extravagance on the part of the curator, who, in my way of seeing, considers this political venue as something merely festive and communal." Fernando Savater, who writes about food when he's not being a professor of philosophy at the University of Madrid, proposed that "the enthronement of Ferran Adrià at the art fair in Kassel adds nothing to his 'genius,' but instead reveals the foolishness of the guardians of modern-day artistic decadence." Robert Hughes pitched in with: "Both Adrià's participation and contribution seem ridiculous to me. Food is food."

Things got worse when Ferran announced that, after long reflection, he had decided to take part in Documenta without leaving Cala Montjoi—which is a good eight hundred and fifty miles from Kassel. He'd given the matter a lot of thought, he said—and he considered that very thinking "about the contextualization of vanguard cuisine in relation to other creative fields" to be the most interesting part of the whole exercise. Anyway, he added, "It wasn't possible to move the team and equipment to another place; that would mean we were merely a catering service." He later told a reporter from *El País*, "It would have been arrogant for me to bring my kitchen into the art world. It is much more logical to bring people from the art world here."

Ferran's idea was that the fifty or so guests who came to El Bulli nightly during the art show's hundred-day run could in fact consider themselves as visitors to Documenta; the restaurant was designated as Pavilion G (five other pavilions in Kassel were labeled A through F), and the appropriate banners and placards were installed. In addition, two diners a day would be selected in Kassel and offered—with one day's notice—round-trip airfare from Frankfurt to Girona, a night's stay at the bare-bones Mar y Sol Hotel in Roses, and a special thirty-eight-course dinner menu. A number of Documenta staff members, critics, and artists were chosen for the honor—the first guests were Chilean artist Juan Dávila and his partner, Graeme Smith—but there were also diners selected at random from among museum-goers and residents of Kassel.

"I was at the Biennale in Venice when I heard what Ferran was going to do," Vicente Todolí told me, "and I sent him a note that just said, 'Brilliant.' It would have been easy for him to fall into a trap. He was sent a smash ball that he could never return, and somehow he did." There is a tradition of artists working with cuisine, he continues, so why not turn things around? "Ferran changed the paradigm," he says.

Performance art—if that's what Ferran's participation in Documenta can be called—often yields "residue," some concrete record of or reference to what is by definition an ephemeral artistic expression. In the case of Pavilion G, the principal residue is a handsome book, published in several languages, called (in English) *Food for Thought/ Thought for Food*, with Richard Hamilton and Vicente Todolí listed as editors. The text includes essays on art and food and the relationship between the two, as well as transcripts of a couple of round-table discussions—held around all-stops-out meals—featuring Heston Blu-menthal, *New Yorker* writer Bill Buford, Catalan artist Antoni Miralda, Austrian experimental filmmaker Peter Kubelka, and other cultural figures. There are no photographs of Ferran in the amply illustrated book, but Matt Groening's portrait of Ferran graces the cover. The book was Ferran's idea—a way, he said, of demystifying his participa-tion in Documenta. Evoking Brillat-Savarin's nineteenth-century clas-sic of gastronomic philosophy, Ferran told me that he considers the book, in a way, to be the new *Physiology of Taste*.

■ ■ ■

Among his many other distinctions, Ferran has been criticized in at least three books. The more prominently marketed of the three is *¡No quiero volver al restaurante! De como la cocina molecular nos sirve cola para papel pintado y polvo extinctor*—"I Don't Want to Go Back to the Restaurant! How Molecular Cuisine Serves Us Wallpaper Paste and Fire-Extinguisher Powder"—by a German-born, Paris-based food and travel writer named Jörg Zipprick.

Zipprick finds a lot to dislike about Ferran: First and most impor-tant, his food is "artificial," based on additives or "chemicals," and his use of those substances threatens the health of his customers (or at the very least induces flatulence and/or diarrhea). That's just the begin-ning, though: Ferran is beholden to large chemical companies and producers of industrial food products, and benefitted unfairly from a European Union initiative known as INICON, which did the dirty work of the chemical industry; he undermines his own credibility by consulting for junk-food producers; he has ridiculous pretensions to being a serious artist; oh, and he didn't really invent all that weird stuff anyway.

Zipprick catalogues the perils posed by various substances used by El Bulli and other avant-garde kitchens: Lecithin is dangerous for people with soy allergies, sodium citrate for those allergic to mold;

agar and gellan can have a laxative effect in large doses; catabolized (broken down) carrageenan cells have affected the immune systems of laboratory animals or caused ulcers in them. . . . Elaborating on the guilt-by-association theme in his subtitle (wallpaper paste is often made with methylcellulose, an ingredient used for texture at El Bulli; citrates, which the restaurant also employs, are an element in some fire retardants), Zipprick quotes Olivier Roellinger—chef at the three-star Les Maisons de Bricourt in Brittany and a vocal foe of "molecular cuisine"—as noting that liquid nitrogen is used in dermatology to remove warts.

Well, yes, and King John famously died of a surfeit of peaches and cider. The condemnation of substances that *might*, under certain circumstances, be dangerous always reminds me of the science-department parody that went around a few years ago warning of the perils of dihydrogen monoxide. This colorless, odorless, tasteless chemical, it was said, kills many thousands of people every year; can cause a host of unpleasant conditions including excessive sweating, frequent urination, and electrolyte imbalance; is capable of corroding many metals; and in one form may cause severe burns. It is also used as an industrial solvent and a fire retardant, and in the production of Styrofoam. Dihydrogen monoxide, of course, is H_2O—water.

The biggest villain in Zipprick's story—the SMERSH or the KAOS of the contemporary European food scene, to hear him tell it—is something called INICON. (The name is a rather tortured acronym for Introduction of Innovative Technologies in Modern Gastronomy for the Modernization of Cooking.) Zipprick identifies INICON as "a research institute of the European Union," and complains that it "helped introduce additives and artificial flavorings into higher gastronomy" and that "many creations relating to molecular chefs [have] been discovered precisely from this . . . research." What he finds particularly galling is that INICON was supported by EU funds; the European taxpayer, in other words, was apparently subsidizing research into a kind of cooking that is (to Zipprick) morally objectionable in the first place. INICON's intention, Zipprick suggests, was to undermine traditional cooking throughout the continent and feed dangerous materials to unwilling diners through the agency of self-styled "genius-chefs"—who hadn't even been smart enough to develop their own techniques

In fact, INICON, whose life span extended from January first, 2003, through December thirty-first, 2005, wasn't an "institute" at all, but a research and development project funded by the European Commission, involving representatives of the commercial food industry and a small number of chefs who exchanged information and worked to develop new food production techniques. The restaurants represented were El Bulli; Heston Blumenthal's Fat Duck; Au Crocodile, a respected establishment with two Michelin stars in Strasbourg; and a little-known, emphatically "nonmolecular" place called Grashoff Bistro in Bremen, the capital of Germany's commercial food industry.

When I asked Ferran about El Bulli's involvement in INICON, he waved his hand dismissively and made a sound very much like "pshaw." "It's nothing," he said. "A project. They asked me to participate. There was money to pay for trips for the kitchen team, that's all. Albert went on some of the trips, but I never went on even one." The *Los Angeles Times* quoted an Italian TV show on which Ferran supposedly admitted having received 25,000 euros (about $37,000 dollars) in INICON funds, but he told me that that simply wasn't true. "It was never, never to make money," he said emphatically. "Albert paid his own way, then got a refund for his expenses." According to Claudia Krines, team leader in bio-process engineering and food technology for TTZ Bremerhaven, a private non-profit research and development organization that was active in INICON, each participating partner received a maximum of 14,500 euros for the whole three-year period, out of which they had to pay all their travel expenses plus the costs of the materials they used in their research and demonstrations. "This would likely consume almost all financial reimbursement," she said.

Among the innovations developed through INICON sessions— eight of them in all over a three-year period—were a way of "frying" foods in water through increased osmotic pressure, a means of making "inverse" ice cream that is solid when warm and melts as it approaches room temperature, and a device for producing more stable emulsions (foams, sauces, etc.). These developments aside, Albert says that he found the meetings "a little stupid, because there was no real working agenda." But, he adds, "I had the opportunity to meet and talk with Heston Blumenthal and Hervé This, among other professionals, and I learned some new things." The gatherings took place in various European cities, in venues including the Écoles Grégoire-Ferrandi, several hotel kitchens, and assorted conference rooms. Typically, says Albert, one chef would present a dish or cooking technique, "Heston with a chocolate soufflé, for example, or me demonstrating the Paco-jet, or somebody else with marmalades. Afterwards, we'd discuss what we'd seen, and plan our work for the future—but in general, there were too many words and not enough work." Blumenthal concurs. "The only good thing about INICON was the chance to develop friendships with other people. Otherwise, nothing came out of it."

■ ■ ■

Another book to take Ferran to task, published two years earlier than ¡No quiero volver al restaurante!, was a curious little volume called Luces y sombras del reinado de Ferran Adrià (Lights and Shadows in the Realm of Ferran Adrià), by a Barcelona-born journalist and author named Miguel Sen. If Zipprick's bête noire is INICON, Sen's is something far more abstract: "normosis"—a syndrome identified and named by the French psychologist and educator Pierre Weil. Following Weil's lead, Sen defines normosis as a sort of mass ultra-conformity that comes to be "when the whole world agrees on one opinion and acts in a certain way, when there is a common consensus because certain behaviors have become customary." He says that "political correctness" is an example of a normosis. So, says Sen, is the adulation accorded to Ferran.

"[T]he Adrià phenomenon is now at its paroxysm," he writes, "and . . . this great enthusiasm is strictly connected to the recent triumph of democracy [in Spain]." The success of El Bulli, in other words, is largely due to the fact that political trends in the post-Franco era "exalted the appeal of novelties and of everything that represented a break with the past." Ferran's fans, Sen writes later in the book, are "loud and obvious. . . . [T]hey sing the praises of his cuisine . . . with nobody raising a hand to question the validity and significance of what the master says. . . . The empire of Adrià knows no criticism that is not eulogy." Sen obviously hadn't reckoned on Santi Santamaria— a celebrated Catalan chef himself, who has lately made a secondary career out of censuring Ferran.

■ ■ ■

Santi Santamaria is a sturdy midsize bear of a man with a generous smile and a balding pate and the shadows of a beard and muttonchop whiskers sometimes framing his rounded face. He is slightly less than five years older than Ferran, born in 1957 in an old farmhouse called Can Fabes—which 'had been in his family for generations—in the small town of Sant Celoni, about thirty miles northeast of Barcelona in the *comarca* (county) of Vallès Oriental. His parents, who were Catalanists and trade-unionists, were regularly harrassed during the Franco regime, and his grandfather, president of the local tenant farmers' union, was jailed in the infamous military prison at Montjuïc Castle in Barcelona; perhaps not surprisingly, Santamaria today is proudly, politically Catalan, and is a vocal and articulate defender of regional traditions, culinary and otherwise, and of the natural environment of rural Catalonia.

A self-taught chef, Santamaria was an industrial designer by profession, and got his culinary start cooking stews and other simple dishes to feed his friends at community political gatherings. When the small enterprise that employed him as a designer went out of business in 1981, he got some severance money, and used it to open an informal bistro that he called El Racó de Can Fabes, in a corner of the family home—where, until he installed a gas line for his kitchen, Santamaria's mother had cooked over a wood fire. Racó means "corner" in Catalan; can, a contraction of ca and en, is more or less the equivalent of the French term chez; as for fabes, though the house is now part of the town, it was originally an agricultural property, and I'd always assumed that the word referred to fava beans (faves in Catalan), a popular crop in the area. "Perhaps," Santamaria says, "but there is another explanation. During the Napoleonic Wars, there was a minor skirmish between French soldiers and local farmers in the plaza in front of the house. Instead of shots being fired, somebody slapped somebody else. In slang, a faba is a slap, so this house became known as 'the house of slaps.'"

Firmly grounded in old-style Catalan cooking but also strongly influenced by nouvelle cuisine, Santamaria had natural talent and quickly developed his own culinary style, growing surer and more sophisticated as a chef every year. In 1988, he was awarded a Michelin star. Two years later—the same year that Ferran won El Bulli its second star back—he got a second one of his own. These parallel events, according to Santamaria, "sowed the seeds of a deep and unjustified professional conflict."

One morning when Ferran and I were having coffee in Barcelona, perched on stools at the counter at the back of Casa Guinart, a well-known food shop at the corner of one entrance to La Boquería, I started to ask him something about Santamaria, and he held up his hand and shook his head a little and said, "There is only one person who knows the real story about Santi and me, and it's not Santi, and it's not me. It's Fermí Puig." So a few days later, sitting in the elegant reception area of his Drolma restaurant, I ask Puig—who was, remember, the one who introduced Ferran to El Bulli in the first place—to fill me in.

"I've known both Ferran and Santi for a long time," Puig begins. "Ferran maybe slightly longer. But I'm from Granollers, which is only about fifteen miles from Sant Celoni, and Santi and I were both correspondents writing political articles for a local magazine, *Comarca al Dia*. I worked in the office for a while, too; you could say that I started by censoring Santi. I had a girlfriend who came from near Sant Celoni and she brought me for the first time to Can Fabes, the first year it opened. I thought, 'It's a little country restaurant and we'll have some grilled meats or something.' I was astonished by the quality of the food. I called Juli and told him to go, which he did."

Soon, Santi started returning the favor, coming to El Bulli on his days off. Everything was cordial. "He would have lunch," says Ferran, "and afterwards we'd talk about food for two or three hours." Puig says, though, that after both restaurants got their second Michelin star, he thought Santi was eating at Cala Montjoi a little too often. "Santi has traveled a lot," says Puig, "and everywhere he goes, when he sees something that can be adapted, he picks it up. That's normal. But he was going to El Bulli more than was prudent. Finally I said to Santi, 'You only need to go twice a year, to show your respect. Otherwise your cooking will be contaminated. What you are starting to do is not what's in your heart.'"

As near-neighbors (Cala Montjoi and Sant Celoni, though as different in landscape and character as could be, are only about fifty miles apart), Santi and Ferran have known each other for decades. But were they ever good friends? I asked Puig. "In 1986," he replied, "I was living in the Canary Islands. I had two restaurants there, in Tenerife, and I was a wealthy man. Every year for four or five years, I invited Santi and Ferran to Tenerife for their holidays, and they'd come at the same time. I'd organize gastronomic weekends, and they'd each cook for me for one day and then spend their vacations there. They both did demonstrations for an annual 'mushroom week' I had, for instance, and Ferran even tried out some of his dishes for the next El Bulli season at my place. I gave them both bungalows with caviar and champagne, and everybody relaxed. Can you say they were friends? No, not in my opinion. They were nice to each other and they talked, but they were not exactly friends. Good colleagues, but not friends." Puig, in fact, was something of a peacemaker between the two men, according to Santamaria. "For years," he has written, "I maintained a more or less cordial professional relationship with Juli Soler and Ferran Adrià. Without Fermí Puig as a catalyst of personal relations, things surely would have gone in another direction, because our characters are diametrically opposed."

Though Santamaria has always expressed the utmost regard for Ferran's talents, it was probably inevitable—by the very fact of their proximity, both geographically and in the culinary rankings—that there would eventually be friction between the two. In 1994, after Santamaria got his third Michelin star—and Ferran didn't—the local food community began to divide itself into Adrianists and Fabists, some preferring Ferran's ever more creative and unexpected cooking, others more attuned to Santamaria's elegant Catalan-inflected nouvelle-style cuisine. It was around this time that the problems between Santamaria and Ferran began in earnest.

Spain had gained its first three-star restaurant only in 1987: the elegant, old-style Zalacaín in Madrid, under chef Benjamin Urdiain. The second Spanish establishment to win the honor was Arzak in San Sebastián, in 1989. Santi was thus only the third three-star chef in the country, and the only one in Catalonia, and the honor to him was immense. "When Santi got his third star," Puig tells me, "he felt himself to be a god. Right away, though, some people of the Barcelona culinary press were a little against him: It was difficult to understand why he had three stars and El Bulli still had only two." At some point, says Puig, Santi started to put some distance between himself and other chefs. "And," he adds, "he didn't show enough respect to Ferran. When he organized a party to celebrate his third star, he invited about a hundred people, including Ferran, to Sant Celoni. But there was only room for fifty or sixty diners at Can Fabes, and the rest went to another restaurant nearby. Now, Ferran *had* to be invited to Can Fabes—but he wasn't. I won't say he was angry, but he was a little sad that day. Santi just didn't understand that he was a leader now and had to use his leadership wisely."

There is a curious, almost certainly apocryphal story about a dramatic moment in the relationship between the two chefs, dating from 1996, when Ferran and Santamaria were both invited to take part in a gastronomic conference sponsored by the International Olive Oil Council at the Barcelona Hilton. Clara Maria Amezúa, founder of Madrid's Alambiquè cooking school, was one of the organizers. "I invited both of them, not knowing that they weren't on good terms," she admits. "I only realized it when I saw some Catalan journalists rubbing their hands in anticipation." According to the Hispanophile American food and wine writer Gerry Dawes, who had volunteered to help translate some of the conference proceedings, the journalists had good reason. Before the panel began, he says, Ferran and Santamaria started sniping at each other. All of a sudden, maintains Dawes, he heard Ferran say to Santamaria, "*Callate! Yo soy genio y tu eres cocinero!*" ("Shut up! I'm a genius and you're a cook!") Dawes swears that this happened, and that some years after the occasion, he reminded Ferran of the incident and Ferran asked, "Did I really say that to Santi?" Yes, said Dawes, and Ferran replied, "I guess I did," with a sheepish smile.

Ferran categorically denies it today. "Furthermore," he adds, "the word *genius* is the one I like least when it's used about me." He has even sometimes been rude to people who use that term about themselves, he says. Fermí Puig wasn't present at the event, but he says, "I have never heard a 'nasty' conversation between Ferran and Santi." Xavier Agulló told me flatly that he didn't believe the story either. "I'll tell you a story of my own about Ferran," he offered. "I thought that it was Santi who was stopping Michelin from giving a third star to him. Santi was very powerful in those days. Ferran and I were sitting on the beach at Cala Montjoi around seven in the evening on a summer evening, and I was mad about Santi. 'I'm going to write something very heavy about that bastard,' I said. 'Xavi,' said Ferran. 'Stop. Don't do anything. Let it be.' I said, 'But, Ferran, you deserve that third star and this SOB is stopping you.' He shook his head and said, 'Calm down, Xavi. Relax. . . .' That is why I don't believe that he'd say something like that to Santi, certainly not in public."

In any case, journalists interviewing Santamaria started bringing up Ferran's name and Santamaria wasn't shy with his opinions. Ferran's cuisine, he told a regional newspaper in the mid-2000s, was "outmoded." Diners at El Bulli couldn't recognize the ingredients they were served, he added, and were offered "flavors that don't exist" (an interesting philosophical concept, it must be said). In 2007, at Madrid Fusión, Santamaria really went on the offensive. Following three days of presentations by an array of Spanish and international culinary stars both traditionalist and avant-garde (among them Ferran, Arzak, Andoni Aduriz, Joan Roca, Tetsuya Wakuda, Grant Achatz, Charlie Trotter, and Dan Barber)—and just before a presentation by Heston Blumenthal that required spectators to don 3-D glasses—he took the stage and delivered an assault on "scientific" cuisine like Ferran's and an impassioned defense of culinary simplicity and traditional values in the kitchen. "How can we be proud of molecular or techno-emotional cuisine that fills dishes with emulsifiers and chemical agents?" he asked, adding that "this trend is crippling haute cuisine." Too many chefs, he continued, have become "a gang of charlatans who work to distract snobs. . . . The only truth that matters is the product that comes out of the earth, passes through the ovens to the mouth of the eater, and is then defecated." He got a standing ovation.

By this time, Santamaria had evolved into a prolific author, having published seven books—both recipe collections and themed culinary works—in as many years. In 2008, his latest book appeared, a thin volume called *La cocina al desnudo* (The Cuisine Stripped Bare). Unlike his previous efforts, this one was pure polemic. *La cocina al desnudo* is obviously a heartfelt work, well written and addressing many issues that need to be addressed—among them genetically modified crops, the industrialization of agriculture, and the proliferation of fast food—but it also sometimes has a self-righteous tone. "One of the basic pillars of democracy is the right of everyone to information," declares Santamaria in his prologue. " . . . This is a book written to encourage the exercise of free speech and to express the wish that so many sleeping consciences will awaken; we cannot live on acceptance, now we have to be ourselves." In the world of postmodern cooking, he adds, "Everything seems reduced to the sound of disco music, the aesthetic of graffiti, and the philosophy of the publicity."

On the place of science in the kitchen, Santamaria writes, "I believe . . . that cuisine, like art, is nourished by experience and a certain mystery. I like to eat a good fried egg, and perhaps it would be helpful to know in addition the physico-chemical processes involved in frying, but I do not appreciate the taste more by knowing the exact temperature of coagulation of the albumen." Like Zipprick, Santamaria questions Ferran's participation in Documenta, writes censoriously about INICON, and criticizes the use of additives—especially methylcellulose, a substance that Santamaria says is used as a laxative (true) and "as false sperm in pornographic films" (this was a new one on me). He also takes a gratuitous swipe at Juli Soler, calling him "an intelligent maître d'hôtel, ironic and talented, who has proven to be an effective public relations man and a manipulator without rival . . . '[t]ouched' by the tramuntana, though with an air of geniality, prisoner of a boundless ambition. . . . I recognize as one of his greatest qualities that he understands that today the media must be behind any great chef."

In a chapter entitled "Letter to Ferran Adrià," Santamaria begins, "Although for many years I have not had the pleasure of eating at El Bulli, you know I respect your culinary work. . . ." Then he continues, "You have said, 'I wouldn't prohibit anyone from eating hamburgers, but would want them to eat one of quality.' However your message of apparent freedom ('I wouldn't prohibit anyone') with a minimal alibi (a hypothetical and difficult to certify 'quality') opens the doors to a model of eating that, in the name of cuisine, today more than ever, we have to combat." He goes on to take Ferran to task for his consulting work—"How is it possible . . . for you to advertise potato chips that belong to the large conglomerate PepsiCo? [i.e., Lay's Mediterráneas Artesanas potato chips] . . . How is this compatible with your proposition, in '100 Ideas for Spain,' published in El País in March of 2008, to teach alimentary education in schools because 'to eat well and to understand what we eat has become an essential subject'?"

Santamaria later told me, "Chefs *must not* make commercials for Pepsi-Cola or sign on with Unilever. We're artisans. There's a limit to what we should do commercially." This is a curious position to take, since famous chefs—including some of the founders of nouvelle cuisine—have worked with commercial food-production firms and touted assorted products for decades. As early as 1976, Michel Guérard became a consultant for Nestlé's Findus frozen food brand. Joël Robuchon recently celebrated twenty years of developing shelf-stable prepared appetizers and main dishes for the immense Fleury Michon concern. Paul Bocuse—who recently opened several Ouest Express fast-food outlets in Lyon—was long the spokesman for Rosier ranges, memorably jumping on an open oven door in TV commercials to prove how sturdily they were built.

But Santamaria seems to hold Ferran up to a higher standard. The "crux of the matter," his "open letter" continues, is as follows: "I don't believe that 'anything goes.' I believe that we have a responsibility to others, and that's why I've been seen to advertise cookware and table-ware in the press and on television but never the snacks of a multinational. . . ." Two weeks after the book was published, in the midst of the uproar it engendered, Santamaria announced—as if to dis-pell any suspicion that he was profiting from his culinary jeremiad—that any money earned by *La cocina al desnudo* would be donated in equal portions to a multiple sclerosis foundation and a consumer rights group.

"Santi has been bad for himself," says Fermí Puig. "When he called me from Madrid a few hours after his speech at Madrid Fusión, he was absolutely happy, very proud of himself. I was mad, and dis-appointed in him, and I told him so. Santi and I have a very intense relationship, but a few days after his book came out I wrote 'In De-fense of Ferran Adrià' in *La Vanguardia*. Santi wouldn't speak to me after that. In truth, though, I would have also written 'In Defense of Santi Santamaria' if somebody had attacked him.

"Everything must be discussed in cuisine, of course, but if you are a chef and you criticize another chef, you must do it with a very fine pencil. Santi painted with a broad brush instead. This is not a war, it's an attack. It's dirty. Ferran has always been so generous, he always tries to bring along colleagues to share the limelight. He doesn't de-serve this. What Santi doesn't realize is that the difference between Ferran and chefs like Santi and myself is that he knows how to do what we do, probably better than we do, but we don't know how to do what he does. Ferran is *hors concours*, someone who appears every hundred years. In the history of cuisine, we will always talk about before and after Ferran Adrià."

On May thirteenth of 2008, the night that I sat down at Inopia in Barcelona with Ferran and talked him into letting me write this book, Santamaria was awarded the Temas de Hoy prize for *La cocina al desnudo,* an honor that comes with a stipend of 60,000 euros (roughly $90,000). In accepting the award, Santamaria stepped up his attack, announcing "a conceptual and ethical divorce" from Ferran and "the avant-garde cuisine he represents," adding that "he and his excellent team are going in a direction contrary to my principals." Then he repeated his accusations that Ferran was endangering the health of his customers—practically poisoning them—through the use of ingredients like methylcellulose. "Can we be proud," he asked rhetorically, "of a cuisine . . . that fills its dishes with laboratory-made emulsifiers and gelificants?" (Santamaria might have a reason to be particularly sensitive about chemicals: Sant Celoni's main industry is chemical production, and local plants have been responsible for several major incidents, including a massive chlorine release into the atmosphere in 1996 and continuing contamination of aquifers along the Tordera River with dioxane and dioxolane.)

Ferran, as a matter of policy, almost never responds to criticisms publically—especially those originating in Sant Celoni—and he says that he has read neither Zipprick's book nor Santamaria's. He did, however, say to me one afternoon at the Taller, "I'm poisoning my customers? Please. A fuet [a thin, dry Catalan sausage] is a thousand times worse for you than anything I have ever made. If you read reports from the scientific world on emulsifiers and texturizers, you'll see that ninety-nine percent of them say what we all know: that these are legal and controlled ingredients, and very safe for the health." He added, "For years, Santi has been attacking me and using me to attack Spanish avant-garde cuisine. I don't like controversy, but what can I do? Things have changed so much in just a few years. Today, untruths are communicated all around the world in an instant on the Internet. There's nothing I can do about that."

A particularly silly example of these untruths, not involving Santamaria, was the story, reported in May of 2009 on Italy's Pizza and Food Web site, that Ferran had decided to close El Bulli and open a pizzeria in Barcelona instead. Under the headline "The super-chef Ferran Adrià wants to become a pizzaiolo," we read that "the Spanish chef who is the most famous in the world . . . [and] who works in the kitchen with a chemist and a nutritionist . . . [and is] a prophet of nouvelle cuisine . . . came to Italy to learn the secrets of the [pizza] masters." He did this, the article continues, because "despite a million requests for tables, he closed in the red last season. Research in haute cuisine doesn't pay." (And apparently research in article writing doesn't matter.) The *Los Angeles Times* was one of a number of other publications that picked up the story. Though that newspaper's staff has been decimated by layoffs to the point that there's practically tumbleweed blowing down the corridors, they assigned two reporters to do original reporting on the story, and the pair turned out a full-length piece, complete with provocative quotes from Albert ("[W]hat's simpler than a disk on which one lays the ingredients of a pizza?") and outraged reactions from traditional pizzaioli in Italy.

Ferran just shakes his head. He hates this kind of thing, but on some level thinks it's pretty funny. "You know why this happened?" he asks. "Because a reporter found Albert eating pizza one day in Italy and asked if we'd ever considered opening a pizzeria. He said, 'Maybe one day.' He was just trying to be nice." What Ferran wants to know, reasonably enough, is "Why didn't those reporters call here and ask *us* about this?" Maybe because it was one of those stories that's so juicy, some people just want it to be true? The Madrid-based writer Lisa Abend reported that more than two months after the pizza story first appeared in Italy, somebody asked her if she knew when the

Adriás' pizza place was going to open. That somebody was a stagiare at El Bulli.

■ ■ ■

If it's difficult to imagine one prominent chef assailing another so powerfully, and publically, in the United States or Great Britain, it's even harder to imagine the kind of reaction that Santamaria statements stirred up. Immediately after the Temas de Hoy award, Euro-Toques, a pan-European organization of about four thousand chefs in seventeen countries, issued a statement condemning Santamaria's remarks, and accusing him of "creating social alarm of incalculable consequences" by questioning the safety of food additives used by Ferran and other avant-garde chefs. The statement also assured the rest of the food world that there was no "war" between Spanish chefs, only one chef's "disrespectful and uneducated opinions." A partially overlapping group of eight hundred Spanish and international chefs issued a statement of its own—and the Spanish president himself, José Luis Rodríguez Zapatero, came out publically in support of Ferran.

Chefs and other members of the food establishment spoke out individually, too. Santamaria himself quotes some of their remarks in the second edition of his book. Juan Mari Arzak, he notes, recommended that Santamaria learn some humility. (When I asked Arzak about the controversy in late 2009, he told me that he didn't want to be quoted on the matter anymore, except to say, "One mustn't speak about Santi. This will go away if we ignore it.") Arzak's fellow Basque chef Andoni Aduriz, of Mugaritz, described Santamaria to the *International Herald-Tribune* as "the Hugo Chávez of gastronomy . . . He loves to spark controversy with his populist talk." Carme Ruscalleda—one of Catalonia's three-star chefs, along with Ferran, Santamaria, and Joan Roca—declared that "Santamaria's arguments are unfortunate and almost terroristic." (She later told me, "It's his opinion, but the world is full of wrong opinions.") José Carlos Capel of Madrid Fusión dismissed *La cocina al desnudo* as "a settling of accounts" and "a show of pent-up frustration and resentment." A number of commentators mentioned the name Salieri.

The Spanish press, of course, loved the flap, dubbing it "Santamariagate" and "the war of the ovens." *El Periódico* gleefully revealed that one of Santamaria's own recipes, for saffron ice cream, called for glycerol and ProCrema, a commercial preparation of milk proteins and six different emulsifiers and stabilizers—a fact that he admitted but dismissed ("one recipe out of many hundreds . . . "). In the second edition of *La cocina al desnudo*, Santamaria complained that "Juli Soler, Ferran Adrià, and Juan Mari Arzak, instead of seeking to collaborate, have raised walls of non-cheflike containment and veto me repeatedly, with the slogan 'If Santi is coming, I'm not going.' A good mutual friend, who prefers to remain anonymous, told me that after a symposium at the Fair of Barcelona, in which he participated with Ferran, Ferran told him that he would never again appear with me in a public debate." ("I've never banned anyone," notes Ferran. "I've just said that I won't come myself.") Santamaria later assured me that "Ferran is a public institution, and he has organized a lobby with enormous power against what I say." Speaking on Spanish television after Santamaria's Temas de Hoy evening, Ferran, for his part, proposed that "these are the saddest weeks in the history of Spanish cuisine." The journalist Lisa Abend told me that Ferran had recently asked her, "Do chefs get along in America?" She told him that, for the most part, they do—a reply that I imagine must have left Ferran a little wistful.

One expression of the Ferran-Santi situation that has elicited laughter instead of some bleaker emotion is a series of skits called "El Millor Cuiner del Mon"—"The Best Cook in the World"—on "Polònia," a popular comedy show on TV3, the main Catalan-language television station in Barcelona. Not all of the segments—many of which may be easily found on YouTube (and are worth watching at least a few of, even if you don't understand Catalan)—involve Santa-maria. Some depict Ferran, portrayed by an actor with an exaggerated speech impediment and a dramatically receding hairline, creating some outlandish new dish with the aid of brightly colored chemicals out of laboratory retorts or appliances like his "spherificating oven." The best ones, though, involve clashes with his supposed archrival. In one episode, Ferran and Santamaria (or rather the actors playing them) bring out dueling books—Santamaria a copy of his weighty *Entre lli-bres i fogons* (Between Books and Ovens), Ferran his even weightier *Un dia en elBulli* (A Day at elBulli). The two proceed to one-up (if that's the right term) each other, with ever smaller and less significant items—custom-designed plate against custom-designed plate, blue-and-white-checked Can Fabes napkin against El Bulli toothpicks, and so on—until they're interrupted by a shrill impersonator of Carme Ruscalleda. The episode ends with Ferran and Santi, brandishing a huge chef's knife and an oversize rolling pin respectively, rushing off to the next-door studio where Ruscalleda has begun to do a cooking demonstration. Another sketch includes a fantasy flashback to a scene of Ferran and Santamaria in their teenage years working together in a burger joint; when a picky customer discards the bun with her burger, an irritated Ferran picks it up and squishes it into a ball—then looks at the round form he's made and says in delight, "My first spherification!" The parody bothered Ferran at first, he admits, but he realized that he had to either get used to it or be constantly upset, and now he says it doesn't offend him at all. In fact, both he and Santamaria—as well as Ruscalleda—have appeared on the show themselves once or twice.

Indeed, Ferran can betray an unexpected sense of humor about the situation. In 2004, he developed a fast-food chain called Fast Good for the Spanish-owned NH Hotels group, followed by a concept for a combination restaurant, bar, and public space called NHube, serving simple traditional Spanish food (hot and cold *bocadillos*, or sandwiches, fried fish, rabbit stew) and offering Internet access and comfortable furniture for lounging and reading. In late 2009, NH Hotels and another Spanish company, the Hesperia hotel group, merged their operations. Santamaria runs several high-profile restaurants in Hesperia properties, including the two-star Santceloni in Madrid and the one-star Evo, which looks straight down on Ferran's birthplace in Hospitalet de Llobregat. "You see," said Ferran with a grin when he told me about the merger, "Santi and I now have the same boss."

■ ■ ■

I've been dining at El Racó de Can Fabes every year or so since the late eighties, and have always found a richness and authenticity to the invariably well-prepared food that I find wonderfully engaging. I've had some of my best meals in Catalonia at the restaurant. The morning after my most recent excellent dinner there, sitting at the long common breakfast table near the restaurant kitchen, I had a long talk with Santamaria about Ferran and about the issues he raised in his book and with his prize acceptance speech. "Look," he said to begin the conversation, "this is not about a confrontation between tradition and modernity. Absolutely not! I find the application of science to cuisine very interesting. It's a good thing. You can't say science isn't good. But in a society of progress, we are obliged to criticize new techniques. One must speak of these things. We need to know about all the possibilities of making things in an artificial manner in order *not* to make them. The most important thing in Mediterranean cuisine is the quality of the ingredients, and after that the conviviality, the joie de vivre. If the quality of the ingredients is hidden, its relation to the environment is broken. I buy most of my raw materials directly from the source, and this is very important to do. There is catastrophe in Spain today. Five thousand small fish shops have disappeared in this country in the last ten years. We are reducing the number of fresh products available every day. The great chefs *have* to resist. The responsibility of chefs has reached a new level in society. We have the chance to speak in the media. This gives us an enormously important voice. We are the new philosophers. People take chefs seriously as they never have before. If a chef says industrial products are good, people believe him.

"The industrial world has a program for gastronomy. It is industry that approaches the chefs, not the other way around. All technology isn't bad. I work with sous-vide, for instance. For keeping the aroma and juices intact over long cooking periods, it's very useful. But it's an intermediate step for me. Chefs aren't chemists. It's a completely different métier. Patisserie led the way in additives. If you're a chef and you send out a mousse to diners, they will eat it within a few minutes, but pastry chefs must make a mousse that will last all day, because you buy something at their shop and take it home and eat it many hours later. Patisserie needs stabilizers to keep the textures of their creations. But chefs don't. If I can put body into a sauce with a Turmix, then why add lecithin?"

I reached for a saltcellar on the table and asked, "What's the difference between sodium chloride like this and, say, calcium chloride—why is one good and the other bad?" "Salt is a natural product!" Santamaria exclaimed. "Okay," I replied, "but so is agar." "Yes," admitted Santamaria, "but so is petroleum, and we don't want to eat that." (If he realized that this was a pretty spectacular piece of circular reasoning, he didn't show it.)

Santamaria thinks that Ferran has lost his way. "El Bulli in the early days," he said, "was full of extraordinary movement, energy, young people who hadn't gone to culinary school but were passionate about cooking. Things changed after the Olympics in Barcelona. This new food goes well with the new generation. Thanks to democracy, the image of Spain has changed. Why does public money go directly into the pockets of chefs? For the worldwide reputation of Spain." He's absolutely right. Spain's newfound place in the gastronomic firmament has been recognized as a powerful lure for both tourism and business, and has full official support: An arm of the Spanish trade commission publishes what is arguably the world's most beautiful food magazine, *Gourmetour*, devoted entirely to Spanish foodstuffs and cuisine; the Spanish government earmarks as much as nine million euros (over twelve million dollars) annually to promote gastronomic tourism and indigenous food products internationally; and Ferran himself, as noted earlier, has been named international "brand ambassador" for Spain by the Spanish tourist agency. There is a certain irony to this, as Santamaria is quick to point out. "The artistic avant-garde," he noted, "has always been outside the establishment, but avant-garde cuisine in Spain is *part* of the establishment; it has been co-opted by the government, by the media, by industry. This is unique in history, an avant-garde that is part of the establishment."

Sitting there at the breakfast table next to the kitchen at his celebrated restaurant, Santamaria seemed more dispirited than aggressive. "Vanguard cuisine has broken the kitchen's relation with local culture," he said. "At some point, I stop. I say no. What is cuisine? We must ask this question, starting from zero. Many people have lost the idea. I think the message is that one must return to cooking."

In the Kitchen

"[A] great chef glorifies natural elements, uses them in ways that enhance their essence, knows how to extract their aromas and set off their consistencies—but he does so by transposing them into a new register, where they disappear only to be reborn as a whole that owes its existence to intelligence."

—Jean-François Revel, *Culture and Cuisine*

The El Bulli kitchen, September seventeenth, 2008: A dozen young men and women stand silently, hunched over a long aluminum worktable, snapping the caps off minuscule golden enoki mushrooms and separating the clumped strands of their stems into individual pieces. These will be cooked like fideus, the short, thin, golden noodles that are Catalonia's favorite pasta, and combined with codium seaweed, ginger jelly, Ibérico ham fat, and abalone as one of the courses in tonight's tasting menu.

The twelve are part of the crew of twenty-five unpaid stagiares who are lucky enough to win a post here every season—Ferran estimates that between five and six thousand people apply for the honor each year—and without whom the intricate and labor-intensive multi-course El Bulli tasting menus could not conceivably be turned out nightly. *Stagiare* is a French term meaning something between culinary apprentice and galley slave. You have to wonder, in fact, whether the young men and women who are chosen quite realized, when they begged and pleaded and called in favors and crossed their fingers for a place in this kitchen, just what they were getting into. Had they been lured here by fantasies of spinning olive juice and puréed peas into solid matter, learning how to ace the Roner and the Pacojet, standing near the Master while he summoned up some new edible impossibility—ahí!—only to find themselves instead hunched over their workstations for hours on end plucking tiny leaves from basil plants, peeling impossible-to-peel pine nuts, shucking inch-wide clams, or cleaving rabbit skulls in two and scooping out the brains?

On the other hand, there must be something intoxicating about being here under any circumstances, about seeing the ingredients they've taken so much time with being transformed—not just cooked or amalgamated into sauces or arranged prettily on plates but utterly *transubstantiated*—into forms neither nature nor Escoffier ever imagined. And of course there's a practical payoff: A stage at El Bulli is a big gold star on a chef's résumé, a bona fides that can be parlayed into an important job at an important restaurant. Stagiares are ambitious or they wouldn't be at El Bulli—and while they're here, they have the chance to nourish their ambition by nagging the full-timers for recommendations and advice, working the line in more ways than one. They also have the chance to meet journalists and high-profile restaurant-goers from around the world and work elbow-to-elbow with celebrated chefs doing "stages" of their own—like Juan Mari Arzak, who spends a few days in the El Bulli kitchen every year. And there's another potential advantage: "We very seldom hire a person to work here full-time who hasn't been a stagiare," says Ferran.

And so they keep separating those little mushroom stems . . .

Then suddenly, it's six P.M.—time for dinner, the "family meal" offered to everyone who works here, whether in the kitchen, in the dining room, or behind the scenes. Activity stops. The aluminum tables are cleared. Three or four stagiares disappear into the rear portion of the dishwashing room and auxiliary kitchen to the left of the main kitchen entrance and come back bearing stacks of plastic chairs, which they quickly slot into place around the tables. A queue forms, winding back into the side room, and soon everybody is perched around one table or another, digging in. Every available surface in the kitchen is taken. (A few of the chefs and stagiares have taken their plates outside the back entrance to sit on the kitchen step so they can smoke.) The food has nothing whatever to do with the specialties that the kitchen has been preparing for diners; it's based on different raw materials and cooked in a different room, and it is certainly different in form. The menu tonight: potato soup with croutons, tiny meatballs with ceps and chanterelles, botifarra sausage with Chinese cloud ear mushrooms, and chocolate ice cream. Bottles of mineral water. No alcohol. Coffee afterward. It's all very, very good. Ferran walks quickly through the kitchen, but doesn't stop. He sees me sitting with the crew and says, as he heads out the door, "Colman! You're eating at El Bulli tonight!" "I know," I reply. "I'm waiting for the next thirty courses. . . ." Then he's gone.

The meal doesn't seem rushed, but it's hardly leisurely. Everybody eats with a certain concentration (it's the only real meal of the day for the stagiares); some of them talk, but there isn't any horseplay (Ferran would not approve); some of them seem lost in their own world. And then, in not much more than twenty minutes, it's over. Suddenly everybody's up, taking dishes back to the service kitchen, scraping the remains of dinner into trash bins, stacking plates and lining up glasses in dishwashing trays. The chairs go back to their storage space, the aluminum tables are wiped down, whatever everyone was working on reappears. The long table that separates the work area from the front of the kitchen is cleared, gets a nice tablecloth, and is set with silver trays for service. Everybody is more focused. They're concentrating now, working faster and with more purpose.

Ferran almost always eats with everybody else, but tonight he has been dealing with some journalists on the terrace and by the time he's finished and comes back into the kitchen, all traces of the family meal have disappeared. A shadow of disappointment crosses his face. Then he goes back into the auxiliary kitchen and forages up a plate of the meatballs with mushrooms and a big, rough-hewn hunk of bread, which he eats quickly, standing at the service bar just inside the kitchen door, beneath a small portrait of Salvador Dalí. "This is rare," he says. "Sitting down to dinner is sacred to me." (He eats a full El Bulli menu about once a week in the early weeks of each season, he tells me, and then less often. "The concentration you need to eat El Bulli cuisine is very strong," he says. "You can't do it every day.")

Serving serious staff meals is a key part of the El Bulli ethos, Ferran tells me. "I guarantee that we feed our people like no other restaurant does," he says. "How else would we convey to a young chef one of the most important principles of our métier: that he must look out for himself in order to look out for others?" He learned this lesson, he says, from the first chef he ever worked for, Miquel Moy at the Hotel Playafels. It's doubtful, though, that Moy took staff feeding to the El Bulli extreme: After he finishes his own quick dinner, Ferran shows me a notebook that lists the details of every single staff meal that will be served for the remaining weeks of this year and for the entire six-month season in 2009. I note that the following year, then, the kitchen tables will be laden with caesar salad and teriyaki pork loin with polenta on July thirtieth; pasta alla bolognese and slow-roasted suckling pig Yucatan style on August twenty-first; gazpacho and risotto with gorgonzola on September nineteenth . . . The food is all traditional, though obviously not all Spanish. Even guacamole, even Waldorf salad, make their appearances.

One chef in the kitchen—the job rotates—does nothing but shop for and prepare the staff meals, but Ferran himself is always looking over his shoulder. "I concern myself with what the staff eats first of all," he says. "No, *really*. I cook traditional food very well." But, I ask, why is it necessary to plan the meals so far in advance? He looks at me as if I should know the answer by now. "Organization," he says firmly. Juli says the same thing on another evening when I sit next to him at the staff table. "Sometimes we even test alternate recipes," he tells me. "This year we tried four or five different ones for pesto, to be sure we had the right one. We did the same thing with spaghetti alla carbonara. We are very, very well organized." He pauses, then taps his finger to his head and adds with a smile, "To the point of madness."

Besides Ferran and the twenty-five or so stagiares, there are typically fifteen full-time chefs and assistants in the kitchen. The stagiares work one whole season of approximately six months, then go their own way. "It's important to have new blood every year, a transfusion," Ferran believes. The full-timers, on the other hand, tend to stay for years, usually leaving only to move into another part of the El Bulli universe, like Marc Puig-Pey, who is now at the Alícia Foundation, or to go off on their own with Ferran's support, like Albert Raurich with his Asian tapas bars, called Dos Palillos, in Barcelona and Berlin.

There have been stagiares at El Bulli almost since the beginning—Ferran was one himself, on his break from the navy—but the current system has been in place only since the early 2000s. The rules for stagiares today are simple but firm: They must be at least twenty-four years old, have professional cooking experience, and speak at least rudimentary Spanish. In return for their service, they are lodged two or three to a room in one of three large apartments in Roses, and get one staff meal a day. (Today, only Ferran, Juli, and the two top chefs—currently Oriol Castro and Eduard Xatruch—sleep at Cala Montjoi.) "The accommodations are pretty basic," remembers Colin Kirby, a stagiare for the 2008 season (now a chef de partie at Frasca Food & Wine in Boulder, Colorado), "but we were barely there. We were either at work or on our way to or from work or having a beer in the café."

It's up to the stagiares to find their own transportation to the restaurant. Some have cars, and typically wait by the front door of their quarters and offer rides to those who don't; some have motorbikes. Kirby says that if he missed a ride, he'd hitchhike. "I got picked up by everybody from complete strangers to Albert Adrià," he says. "Ferran and Juli understand the chaos involved in getting seventy people to and from the restaurant every day," he continues, "but even so, you hear these rumors that if you're even thirty seconds late, you're fired. I never knew whether that was a myth or not." It's not, says Albert Raurich. "If anybody, not just a stagiare but anyone who works there, is even two minutes late," he says, "they'll get a warning the first time. The second time, they're gone." Some of the younger stagiares probably still go out after work and party, adds Raurich, like Ferran and most of the other chefs did in the old days. "That's fine," he says, "as long as they get back to the restaurant when they're supposed to and are ready to work. But Ferran likes his employees to have a life during the day. He likes them to go to the beach, or play sports, and then get to the restaurant with an active mind, not having just woken up."

Stagiares start at the restaurant about a week before the annual opening each year, and pull twelve- or thirteen-hour shifts for most of the season, arriving at noon every day and working until midnight or one in the morning. When they first arrive, they spend a lot of time doing general housekeeping. "The place has been closed for six months, with all the furniture and equipment in storage," says Kirby, "so you have to put everything back out and clean everything. You even go out and hand-wash and organize the rocks by the entrance." (On the last day of the season, the stagiares clean everything again and put it back in storage.) "When all that has been done," Kirby continues, "*then* we start learning all the basic techniques, spherification, how to make the foams, and so on. They pretty much go over everything and explain it to you."

Ferran has said that it's probably harder to get hired as a stagiare at El Bulli than it is to get a reservation. Candidates who come with a strong recommendation from one of the chefs Ferran knows well and trusts—Arzak, Andoni Aduriz, and José Andrés among them—get preferential treatment. Perseverance also helps. In 1998, before the formal stagiare program had started, a young Englishman named Jason Atherton showed up at El Bulli on a bicycle and begged for a slot in the kitchen. Atherton didn't speak Spanish, so Ferran said no. He pleaded, offering to wash dishes, sweep the floors, anything that would get him into the kitchen. Finally, Ferran relented. (Today Atherton has a Michelin star at his Maze in London.) A young Japanese man, remembered only as Tomo-san, reportedly sent then-head chef Albert Raurich an e-mail begging for a place once a week for three years before being accepted for the 2004 season. In 2009, a young South Korean chef named Myungsun "Luke" Jang pitched a tent by a palm tree ("Because I needed something to protect me from the wind," he told me) on the beach at Roses and started walking up the hill to El Bulli every morning hoping to encounter Ferran and talk his way into a stage. He was eventually successful. Another 2009 stagiare applied for four years in a row before getting in.

All the stagiares, whether they are working chefs or relative beginners in their other lives, are treated as equals—at least to begin with. "Eventually, over time," says Colin Kirby, "you can start to tell the people who are really good, or really have the solid background. Their technique and level of discipline eventually take over—and the best people get the big jobs. The whole time you're at El Bulli, you're aware that you're being watched. They notice everything, and if you're doing well, they'll let you do, say, some spherification. But you also need to do the mushroom stems. Those kinds of jobs are endlessly repetitive, but after a while they become sort of soothing, and you realize that the sooner you accept the beauty of separating mushroom stems, the sooner you can move on to the next task. It's like when Ferran says that there's no difference between a peach and a truffle.

There's no difference between separating mushroom stems and spherifying peas. You have to do them all. You have to be comfortable with either one. When I was there, there were kids who'd say, 'Let me do this or that,' but you had to earn it, and the way you earned it was by doing anything they asked you to do." (Not everybody gets it. Another 2008 stagiare told me that he asked himself more than once, "Why am I standing here fourteen hours a day doing this stuff?" He added, "I respect Ferran, but as food, that stuff is weird." He sounds as if he considers his stage at El Bulli to have been a waste of time, which for him it probably was.)

Every Thursday, "more or less," while he was there, says Kirby, the stagiares were invited to join in a creativity session. "Ferran would come for thirty or forty-five minutes," he continues, "just playing with ideas. He'd give us two ingredients and the next week everyone was allowed to share their ideas with him, no matter how crazy or irrelevant." Sometimes, an idea would make the cut and end up being incorporated or adapted into the menu.

As I write this, the full-time creative team, under Ferran, is headed by Oriol Castro. Castro, a slender young man with close-cropped black hair and a serious mien—he seems to be perpetually in a state of intense concentration, even when he's relaxed and eating lunch—is also the leading light at the Taller in the months when the restaurant is closed. Castro came to work at El Bulli in 1996 as a stagiare, after studying pastry-making in Barcelona and working for Martín Berasategui and several other chefs, joining the staff officially the following year. He and Ferran clicked almost instantly, and he became indispensible. "If Oriol leaves," Ferran told me one day, "El Bulli is finished. For me, he is the fifth most creative chef in the world." (He declines to enumerate the other four.) In the El Bulli kitchen hierarchy, Eduard Xatruch is in charge of production, which means turning out the menus every night. ("Creation and production are two completely different things," Ferran stresses. "Creation is fantastic, but production is hard.") Ferran has called Xatruch "the most Bulli-ized of the kitchen team, because he came to us practically as a boy and has been very little influenced by other restaurants and ways of working." Xatruch, who still has a boyish look about him, is also responsible for buying the raw materials, and Ferran says that he knows and understands intimately the ingredients the kitchen uses, both familiar and exotic. Then he adds, "My principal job here is as an idealogue. My job is to control Oriol and Eduard."

■ ■ ■

The old El Bulli kitchen was small, less than nine hundred square feet in area, and awkwardly laid out. In 1992, when they decided to rebuild and expand it, Ferran and Juli started making excursions to look at kitchens in Barcelona and the Basque country and also in France; the recently enlarged facility at Troisgros in Roanne was one model. Then, working with a young Barcelona architect named Dolors Andreu, they started sketching out plans and making models. The idea was to uproot and level part of the garden on the west side of the building, clearing enough land to be able to roughly quadruple the size of the existing facility. By the time construction began in 1993, Ferran knew exactly what he wanted: a bright, open space with definitively separated "hot" and "cold" sections; a separate area for what was to become known as "the sweet world"; a combination of modern and traditional materials (perforated concrete, slate from nearby Cap de Creus); a mix of halogen, fluorescent, and natural light, the last of these streaming through the floor-to-ceiling window on one side; all shelves and storage areas at a convenient level (no high shelves or low drawers); an ample but not oversize chef's table, where Ferran could serve meals to special guests on occasion but mostly where he could work and from which he could survey the entire kitchen; plenty of smaller refrigeration units and an independent cold room; and Thirode induction cooktops (more than twice as energy-efficient as gas).

A wine serving area and service bar were installed near the entrance, and a long, narrow wooden table was positioned to separate the cooks from the serving staff; trays of food destined for the dining room crowd the space at mealtime. A heroic bull's head sculpture, by Xavier Medina-Campeny, is embedded into the middle of the table—no doubt confusing at least some visitors to the kitchen, who may have only recently learned that *bulli* isn't the Spanish word for bull. The entire project, says Ferran, cost about a million dollars, but was well worth it. "The new kitchen was absolutely essential to our development," he says. "El Bulli couldn't be the restaurant it is today without it."

Giles Coren, restaurant critic for *The Times* in London, described the kitchen as being "reminiscent of the laboratories you see in shampoo adverts." I'm not sure which shampoo adverts he's talking about, but in fact there's nothing laboratory-like about Ferran's kitchen at all. It is certainly contemporary in appearance, but no more so than recently built showplace kitchens in scores of other top contemporary restaurants in Spain, France, Italy, Germany, and beyond. Visitors expecting to see mini–particle colliders and walls full of electronic monitors will be sadly disappointed. The only vaguely unsettling aspect of the kitchen to me is the smell: There is often a sourish, faintly sulfurous aroma in the air (I've never figured out what it is, and the people who work in the kitchen don't notice it), especially before restaurant service begins; at that point, as food is being plated, scents recognizable as cooking food become apparent.

Ferran gives me the run of the place. "Go on," he says. "Go anywhere you want. Ask questions." I do, but I watch my step: Cooks are walking quickly through the kitchen (they're only supposed to move in one direction around the work stations), and the cry of "*Quemo!*"—

literally "I burn," meaning "hot stuff coming through"—echoes frequently. (I notice that the term is used broadly; often what someone is coming through with isn't hot at all.)

One chef is cutting what look like rounds of thick plastic wrap with a cookie cutter on a laminate cafeteria tray, then carefully lifting them off and arranging them neatly on sheets of wax paper, which is in turn laid onto the stacking rounds of a large dehydrator. The rounds turn out to be parmigiano gel: Once they're dried, they'll become pasta wrappers for baby clams; the finished dish will look like Chinese dumplings.

There are three tall red roses in separate bud vases on the service counter, and I notice Ferran walking over and plucking a petal off one of them. I wonder for a moment if he's so obsessive in his "organization" that he's grooming the flowers before they go into the dining room—but no, he takes it over to one of the chefs and shows it to him. The chef is working on beet crisps in the form of rose petals, and Ferran is reminding him of the contours of the original.

Xatruch, meanwhile, is working on a concept that won't make its official debut until the following year: Using a large plastic syringe, he injects a mixture of coconut milk and xanthan into a balloon—an ordinary toy-shop one; a little plastic bag full of them rests nearby on the counter. Then he blows it up and rotates it in what looks like a truncated ice bucket filled with liquid nitrogen, billowing smoke at 321 degrees Fahrenheit. His hand dips into the smoke. "It's not cold if you're not stupid about it," he says, "but if you're wearing a ring, it will absorb the cold and you might lose a finger." When he carefully strips the balloon away, the coconut milk has formed into a round ball, thinner than an eggshell. (Later, he will try the same technique with melted and diluted gorgonzola and with a pine-nut infusion.) Ferran walks by and stops to watch. He nods approvingly at the sheer white perfection of the coconut-milk globe. Then he points to the plastic syringe and says, "Scientific, yes? High-tech?" He turns to the chef's table and tears a piece of paper out of one of his notebooks, curls it into a cone, and inserts it into the end of another balloon. "This would work, too," he says with a smirk. "Very scientific . . ." (The balloon idea, it turns out, was suggested by a stagiare, Lee Wolan, at one of the creative sessions. It was a technique used by Homaro Cantu at Moto in Chicago, where Wolan had once worked.)

A few minutes later, I see Ferran swigging from a tiny bottle of Underberg bitters. "I'm not drinking this because my food has made me sick!" he jokes. I walk over to one of the induction cooktops, where something very traditional looking, and very fragrant in an old-fashioned, heart-stirring way, is bubbling away in two immense cauldrons. Ferran comes over and explains: It's a traditional French *civet de lièvre*, a rich blood-thickened stew of hare, he tells me—but, he adds, the solids will be discarded and the liquid reduced down to a couple of quarts of strong essence. (I think of the story of the Chinese chef who was berated by his master for having invoiced him for seven hams but served only one. "The other six," the chef replied, "were for the sauce.") Ferran likes stocks with plenty of flavor. "I make chicken stock with whole farm chickens," he says, "and veal stock from meat, not just bones." He never makes courtbouillon or fond de poisson, he adds, because he doesn't care for their fishy flavor.

On one worktable, I see bowls of something dark and sinuous, a tangle of mysterious curls. "Seaweed from Galicia," says Ferran. "We use five kinds. If I could find it out there"—he gestures toward the window and the beach below—"I would, but this doesn't exist here. I will use products from here or as near as possible if I can. Otherwise I will get them from wherever they're best."

We move to another part of the kitchen. Ferran reaches into a round plastic container, some Spanish Tupperware clone lined with paper towels, and pulls out perfect disks, dark red and slightly scalloped. "'Pringles' of tomato," he says proudly, giving me one to taste. It is exactly the texture of Pringles, crisp but immediately softening in the mouth, and it has a tomato flavor as intense as that of a ripe beef-steak on a summer afternoon.

"Come over here," he says next, leading back to one of the cook-tops. "Oriol is going to show you something." There are two small pots of water simmering on the stove. Castro whisks cornstarch into one, pouring it in a small, steady stream, tablespoons of it, until the water gradually thickens to a syrupy consistency. Then he adds less than a teaspoon of another substance to the other pot, and with a flick of the wrist it thickens to the same point. "This is xanthan," says Ferran. "It takes a tiny fraction of the amount of cornstarch or flour you'd need, and it will even thicken cold liquids. It's a wonderful thing. Why shouldn't we use it? Is it a 'chemical'? Yes, like cornstarch." (In fact, xanthan, often called xanthan gum, is a polysaccharide produced by fermenting sugars with a plant bacterium called *Xanthomonas camp-estris*. Cornstarch, literally the starch from corn, is extracted through a process that involves slight fermentation, soaking, separation from other substances by centrifuge or hydrocyclone, and drying. Which of the two substances is more "natural" could certainly be argued.) It dawns on me that, unlike the civet or the Pringles, the little pots of thickened water have no application to any dish. Ferran has arranged a demonstration for me, just to make a point.

We sit back down at the chef's table, and Ferran returns to an ear-lier theme: "Do you see the 'science' here? Do you see the 'molecular gastronomy'? We are *cooking*." He opens one of his omnipresent note-books, pulls out a pen, and—with unexpected vehemence—starts sketching out a chart to *prove*, he says, that he has never used the term "molecular gastronomy" and that it has nothing whatever to do with him. I tell him that he's preaching to the choir—not adding that that's just as well because I can't begin to make sense of his chart.

"Food," he offers, changing the subject, "may be *productist*, like a *suquet* [a traditional Catalan fish and potato stew], where the raw materials appear in an obvious and recognizable form, or *elaborationist*, like cannelloni Rossini, where the appearance of the raw materials has been transformed. Here I would say we're about thirty percent the former and seventy percent the latter."

"What do you do during the day, before you come to the restaurant?" I ask him. He looks surprised at the question. "*Creativity*," he says, miming a look of concentration, staring straight down at the table, his hands held up like horses' blinders at the sides of his face, then moving in tight circles, like wheels turning. "I'm *thinking*, from the morning until the service begins. I start upstairs at nine A.M. and come downstairs at eleven. I stay until one A.M. And when I'm not here, I'm across the road in the house, all alone, thinking. Creativity is at the center of everything else. If we didn't have it, we'd close tomorrow. The challenge of creativity is what makes El Bulli continue." At the same time, he adds, it's a mistake to think that all he does is the creative part. "I'm involved in the consulting and the advisory functions," he says, "and probably because of my past as a student of economics I'm involved in doing budgets and budgetary control, and with Juli I deal with banks, accounting, the wine inventory, and so on."

He abruptly gets up, leaving me behind, and prowls around the kitchen, stopping to taste, to talk. He's a relatively quiet chef, not a shouter (at least I've never heard him raise his voice above a level of forceful urgency in the kitchen). He paces a little. He steps over to the service bar and leafs distractedly through the reservation book. He seems almost at sixes and sevens. He seems almost bored. Then he comes back to the table, sits back down, and says, "I'm thinking about next year." "That's good," I reply. He shrugs. Then he points to the middle of the kitchen. "It's like a ballet," he says. "Now, at the end of the season, it was a well-oiled machine. When we open, it's a challenge. You can't imagine how different it is now from when we first open."

In the Kitchen

■ ■ ■

The El Bulli kitchen, June sixteenth, 2009. Opening night. Even in its earliest days, El Bulli closed every winter—originally from mid-January to mid-March. This was purely a practical matter: The road to Cala Montjoi was frequently impassable during that period, and nobody would have come anyway. In 1987, again for practical reasons, the decision was made to extend the closing period to five months; this was lengthened to six months in 1999, with the restaurant opening April through October. This year, Ferran has decided to do things differently: In order to be able to work in the restaurant, for the first time in decades, with game birds, wild mushrooms, and other foods of late autumn and early winter, he has decided to push the season back so that it will run from June to December—and tonight the El Bulli year begins.

Ferran is right, of course: The kitchen feels noticeably different than it did the last time I was here, in the final weeks of the 2008 season. The stagiares are arrayed as usual at their workstations—the ones gathered around the long table are peeling battalions of fat white asparagus—but they're aligned a bit raggedly, and their motions lack fluidity, coordination. They're still a bunch of individuals, not yet a team; when they move around the kitchen—"*Quemo! Quemo!*"—it's obvious that they don't quite have the ant patterns figured out yet. The regular chefs, meanwhile, are supervising everything especially closely, instructing, correcting, sometimes approving and sometimes not. Meanwhile, a small film crew—a cameraman, a director, a couple of assistants—have set up on one side of the room and make sorties into the thick of things. They're filming the final part of what is to be a ten-part DVD record of the history, development, and daily workings of the restaurant; this portion is a video interpretation of the massive book *A Day at elBulli.*

Ferran is so often surrounded by photographers and videographers

261

these days that he hardly pays attention to the crew. He just lets them do what they're doing. He sits at the chef's table, meanwhile, notebook open, tense, surveying the kitchen, head turning back and forth, as if he's searching for something, looking as if he's about to jump up at any moment. ("To follow the gaze of Ferran requires the training of a triathelete," wrote Daniel Vázquez Sallés in *El Mundo*.) Then he does jump up, goes over to where Castro is working, peers at something closely, says something sotto voce, then comes back and sits back down. He's wearing scuffed athletic shoes, frayed black jeans, and a white chef's coat bearing the two-red-chopsticks logo of Albert Raurich's Barcelona restaurant, Dos Palillos. There's a pencil with a little green rubber apple on the end stuck behind his ear; from certain angles, it looks disconcertingly like some kind of growth protruding from his head.

I sit down next to him and ask how many new dishes are on the menu tonight. He shakes his head and wags his finger. "No, no, none," he replies. "Every year it's the last year's menu when we start. After the first few weeks we begin replacing them one by one. It would be too much otherwise. Remember, more than half the staff, the stagiares, are new every year. They still have to learn the rules, the techniques, the philosophy." Castro and his team are working on the new dishes on one side of the kitchen anyway, even though they won't be served yet, bringing them or parts of them over to Ferran every few minutes for him to taste. "Things that we develop at the Taller are refined here," says Ferran. "Now is the moment when we see whether our ideas are magic or not."

"There are two Ferran Adriàs," he says between tastings. "One during the months when we are open, one when we are closed." I suggest that there are three, that in the open months he is very different at the beginning and the end of the season. "Yes, yes," he admits. "I am a cook the first month, always here. I'm in a trance now. For now, it's cuisine, cuisine, cuisine. For three months every season we work at an intense level, then for two months it's normal. The last month every year is very tranquil." He falls silent and scribbles a few sentences in his notebook.

I can see something that looks interesting going on over in the "sweet world," so I go to take a closer look. Standing just across their worktable, I watch as two stagiares, working under small heat lamps with a concentration that suggests that of watchmakers or one of those pretty-boy technicians on *CSI*, somehow spin sugar into fine thread coiled around a white cylinder stuck on the end of an electric screwdriver—the result being a series of light, translucent helixes, Slinky-like, so delicate that they look as if they'd collapse if you breathed on them. These are the virgin olive oil caramel springs, made with olive oil and isomalt (a disaccharide sugar substitute); each one will be presented at the table inside a shiny black box, like a piece of jewelry (servers suggest that diners put the springs on their fingers like a ring and nibble them off). Each spring takes two people three or four minutes to finish, and I realize that they'll probably be consumed in a few seconds.

A friend of Ferran's and some of the other chefs, Manel Vehí from the Bar Boia in Cadaqués—once Dalí's favorite hometown hangout—arrives with a gift for dessert for the family meal: two big bags of *taps de Cadaqués*, "Cadaqués corks," chewy, sugar-glazed little babas, traditionally soaked in rum but also delicious on their own. Ferran gets up and shakes Vehí's hand and clasps his shoulder, then goes back to the table while one of the stagiares takes the taps into the back kitchen. Castro comes over with a small bowl of little spheres that look like those faux ice cream confections called Dippin' Dots but shake like very soft marshmallows. "Hazelnuts," says Ferran, in a tone of voice that reminds me that they aren't really. He pops one into his mouth, then shakes his head no. Castro goes back to try again. "Our system is very, very complex," he tells me. "This model is very, very, very difficult to reproduce. It's unique. It's a model *asesino* [assassin] when other chefs try it and it doesn't work."

From the table, I can see Xatruch showing a scrum of stagiares how to plate some of the preliminary dishes. This year, there are stagiares from five national hotel and restaurant schools around Spain, in Barcelona, Lleida, Girona, Valencia, and Cambrils, and two imported culinary students, one each from Mexico and Argentina. There are a few who have been recommended by Arzak and Aduriz, too. There are a few Americans—and a Korean, the one who camped outside to win a spot. A testament to the international nature of the team may be found in a clump of cactus outside the restaurant, overlooking the cove: Departing stagiares at the end of each season traditionally carve their names and dates of service into the ancient cactus paddles, and easily a score of nationalities seem to be represented.

"The four women we have this year are the best of the stagiares," Ferran tells me in 2009. Albert Raurich later adds that that's usually the case. "I think it's because they have to work twice as hard in the first place to get this far," he says, "so when they do, they are much better able to handle the pressure than most of the men."

Now Ferran gets up yet again. He disappears for a minute, then walks back through the kitchen eating a peach—not a spherified one, but the genuine article, big, sulfur-yellow, ripe; a ribbon of juice drips down his chin.

Juli darts into the kitchen and gestures with his head toward the clock on the wall. It's seven thirty, when the first customers are due. It is unheard-of in Spain for a restaurant, at least outside of the tourist traps and big hotels, to open for dinner before eight thirty or nine, but then, of course, El Bulli isn't like other restaurants, and since a meal here might last four hours or more, this doesn't really seem too early to begin. Ferran stands up, walks to the near side of the long service table, claps his hands, and says, "*¡Silencio! ¿Okay?*" There had been very little chatter to begin with, but now there's none.

The first three waves of diners arrive for their visit to the kitchen. All are Americans—women in pricey sundresses, men in golf slacks, a blond in a peasant top and capris, junior sporting shades and sandals. One asks for an autograph. Cameras flash. Between visitors, Ferran is up and in charge, standing at the end of the service table checking order slips, scrutinizing the customized menus he has earlier sketched out for each table, watching everything, occasionally barking out a warning or a command. Xatruch, meanwhile, is very carefully watching as the first small delights are carefully laid on their serving dishes ("plating" seems too generic and inexact a term). Black-suited servers stand in a line alongside the service bar, waiting to convey the first amazements and delights into the dining room. Xatruch nods to the first two, and they silently pick up trays and head out of the kitchen. The show begins.

Morphing

"Never leave well enough alone."

—Raymond Loewy, used as the title of his autobiography

Do you ever think about closing El Bulli?" I ask Ferran one afternoon in mid-2009, as we sit outside in the small garden behind the Taller. "Every day," he replies almost before I've finished posing the question. Then he smiles and says, "That's a metaphor." I'm not sure "metaphor" is exactly the right word, but I get the idea.

As early as 2004, Ferran had told an interviewer that he was considering taking a one-year sabbatical. In 2006, a story in *Nation's Restaurant News* stated unequivocally, "This past season [i.e., 2005] was Adrià's last in the kitchen—at least until 2008, when he will decide what to do next." In 2007, Ferran announced that "at the end of 2008, I am leaving my diary empty." ("There was a moment in my life in 2003 or 2004," he later told me, "when I asked myself how much money I really needed to live, and I thought when I got that amount I would close the business, maybe in 2008.") Albert, of course, actually did retire from the organization. "I'm finished with El Bulli now, definitely," he insisted, after he'd signed out of the Taller in 2008. "I don't even know what they're doing this year." Ferran, though, kept coming back, to both the Taller and El Bulli, remaining as involved as ever. He was working hard, but he was having too much fun to stop. "The years from 2003 to 2009," he told me in 2010, "were just *fantastic!*"

But he had also told me, in 2009, that he was taking things year by year. "I want to continue as long as I have the dream and the passion," he said, "but I want to reinvent myself. The one hundred sixty or so days that we keep the restaurant open are very hard. There are those who think we're privileged because we open for only six months a year, but when you make creative cuisine, the pressure is very strong. If we didn't do it this way, I could sit on the beach in peace all day and just go to the restaurant every afternoon at six, no problem." At the time, he dropped some tantalizing hints as to what the future might hold. "The structure of the restaurant continues to change," he said. "It's possible that next year we will be open only three months, but seven days a week. Or maybe we need ten months of creativity and just two months of restaurant. For me it would be the same. We could also have just one, two, three tables only, and take no reservations at all. We would select the people who would come, gastronomes who appreciate our cooking. It would be only a way to show how we are evolving. This is all just something I'm thinking about. In any case, El Bulli exactly as it is today will not continue for more than two or three more years. We have to always raise the level. There are fifty possibilities."

He also said, "Maybe I'll take a sabbatical not just from El Bulli but from everything. El Bulli and I will both be fifty, more or less, in 2012. It opened as a mini-golf in 1961, but the *chiringuito* was built and they started serving food in 1962, the year I was born. That would be a good date for me to close the restaurant, but not permanently. I'd like to be able to travel, not for work, maybe to spend six months in

Japan and six months in China with my wife. Of course, that's just what I think today. And then sometimes I think 2012 will be the end, period. Look, Juli's sixty. He will want to retire at some point. El Bulli can't exist without Ferran and Juli. *Me* without Juli is difficult to contemplate. And my moral contracts—I call them that because they're not written down—with Oriol and the other top chefs run until 2012. It's possible, then, that 2012, when I'm fifty, will be the end."

That Ferran would seriously consider shutting down his legendary establishment didn't entirely surprise me. Sure, everything was up to date in Cala Montjoi, but had they gone about as far as they can go? Ferran proved that there was more to be discovered in the world of food, that there were techniques that no chef had yet employed, flavors and textures that no chef had yet offered diners. But there *is* a finite number of foodstuffs in the world, and maybe there's also a finite number of ways a kitchen can manipulate and present them. Ferran himself had admitted frequently that his creative pace was lagging. "Every time, it takes more to innovate," he remarked to me one day. "Today to create new things takes four times as long as it did ten years ago." Maybe the rise of El Bulli, I thought, would turn out to have been like the uncovering of some vast new oil reserves; they'd keep our internal combustion engines going for a few more decades, but ultimately, they were a nonrenewable resource.

■ ■ ■

Ferran's obsession with documenting the history and accomplishments of El Bulli and his creative team found a new expression in 2008 with the publication of a massive tome, rivaling one of the General Catalogue volumes in size, called *A Day at elBulli: An Insight into the Ideas, Methods and Creativity of Ferran Adrià*. Available not just in English but in French, Italian, German, Dutch, and Japanese translations, this was a completely redesigned and expanded hardcover edition of a large-format 2007 paperback called *Un dia en elBulli,* available only in Spanish and Catalan. *A Day at elBulli* is a treasure trove of information, recipes, and above all photographs, covering virtually every aspect of the restaurant; if you've ever wanted to know what a page of the reservation book looks like, or how the parking lot gate is opened, this volume won't disappoint you.

An even more exhaustive visual record of El Bulli, announced by Ferran at Madrid Fusión in January of 2009, was an on-screen parallel to the General Catalogue—a ten-part film, running more than eight hours in all. "History is what really helps us to be objective," he explained to the audience. "We have no real history of cuisine. We work on what we think we know. We need some sort of archive for creative cuisine, and this will be a beginning." He then screened a four-minute trailer for the film. We probably shouldn't make too much of the fact, I thought at the time, that the soundtrack was David Bowie's "Space Odyssey," which, as you may recall, is about a disaffected astronaut who cuts his lifeline and drifts off into space.

A short (two-hour) version of the film was shown over two consecutive evenings on TVE, the state-owned Spanish public television channel, in early 2009, and got very good ratings. The long version, called *elBulli, historia de un sueño* [Story of a Dream]: *Catálogo audiovisual 1963–2009,* came out in DVD form late in the year. The first nine segments were directed by a young Catalan filmmaker, born in Andorra and raised in Barcelona, named David Pujol, previously best-known for a well-received documentary called *Cadaqués: The Exception,* about the art community in that little village just around the cape from Cala Montjoi. The tenth segment, a visual version of *A Day at elBulli,* was directed by Albert Adrià, with great energy and style. (When I saw it, I suggested to him that maybe he had a future in cinema. "Yes," he replied with a grin, "maybe I'll be the first filmmaker-chef!") Pujol told me, "Ferran thinks, 'If I decide to quit, now people will have, between the General Catalogue and this film, an understanding of what we did here.'"

At Madrid Fusión, Ferran also mused about the international economic crisis. "The downturn," he said, "will accomplish this: People will now know that an avant-garde creative restaurant can't be set up as a financially viable business. We need to understand what avant-garde cuisine represents. It accounts for less than one tenth of one percent of what people eat. Of course, avant-garde cuisine will continue to be featured in the media, which means that people will be interested in it, but in the same way that they are interested in Formula One racing or haute couture, from a distance. . . ."

In January of 2010, again at Madrid Fusión, Ferran made another announcement—or rather, as more than one story reporting the event put it, "dropped a bombshell": He announced that at the end of the 2011 season, he and Juli would close El Bulli for two years, reopening the place in a different form entirely in 2014. The press release that accompanied Ferran's announcement called the hiatus "the closure of one cycle and the beginning of a new phase, in which a radical approach to the creative process and the pursuit of new challenges and stimulus will be the main priority." The years 2012 and 2013, the document continued, "will be devoted to thinking, planning and preparing the new format for subsequent years."

His decision was not so much a break with the past, Ferran told reporters, as it was a logical extension of the restaurant's evolution—the sixth in a progression of fundamental changes to the place over the years, the others (not exactly on the "bombshell" level) having been the inauguration of a half-year season in 1987, the design and construction of the new kitchen in 1993, the creation of the Taller in 1998, the abolition of lunch service in 2001, and the disappearance of the à la carte menu in 2002.

The original announcement seemed to promise that El Bulli would reopen, presumably as a restaurant of some kind. A few weeks after Madrid Fusión, though, on February twelfth, just when the international hubbub about the hiatus was beginning to die down, Ferran made a new announcement: According to the next day's *New York*

Times, "On Friday, Mr. Adrià said he had decided that the restaurant would close for good in December 2011. He says he made the decision because he and his partner, Juli Soler, had been losing a half-million euros a year on the restaurant and his cooking workshop in Barcelona. 'At the level of contribution,' Mr. Adrià said, 'I think we would rather see the money go to something larger that expands the concept and spirit of what El Bulli represents.'" That, said the *Times,* would be not a restaurant at all but an academy for advanced culinary study, organized as a foundation. I e-mailed Ferran immediately to ask if this was true. "The article was not well reported," he replied almost instantly. "Come to Barcelona and I'll explain everything calmly and in detail." I was on a plane the following week.

■ ■ ■

Ferran is taking off his shirt as I arrive at the Taller on a Saturday morning in mid-February. There is photographic equipment set up near the glass doors giving onto the terrace—I don't think I've ever been at the Taller or in the kitchen at the restaurant when there hasn't been a photographer or a videographer at work—and an assistant pulls a stool up for Ferran to perch on. Pedro Madueño, the graphics editor of *La Vanguardia* and a noted photographer himself, is making a portrait of Ferran with an old photographic technique called ambrotype. It takes about three minutes for one exposure. (Ferran isn't shy; a feature about him in the same weekend's *Vanguardia* Sunday magazine includes photos of him standing shirtless and squatting in exercise clothes; the cover is a head shot of him under the shower.) The assistant takes the plate off to the bathroom to develop it, and shortly reappears with the finished work. It is an unsettling image, in chiaroscuro sepia: Ferran's torso is vignetted, and his eyes are in shadow; his face seems preternaturally elongated and his expression is grim; the ambrotype could be a still from some silent movie about werewolves or a malevolent hypnotist.

Ferran in real life, on the other hand, is amiable and bright today. He pulls on his shirt and with a trace of a smile says, "Let's go over to Carmen." We walk downstairs, along the tail end of the Carrer de la Portaferrissa, across the Ramblas, down the Carrer del Carme, and up one flight to the El Bulli business headquarters. We sit down at a big worktable near the back of the office, near the window overlooking the side of the Boqueria and the outdoor area where small farmers sell their produce. I take out my notebook. "Okay," Ferran begins. "El Bulli is finished." There is an instant of what feels like momentous silence in the room.

Then he continues. "I mean El Bulli as a gastronomic, avant-garde restaurant on the current model. But what it will evolve into is something nice. Our decision is logical, and very, very pretty. It is a radicalization of the model of El Bulli. We are very happy." That radicalization, as he told a jam-packed session at Madrid Fusión, will come in the form of a non-profit foundation. "When I made my announcement," he says, "it was 'tragedy' in Spain. Immediately everyone was saying, 'It's the end of an era!' 'The vanguard is finished!' Even people who have always said they don't like El Bulli were . . ."—he mimes rubbing tears from his eyes—"and saying, 'Please don't leave.'" The prominent Spanish novelist Juan José Millás opined that "closing El Bulli is like putting a sign in front of [the Velázquez masterpiece] *Las Meninas* in the Prado saying 'Closed for Reflection.'"

There are those who think that Ferran handled the announcement badly—that he should have just told everybody that he was closing the restaurant for a sabbatical and then thought the whole thing through, keeping quiet about his future plans. "Instead," says one observer close to Ferran who prefers not to be named, "he went around Spain like a retiring bullfighter, receiving kudos from one and all, which took on the trappings of vacating the throne." The American writer Gerry Dawes, who has followed Ferran for at least fifteen years, evokes the Spanish saying *"Rey muerto, rey puesto"*—"When the king dies, another is put in his place." "I think that personally and professionally," he says, "Ferran may have reached his apogee and by abdicating the way he did, he opened up the seat for the next king of Spanish cuisine." (For the record, Dawes thinks that title should go not to any of the obvious candidates now working in Spain—they don't have enough of a worldview, he says—but, based on what he is doing at his Bazaar in Los Angeles, to José Andrés.) Ferran, as usual, seems immune to criticism. All his professional colleagues, he told me, support his decision and the way he revealed it. "They all told me," he says, "whatever you do will be the right thing."

The big news so far—which Ferran has not officially announced as I write this—is that the restaurant, which will have reopened for 2010 on June fifteenth, will not close in December of the year as originally planned, but will stay open for one long final season, straight through (except for a two-week break somewhere along the line) until July thirty-first of 2011. That will be the last night of El Bulli as purely a restaurant. "I know for certain that I will never have another restaurant after that," he says. "I mean a gastronomic restaurant, haute cuisine, vanguardia. For me that business is finished. From now on, there is only the foundation for me."

What will Ferran do for two years? The popular impression has always been that for the six months a year when the place was not open, Ferran could be found almost daily at the Taller, whipping up new wonderments for the coming season. In fact, at least since he became an international celebrity, circa 2003, Ferran has filled his off-months with almost incessant travel, promoting his books and other products, taking part in conferences, giving talks and demonstrations. Between the seasonal closing of the restaurant in October of 2008 and its reopening in June of 2009, for instance, he made journeys to Australia, South Africa, Brazil, the U.S. (several times, and both coasts), Madagascar (for Christmas), the Dominican Republic, Tokyo, Seoul, and assorted cities all over Europe—plus probably a few other places. And both at home and away, he talks almost constantly to reporters and food writers. He once computed that in 2005, a particularly busy year, he gave more than a thousand interviews, including as many as thirty-five a day at Slow Food's Salone del Gusto in Turin. "A quarter of my time today goes to the press," he complained to me one day, "and it's too much. I can devote one month a year to interviews, but not the whole year." Everybody wants a piece of Ferran, and he seems to want to try to satisfy them all. He once told a French trade magazine that he works 17 hours a day, 345 days a year.

Now he promises that his pace will slow down. "I need two years to think," he says. "Maybe right after the last season ends, I'll take a long trip with Isabel, going places I haven't been. Then, in 2012, I will do nothing. No interviews, no conferences. For me it will be a year off. A year for nettoyage [cleansing]." He waves his hand past his temple, as if brushing away cobwebs.

And in 2014? The foundation Ferran envisions, he stresses, will not be a school in any conventional sense. There will be no cooking classes. According to an official statement appearing on the El Bulli Web site, the foundation will be "open to . . . all avant-garde gastronomy lovers: chefs, sommeliers, front of the house professionals, gourmets, creative thinkers or solely enthusiasts of our dream . . ." It will be, says Ferran, "a new paradigm." He calls it a "think tank," using the English phrase. "Until now," he says, "El Bulli has been an experience. After 2014, it will be an exploration and a revelation."

The idea is to grant scholarships annually for a one-year course of study to about twenty-five applicants, to be divided into five or six groups of four or five people each, with each group headed by a member of Ferran's creative team—which might include Ferran himself, Juli, Albert, Oriol Castro, Eduard Xatruch, Mateu Castañas, and/or Marc Cuspinera, among other El Bulli stalwarts. "We will deal not only with vanguard cuisine," he stresses. "It will be a complete gastronomic formation. If one fantastic chef comes out of the foundation each year, that will be enough for me." He also envisions inviting members of the press to come for one week each year—"But," he says, "they will have to spend one day of the week in the kitchen." The possibilities, he adds, are infinite.

The foundation, Ferran continues, will be "a place dedicated to creativity first of all. We will work with art, design, culinary history, and other disciplines, with the lessons later applied to cuisine. We'll be allied very closely with Alícia. It will be a little like Stone Barns and Copia." (He's talking about the Stone Barns Center for Food & Agriculture, a non-profit farm, educational center, and restaurant on an old Rockefeller estate in New York's Westchester County, and about the Copia food and wine "discovery center" in the Napa Valley, promoted by the late Robert Mondavi—which Ferran may not realize is now bankrupt and shuttered.) "We will maintain a strong connection to gastronomy, but also to agricultural production, health, and socioeconomic position of cuisine," he says. "The name of the foundation may change, but for now, I think we are going to call it, in English, 'El Bulli Food for Thought / Thought for Food.'" This echoes the title of the book edited by Vicente Todolí and Richard Hamilton to commemorate Ferran's participation in Documenta 12. Though there have been reports of corporate interest in the project, Ferran thinks that it can be self-sustaining, with additional income drawn from the various El Bulli consulting projects. "Now we spend three hundred thousand euros on the restaurant every year and two hundred thousand on the Taller," he says. "We will spend the same amount on the foundation, so it should be possible to do this with no outside sponsorship."

Ferran wants to take a break from our conversation at Carmen. He gets up from the table and motions for me to follow him. He goes into the office next door to where we've been sitting and he picks up an inch-and-a-half-thick folder of e-mails that have been printed out for him to read, and translated if they're in languages other than Spanish or Catalan. "Is that one day's worth?" I ask. "No," he replies, "that's just from this morning." (It is about noon.) The e-mails are a combination of invitations, most of which he turns down for purely practical reasons (he simply doesn't have the time), communications from fellow chefs wanting to place stagiares at El Bulli, and expressions of sadness at the forthcoming changes ("PLEASE don't do this!" reads one, from a fan in Tokyo). He also receives, he says, questions about creativity from the heads of big companies and government ministries. "If the e-mails and letters we get aren't idiotic," he says, "we answer all of them." He pulls three or four out of the folder and sets them aside. "I keep some every day to think about," he says.

Back at our table, Ferran hands me a photocopy of one of his freehand sketches, a rough diagram of the El Bulli property as he currently envisions it, drawn on a page with a few lines of type from one of his e-mail printouts. The sketch shows the front dining room and the kitchen left intact; a note in the former says "8–9 *mesas* [tables]," and breaks down the seating into tables for two, four, and six—holding thirty diners in all. The second dining room is a "possible museum"—though Ferran says that he hates that word. A wing off the kitchen is divided into a library and an audiovisual center. The famous terrace will probably be covered over, with a second story added to hold a shop; "Maybe there'll be a gallery, as in Marrakesh," says Ferran. The parking lot will be moved, and in its place will rise a new building, to function as the main study center, with a "possible bungalow" with accommodations for two attached. "Of course," says Ferran, "all this is in my head. It could change." He scrawls his signature at the bottom of the photocopy and hands it to me. "Remember when I signed the place mat for you at Inopia?" he asks. (I'm astonished that he himself remembers, but I probably shouldn't be.)

Of course, the goings-on at the foundation will be extensively documented. As an explanation of the foundation on the El Bulli Web site puts it, "Each year's progress will be divulged via books in traditional and/or electronic format, audiovisual productions, internet and whatever other technological medium that we believe suitable for their disclosure. Also, in congresses and gastronomy schools." And there will be, Ferran tells me, a long-term undertaking to produce a forty-volume history of contemporary cuisine, "a work that will take fifteen years." Another foundation project, which he will work on himself, is a book about "all the products used in haute cuisine, from Escoffier to today." This is apart from a collaboration now in the works between Ferran and the art photographer Hannah Collins, a book and traveling exhibition to be called *Every Ingredient Is Its Own Universe*. This is a photographic record of the origins of every ingredient in a thirty-five-course El Bulli meal, shot all over the world, from Japan to Ecuador.

Ferran has always encouraged his top people to develop side businesses of their own. Albert Raurich, who ran the El Bulli kitchen for six years alongside Oriol Castro, has opened Dos Palillos, an Asian tapas bar in Barcelona with a new offshoot in Berlin; Castro himself, meanwhile, along with Eduard Xatruch and Mateu Casañas—the core of the El Bulli kitchen team—are working with Marc Calabuig at International Cooking Concepts to discover and market a new line of gourmet food products from around the world. The new configuration of El Bulli will give everyone more time to pursue their own projects, says Ferran. "Oriol is one of the best chefs in the world," says Ferran, "and he and the rest of the creative team deserve something better, more time for themselves."

Of course, Ferran, *nettoyage* quite aside, continues to have projects, too. At one point, he told me, he was considering doing something in Qatar—"Not an El Bulli, but an educational project, a university of gastronomy." (Discussions with his putative patrons there stalled.) And in June 2010, he announced that he and Albert were going to open what he described to me as "a place which we want to become a cultural world around the theme of tapas"—in other words, a sort of super–tapas bar—in Barcelona, in collaboration with the owners of a highly respected local seafood restaurant called Rías de Galicia. "The idea," Ferran told me, "is that Albert and I will open ten sites worldwide with support from the Spanish government and local operators. These will be cultural embassies based on tapas." He will, in other words, be getting a head start on his dream of one day seeing ten thousand tapas bars around the globe. ("Don't forget," Ferran couldn't resist adding when he told me about his plans, "that in 1991 we incorporated the world of tapas into El Bulli—something that, like many things that have happened there, was never given the importance it actually had.")

Albert, meanwhile, is full of other ideas, too. He might do something with Oriol Castro, as yet unspecified, he says. He also has an idea for a shop combining fruit and chocolate. "I imagine a place where you take a perfect raspberry and watch the chocolate go on," he says. In 2003, Albert and Ferran had told me about a notion they'd had of launching a series of very simple restaurants based on *guisats*—stews—with everything cooked in a pot. That's still a possibility, says Albert. "There would be six big casseroles, each with a different guisat," he explains. "Things like squid with peas, roast chicken with *samfaina* [the Catalan equivalent of ratatouille]. . . . The problem is that if you make things of quality, using the best ingredients, the stews will cost too much. This is a problem we have to work out."

He has an idea for a book, too, he says—"a manual for young cooks at home, very realistic, with basic recipes, things you can make in twenty to forty minutes, with weights and measurements given. There will be photographs of everything, photographs made in my home kitchen. I don't have a lot of equipment in my home kitchen, just a little stove and an immersion blender. That's all. There's lots of information on the Internet, but that's the problem: There's too much. If you search for a recipe, you get too many answers. How can you know which one is best? That's what my book will tell you, the right way to make things." Having directed the final part of the El Bulli DVD, Albert is also thinking about making another film, possibly with the celebrated Barcelona artist and designer Javier Mariscal.

What everybody really wants to know, of course, is whether people will still be able to eat at El Bulli—or, rather, will serving food in a restaurant context be one of the foundation's activities. "Yes, of course," says Ferran. "At one time, we considered closing the restaurant side of things completely, permanently, and devoting our time to conferences, lectures, the activities at Alícia, and so on—but we are chefs, after all. That's what we love to do, not the theory." But, he quickly adds, "Every year will be different, with different opening dates, different reservation policies, different programs. Maybe we will serve breakfasts for a while, which is a meal I'm passionate about but one that restaurants traditionally forget. Maybe we'll experiment with a bar serving only cocktails and snacks. One idea is that we will open as a gastronomic restaurant for two months a year, with only twenty-five or thirty covers a night. I need feedback, at least from a few tables of diners."

I ask if he will serve food on the level of what he has been serving at El Bulli. "It will be *better*," he replies. "A higher level. The meals will be like the ones we did for the Documenta book, which were the best meals we've ever made." In one scenario, he adds, people might have dinner first, then "an experience in the kitchen," the exact nature of which he hasn't yet figured out. The new format would also allow him to host guest chefs. "With the foundation, for instance, we can invite Mibu [i.e., Japanese master chef Hiroyoshi Ishida] back, or maybe Thomas Keller, or . . ." What is clear, adds Ferran, is that there will be no more Michelin stars. "We won't be in any of the guidebooks," he says. (That I doubt, incidentally; the guides will figure out a way to include El Bulli, foundation or not.) Beyond that, as the online statement says, "At present we are unable to give more specific details as we are currently studying the most adequate model for this new operative." Or, in the words of Ferran to me at Carmen, "These are some of the ideas. I'm still brainstorming."

■ ■ ■

We're sitting on the terrace at El Bulli on a warm October afternoon three months before Ferran is to announce the closing of the restaurant and the creation of the foundation. The wood-slat outdoor tables are bare, the comfortable big wooden chairs positioned around the terrace at various informal angles; it will be three or four hours before the first guests arrive. There's a faint, teasing breeze bearing a hint of the sea. We're shaded from the afternoon sun by a tile-roofed overhang, and I'm thinking how easily this terrace could be part of some casual restaurant in Provence or on the Ligurian coast where you'd want to waste the afternoon drinking rosé and nibbling non-spherified olives in the soft light and sweet-smelling air—the kind of place, in a way, that it was at the beginning.

Ferran, the man who has taken El Bulli out of that league, seems relaxed this afternoon, but he's also pensive, philosophical. "To keep a cool head is very, very hard when everybody is saying that you're the greatest chef in the world," he says, "but I have to try. I have a sense of humor. I can't control 'Ferran Adrià.' People say things about me that aren't true. There are lots of opinions about El Bulli, lots of idiotic problems. I'm vaccinated now against everything. El Bulli has become a monster, impossible to tame." He stops and leans forward. "Look," he says, "I don't make an effort to be different. And I don't think I'm better for being different. You could say I have a business where I don't *want* to be different. What we want at El Bulli is to wake up in the morning and have the unique excitement of seeing if we're able to do something new. I don't work for ego or money anymore. I work to have fun. And having fun requires that excitement that you get from making something new." He shakes his head. "I have a problem and an opportunity," he says. "The problem is that I'm already forty-seven, so I don't have my whole lifetime left. The opportunity is that I'm *only* forty-seven. Robuchon is my model. He retired, but he still kept active. He's a mirror for me."

I ask Ferran if he's religious. "Oh," he replies, waving his hand. "No. Like anybody. I pray only when things go badly. My mother is religious." Superstitious? "No," he says, "but I am aware that there were *so many* coincidences that put me where I am today. If Marketta had had a family, we wouldn't be here now, or if Dr. Schilling had sold the restaurant to Neichel, who should have been the proprietor. If the restaurant had been in a big town instead of Cala Montjoi, I wouldn't have had the same perspective and wouldn't have developed in the same way; for fifteen years, it was hard, but it was calm, almost nobody came, so we had the time to work, to explore, to grow. All the young chefs today, they shoot up like rockets." (He demonstrates, flinging his arms skyward.) "There were fifty variables. Robuchon's comments were *so* important. So was the Gault/Millau guide, the three Michelin stars, *The New York Times*. . . . All this could happen only once. I never imagined when I began that I would end up like this. I thought maybe I'd have, at the most, one of the best restaurants in Catalonia, maybe in Spain. Having three stars from Michelin, that's the maximum I could have imagined. What happened? I never wanted to be the 'best chef in the world.' For me, it's a gift. All this adulation? Two Doctor Honoris Causa degrees? Documenta? It's *impossible*." He's right, of course. Nothing in Ferran's ancestry, early training or home life, or first forays into cooking would have suggested or predicted what he would become. He is a good argument for the theory that some people are simply chosen by the gods—or at least touched by (that word he hates) genius. I remember talking to Albert one day at the Taller about the improbable rise of El Bulli, and he nodded. "I think about that all the time," he said. "'Why us?' That could be the title of your book, Colman. *Why Us?*"

Morphing

∎ ∎ ∎

Since 2002, meals at El Bulli have concluded with what the menu terms—always in English—"Morphings." As a verb of fairly recent coinage, *to morph*, derived from *metamorphose*, means to be transformed or to change from one thing to another; *morphing* is a term used primarily in the fields of animation and special effects to mean specifically a seamless transformation of one image into another. Morphings in Ferran's sense are transitional bites between the body of the meal and the after-dinner relaxation of coffee and liqueurs (and the perhaps less relaxing trip down the hill to Roses, back to real life). Ferran makes it clear that he would like the impending transition of El Bulli, and of his own career, to the next stage to be seamless, too. "Whatever happens," he says, "it's very important for me to end well. El Bulli has been something very beautiful. It must have a beautiful finish."

Bibliography

Documenta Kassel 16/06—23/09 2007. Köln: Taschen GmbH, 2007.

Guide of Catalonia: Journeys and Fun 1987. Espulgues de Llobregat, Barcelona: Plaza & Janés Editores, S.A., 1987.

Adrià, Albert. *Los postres de El Bulli*. Madrid: Ediciones Península, 1998.

———. *Natura*. Cala Montjoi: elBulli Books, 2008.

Adrià, Ferran. *Espumas de Ferran Adrià: Restaurante El Bulli*. Barcelona: DCI, S.A., 1998.

———. *Las 50 nuevas tapas de Ferran Adrià*. Barcelona: Editorial Formentera, S.A. / Woman, n.d., 1998.

———. *Los secretos de El Bulli: Recetas, téchnicas y reflexiones*. Barcelona: Ediciones Altaya, S.A., 1998.

Adrià, Ferran, et al. *El Bulli: El sabor del Mediterráneo*. Barcelona: Editorial Antártida/Empúries, 1993.

Adrià, Ferran, Juli Soler, and Albert Adrià. *Cuinar a casa amb Caprabo i Ferran Adrià*. Cala Montjoi: elBullibooks, 2003.

Bibliography

———. *A Day at elBulli: An Insight into the Ideas, Methods and Creativity of Ferran Adrià*, trans. by Equip de Edicion and Cillero & de Motta. London: Phaidon Press Limited and New York: Phaidon Press, Inc., 2008.

———. *elBulli 1983–1993*. Cala Montjoi: elBullibooks, 2004.

———. *elBulli 1994–1997*. Cala Montjoi: elBullibooks, 2003.

———. *elBulli 1998–2002*. Cala Montjoi: elBullibooks, 2002.

———. *elBulli 2003–2004*. Cala Montjoi: elBullibooks, 2005.

———. *elBulli 2005*. Cala Montjoi: elBullibooks, 2006.

Alícia & elBullitaller. *Diálogo entre ciencia y cocina*. Barcelona: Editorial Planeta, S.A., 2006.

———. *Lèxic científic gastronòmic: Les Claus per entendre la cuina d'avui*. Barcelona: Editorial Planeta, S.A., 2006.

Arenós, Pau. *Els genis del foc: Qui són, com creen i què cuinen 10 xefs catalans d'avantguarda*, 2nd edition. Barcelona: Editorial Empúries, S.A., 2002.

Bàguena i Maranges, Núria. *Cuinar i menjar a Barcelona (1850–1900)*. Barcelona: DIM Ediciones, S.L., 2007.

Bourdain, Anthony. *The Nasty Bits: Collected Varietal Cuts, Usable Trim, Scraps, and Bones*. New York and London: Bloomsbury Publishing, 2006.

———. *Kitchen Confidential: Adventures in the Culinary Underbelly*, updated edition. New York: Harper Perennial, 2007.

Caballero, Óscar. *Quand la cuisine fait date*. Paris: Les Éditions du Bottin Gourmand, 2007.

Casas, Carmen. *Comer in Catalunya*. Madrid: Penthalon Ediciones, 1980.

Dalí, Salvador. *Les dîners de Gala*, trans. by Captain J. Peter Moore. New York: Felicie, Inc., 1971.

———. *The Secret Life of Salvador Dalí*, trans. by Haakon M. Chevalier. New York: Burton C. Hoffman/Dial Press, 1942.

Friedland, Susan R., ed. *Food and Morality: Proceedings of the Oxford Symposium on Food and Cookery 2007*. Tutnes, Devon: Prospect Books, 2008.

Hadjidakis, P. J. *Delos*. Athens: Latsis Group, Editions Oikos, 2003.

Hamilton, Richard, and Vicente Todolí, eds. *Food for Thought/Thought for Food*. Barcelona and New York: Actar, 2009.

Hamley, I. *Introduction to Soft Matter*, 2nd edition. Chichester: J. Wiley, 2000.

Bibliography

Kellogg, Ella Eaton. *Science in the Kitchen. A Scientific Treatise on Food Substances and their Dietetic Properties, Together with a Practical Explanation of the Principles of Healthful Cookery, and a Large Number of Original, Palatable, and Wholesome Recipes.* Chicago: Modern Medicine Publishing Co., 1893.

Kurti, Nicholas, and Giana Kurti, eds. *But the Crackling Is Superb: An Anthology on Food and Drink by Fellows and Foreign Members of the Royal Society.* Bristol and Philadelphia: Adam Hilger, 1988.

Lévi-Strauss, Claude. *The Raw and the Cooked: Introduction to a Science of Mythology I*, trans. by John and Doreen Weightman. New York and Evanston: Harper & Row, 1969.

Lowe, Belle. *Experimental Cookery from the Chemical and Physical Standpoint.* New York: John Wiley & Sons, Inc., and London: Chapman & Hall, Limited, 1932.

Luján, Nèstor. *Diccionari Luján de gastronomia catalana.* Barcelona: Ediciones La Campana, 1990.

MacDonough, Giles. *A Palate in Revolution: Grimod de La Reynière and the "Almanach des Gourmands."* London: Robin Clark, 1987.

Mans, Claudi. *La Truita cremada: 24 lliçons de química*, 8th edition. Barcelona: Collegi Oficial de Químics de Catalunya, 2008.

———. *La vaca esfèrica: Conceptes cientifics quotidians que, d'entrada, jo no devia entendre prou bé.* Barcelona: Rubes Editorial, 2008.

Marinetti, F. T. *The Futurist Cookbook*, trans. by Suzanne Brill, edited with an introduction by Lesley Chamberlain. San Francisco: Bedford Arts Publishers, 1989.

McGee, Harold. *On Food and Cooking: The Science and Lore of the Kitchen*, revised and updated edition. New York: Scribner, 2004.

Michener, James A. *Iberia.* New York: Random House, 1968.

Moret, Xavier. *elBulli des de dins: Biografia d'un restaurant.* Barcelona: La Magrana, 2007.

Pla, Josep. *Alguns grans cuiners de l'Empordà.* Barcelona: Libres a Mà/ Ediciones Destino i Ediciones 62, 1984.

Revel, Jean-François. *Culture and Cuisine: A Journey Through the History of Food*, trans. by Helen R. Lane. New York: Doubleday, 1982.

Sagristà, Xavier. *Entre mar i muntanya: Apunts de cuina a l'Empordà.* Barcelona: Editorial Empúries, S.L., 2002.

Santamaria, Santi. *La cocina al desnudo*, revised edition. Madrid: Ediciones Temas de Hoy, S.A., 2009.

Schechter, Peter. *Pipeline*. New York: William Morrow and Company, 2009.

Sen, Miguel. *Luces y sombras del reinado de Ferran Adrià*. Barcelona: La Esfera de los Libros, S.L., 2007.

Shatner, William, and David Fisher. *Up Till Now: The Autobiography*. New York: Thomas Dunne Books, 2008.

Soler, Juli, Ferran Adrià, and Albert Adrià. *Un dia en elBulli*. Roses: elBulli Books, 2007.

Symons, Michael. *A History of Cooks and Cooking*. Urbana and Chicago: University of Illinois Press, 2000.

This, Hervé. *Molecular Gastronomy: Exploring the Science of Flavor*, trans. M. B. Debevoise. New York: Columbia University Press, 2006.

Weber-Lamberdière, Manfred. *Die Revolutionen des Ferran Adrià: Wie ein Katalane das Kochen zur Kunst machte*. Berlin: Bloomsbury Berlin, 2007.

Witherspoon, Kimberly, and Andrew Friedman, eds. *Don't Try This at Home: Culinary Catastrophes from the World's Greatest Chefs*. New York and London: Bloomsbury, 2005.

Wrangham, Richard. *Catching Fire: How Cooking Made Us Human*. New York: Basic Books, 2009.

Zipprick, Jörg. *¡No quiero volver al restaurante! De como la cocina molecular nos sirve cola para papel pintado y polvo extinctor*, trans. by Alfredo Brotuns. Madrid: Foca, 2009.

DVDs

Decoding Ferran Adria, hosted by Anthony Bourdain, produced and directed by Chris Collins and Lydia Tenaglia. A Zero Point Zero Production, 2004.

elBulli, historia de un sueño: Catálogo audiovisual 1963–2009, by Ferran Adrià, Juli Soler, and Albert Adrià, directed by David Pujol. Visual 13, 2009.

Acknowledgments

My thanks go first and most of all to my main character, Ferran Adrià. For more than two years, from the time he first gave this project his blessing, he granted me unrestricted access to the El Bulli kitchen and dining room in Cala Montjoi and to his Taller, or workshop, in Barcelona; he let me watch him and his chefs at work, explained and illuminated his creative processes, pointed me in directions I might not otherwise have taken, and responded promptly and candidly to my ceaseless queries (even the complicated and the discomfiting ones); best of all, though, he did all this without interfering in the least with my research or asking for approval of the results. *Moltes gràcies per tot, amic meu.*

Ferran's family was generous and forthcoming, as well. His parents, Pepi (Josefa) Acosta Sanchez and Ginés Adrià Muñoz, chatted freely with me and answered my questions frankly and charmingly.

His brother and longtime collaborator, Albert, gave me fresh perspectives on the phenomenon of El Bulli—and on his famous sibling—with unfailingly good humor. Ferran's wife, Isabel Pérez, was helpful in a dozen ways, and always a pleasure to encounter (and to dine with). And Juli Soler, whom I think must be counted as a member of the family (I doubt that Ferran would disagree) was . . . well, Juli Soler—which is to say funny, incisive, unpredictable, and practically omniscient about anything concerning El Bulli, past or present.

I owe immense gratitude to José Andrés, who has long been Ferran's most tireless and eloquent champion in America, and who initially introduced me (in person) to him. José was the godfather of this book: He planted the idea in Ferran's crowded mind, then kept after him until he finally agreed to consider it. Ultimately, José made the book happen. Fermí Puig, who knew Ferran "when," and who first brought him to El Bulli, was a wonderful source of information and insight. In addition to Puig and Andrés, a number of other alumni of the restaurant were generous with their time, their recollections, and their opinions. Sincere thanks, in particular, are due to Jean-Louis Neichel, Jean-Paul Vinay, Kristian Lutaud, Xavier Sagristà, Albert Raurich, Carles Abellán, Sergi Arola, Isidre Soler, Joan Roca, and Andoni Aduriz. Thanks, too, to Toni Gerez, Artur Sagués, and Félix Maena, veterans of the El Bulli dining room.

The present-day staff at El Bulli could not have been more accommodating. Oriol Castro, above all, was endlessly informative and hospitable, and I owe thanks as well to Eduard Xatruch, Mateu Casañas, Lluís García, Lluís Biosca, Pol Perelló, Ferran Centelles, David Seijas, David López, and all the rest—not forgetting the stagiares Lee Wolin, Myungsun Jang, and especially Colin Kirby. Thanks, too, to Marc Cuspinera at elBullicarmen and to Marc Puig-Pey, Pere Castells, and especially Toni Massenés at the Alícia Foundation.

Santi Santamaria, the first Michelin three-star chef in Catalonia, who has emerged as Ferran's harshest but most articulate critic, explained his point of view to me in detail and gave me a lot to chew on. Juan Mari Arzak, who set Spain on its path to contemporary culinary greatness, spoke to me about Ferran and his importance with great affection and authority. Heston Blumenthal in Bray and Vicente Todolí in London explained much and helped put Ferran's achievements in context. Spain's most celebrated pastry chefs, Christian Escribà and Paco Torreblanca, offered invaluable details about Ferran's culinary development (and personal character)—Albert's, too. In Alicante, Maria José San Roman connected me with several people key to my story, and took me to meet Jorge Marin, Ferran's "boss" from his navy days. My thanks to all.

The filmmaker David Pujol gave me many useful insights into Ferran's personality and much inside information about the history of El Bulli, both in conversation and through his superb multi-part video documentary *elBulli, historia de un sueño: catálogo audiovisual 1963–2009.*

Many other men and women who count themselves as friends of Ferran's, and/or who have worked with him or observed him closely over the years, were willing to share their perceptions, and in some cases to tell me the kinds of wonderful stories that add essential life to a book like this. Among these are sculptor Xavier Medina-Campeny; journalists and authors Pau Arenós, Óscar Caballero, Xavier Agulló, and Carmen Casas; the estimable hotelier and chef-restaurateur Jaume Subirós; chef Carme Ruscalleda (proprietor of another of Catalonia's three-star restaurants); Llorenç Petràs (the mushroom king of La Boqueria); and Valentin Fuster, Bob and Antonella Noto, Juan Solé, Marc Calabuix, Cristina Giménez, Rafael Ansón, José Luis Muguiro Aznar, Carlo Petrini, Annette Abstoss, Lluís Debuen, Michèle Nibert, and Catherine Perrot.

My good friends in Barcelona, Agustí and Lluïsa Jausas and George and Lucy Semler, clarified many matters both linguistic and cultural. In America, I got much good information from Gerry Dawes, Arthur Lubow, David Weiss and Otger Campàs at Harvard University, Jeff Cerciello, Harold McGee, Ted Russin and his colleagues at CP Kelco, Thomas Keller, and Ken Oringer.

Teresa Baranchea, Claudia Krines, Lisa Abend, Ross Lewis, Clara Maria de Amezúa, Dorothy Kalins, Kim Yorio, Corby Kummer, Amanda Hesser, Bruno Mantovani, Lizette Gratacós Wys, Fabrizio Aielli, Erin Swing Romanos, and Susana Nieto all assisted in various ways. Special thanks to Pilar Vico and the Tourist Office of Spain in New York City. And my loving gratitude to Erin for her patience and support (in more ways than one).

Finally, my thanks to my agent, Michael Psaltis of the Culinary Cooperative, for having helped me organize my thoughts on this challenging project and for making not one but two deals to help it become a reality; to William Shinker, Lucia Watson, Lisa Johnson, and (just for a minute there) Erin Moore at Gotham Books; and to Richard Schlagman (who discovered me and this project when he found me working on my laptop in the kitchen at El Bulli), Emilia Teragni, and Laura Gladwin at Phaidon Press.

Index

Abellán, Carles, 121, 122, 152
Abend, Lisa, 240, 242
Achatz, Grant, 29, 215, 235
Additives, 10, 185, 187, 226, 227,
    237, 239, 241, 245, 259
Adrià, Albert, 5, 7, 70–73, 77, 78,
    106–108, 114, 120, 125,
    126, 156, 163, 174, 182–183,
    185, 186, 192, 202, 228,
    229, 240, 267–268, 270,
    275, 278–280, 282
Adrià, Ferran (see also El Bulli
    restaurant)
  additives, use of, 10, 185, 187,
    226, 227, 239, 241, 259
  Alícia Foundation and, 207–210
  austerity of, 15
  birth of, 69
  Bistro del Bulli and, 109–110
  books by, 46, 83–84, 130–131,
    132, 144, 158–161, 200–202,
    221, 243, 261, 269–270
  brother Albert and, 106,
    156, 174
  business partnership with Juli,
    123, 129
  as Chef of the Year (1999), 22
  childhood of, 71–73
  clothing of, 14–15
  criticism of, 10–11, 13, 125,
    167, 183, 204, 219–223,
    226–227, 229–246
  culinary philosophy of, 20,
    23–26, 114, 147–148, 152,
    153, 159, 161–162
  deconstructions and, 26–27
  degrees awarded to,
    211–212, 282

Adrià, Ferran (*cont.*)
Documenta 12 (2007) and,
223–226, 236, 276, 282
early employment of, 74–77
early meetings with author, 4–11
education of, 73–74
favorite foods of, 6, 70, 71, 73
first works at El Bulli, 85–86
foams and airs and, 114,
126–127, 158, 189–194
fonds, redefinition of, 127
generosity of, 18, 185, 190
as genius, 25
Harvard University and,
212–215
influence of, 28–33, 132
influence of Gagnaire and Bras
on, 124–125
Ishida and, 205–206
in Japan, 205–206
Juli and, 95, 97, 100, 104
Mantovani's composition and,
215–218
marriage of, 195–196
Maximin's impression on, 112,
113, 141
Medina-Campeny and,
127–128, 191
Mercader and, 143, 144
military service of, 79–84
molecular gastronomy and,
175–177, 182, 189, 213, 259
name change, 132–133
nouvelle cuisine and, 9,
143–145
parents of, 70–71, 77–78
personality of, 16–19
physical appearance of, 14, 81
presentations of, 17, 24,
188–189, 205, 213
professional evolution of,
111–119, 201

proposed foundation of, 272,
275–277, 280–281
"provocation of 1997" and,
157–158
Puig and, 82, 99, 100, 114
redefinition of restaurant
experience by, 27–28
Robuchon on, 154–155
Santamaria and, 230–246
seminars run by, 148
spherification and, 29–31,
182–185
sports and, 73, 75
stages in French restaurants
of, 106
Talaia Mar and, 152–153, 156
travels of, 205–206, 274–275
voice and speech of, 16
writings on, 21–23, 48, 120,
203–205, 275, 282
Adrià, Isabel Pérez Barceló, 8, 9,
70, 72, 195–197, 213
Adrià, Pepi (Josefa Acosta
Sanchez), 70–74,
77–78, 106
Adrià Muñoz, Ginés, 15, 70–71,
74, 76–78
Aduriz, Andoni, 235, 241, 253, 264
Agulló, Xavier, 116, 122, 129, 148,
150, 198, 235
Aielli, Fabrizio, 32
Ali, 101
Alícia Foundation, 207–210,
212, 276
Amezúa, Clara Maria, 234
Anaxippus, 137
Andrés, José, 5, 7, 29, 76, 101,
116–122, 154, 185, 206–207,
215, 253, 274
Andreu, Dolors, 255
Aneiros, Fernando, 76
Apicius, 137

Arenós, Pau, 3, 13, 16, 143, 152–153, 155, 158, 177, 219

Arguiñano, Karlos, 142

Arola, Sergi, 109, 152

Arzak, Juan Mari, 6, 41, 141–144, 153–154, 206–207, 233, 235, 241, 242, 248, 253, 264

Arzak, Marta, 223

Asimov, Eric, 24, 188

Atherton, Jason, 253

Balaguer, Oriol, 152

Barber, Dan, 235

Baumé, Antoine, 178

Beauvilliers, Antoine, 137

Beeton, Mrs., 178

Berasategui, Martín, 254

Bettónica, Luis, 3, 4, 120

Biarnés, Jaume, 209

Bistro del Bulli, 109–110

Bittman, Mark, 21

Blanco Negro magazine, 122–123

Blumenthal, Heston, 181, 186, 192, 196, 226, 228, 229, 235

Bocuse, Paul, 82, 112, 139–142, 154, 190, 238

Bofill, Ricardo, 19

Bonodo, Feggy, 55

Borja-Villel, Manuel, 224

Bosch, Eduard, 164

Bouillard, Octaaf "Oki," 58

Bourdain, Anthony, 24, 32, 47–48, 50, 188, 202, 221

Bowie, David, 270

Bras, Michel, 124

Bremzen, Anya von, 28

Breuer, Silvia, 65, 90

Brillat-Savarin, Anthelme, 120, 226

Brooks, James, 166

Buford, Bill, 226

Buj, Ramiro, 84

Burgos, Antonio, 220–221

Caballero, Óscar, 15, 48, 52, 112, 135, 143

Cabau, Ramón, 144

Calabuig, Marc, 193, 278

Campàs, Otger, 187, 212–215

Cantero, Rafael, 115

Cantu, Homaro, 29, 258

Capel, José Carlos, 241–242

Carême, Marie Antoine, 24

Casañas, Mateu, 172, 275, 278

Casas, Carmen, 23, 43, 59, 63, 111, 158, 196

Cassi, Davide, 182

Castells, Pere, 176–177, 209

Castillo, José Juan, 142

Castro, Oriol, 156, 172–174, 182–183, 251, 254–255, 259, 262, 263, 275, 278, 279

Catalan cuisine, defined, 62

Catalan Cuisine (Andrews), 3, 4

Catalans, description of, 19

Centelles, Ferran, 200

Cerciello, Jeff, 163

Chantecler, Nice, 111–112

Chapel, Alain, 82, 132, 139

Chua-Eoan, Howard, 213

Ciardi, John, 20

Club des Gourmets magazine, 107–108

Cocina al desnudo, La (Santamaria), 10, 236–239, 242

Cocinar en 10 minutos con Ferran Adrià, 160, 202

Colette, 35

Collins, Hannah, 278

Copia, 276

Coren, Giles, 48, 256
Cracco, Carlo, 28
Cruanyas, Lluís, 144
Cruyff, Johan, 73
Cuinar a casa amb Caprabo i
    Ferran Adrià (Cook at Home
    with Caprabo and Ferran
    Adrià), 202–203
Cuspinera, Marc, 162, 275

Dacosta, Quique, 6
Dalí, Salvador, 19, 56–58, 250,
    263
Damoxenus of Rhodes, 137
Darwin, Charles, 135
Dávila, Juan, 225
Dawes, Gerry, 21, 234,
    273–274
Day at elBulli, A: An Insight into
    the Ideas, Methods and
    Creativity of Ferran Adrià,
    46, 269–270
de Diego, Eugeni, 172
de La Reynière, Alexandre
    Grimod, 178
Delaveyne, Jean, 139
de Lune, Pierre, 131
Derrida, Jacques, 26
Dia en elBulli, Un (A Day at
    elBulli) (Adrià), 46, 243,
    261, 269
Documenta 12 (2007), 223–226,
    236, 276, 282
Ducasse, Alain, 155
Duchamp, Marcel, 56
Dufresne, Wylie, 29, 215

El Bulli: El sabor del Mediterráneo
    (The Flavor of the
    Mediterranean) (Adrià),
    83–84, 130–131, 132,
    144, 221
elBullicarmen, 199
elBullicatering, 151
elBulli des de dins (El Bulli from
    Within) (Moret), 42
El Bulli restaurant (see also Adrià,
    Ferran)
  appearance of, 44–45, 127,
    129, 198
  author's first visit to, 3–4
  beginnings of, 53–58, 61–67
  Bosch as chef at, 164
  Castro as chef at, 254
  catering by, 150–151, 161, 200
  consulting business, 198–200
  desserts at, 94, 120, 125–126
  dining experience at, 45–50
  economic issues, 120–122, 129,
    149–150, 197–200, 260, 272
  example of menu, 35–42, 48–50
  Ferran and Lutaud as co-chefs,
    104–109
  Ferran takes over, 21
  film on, 270
  first chefs at, 58
  future of, 267–269, 271–274,
    280, 283
  General Catalogue, 201–202,
    269, 270
  Horta's involvement with,
    149–150
  INICON, involvement in,
    226–229
  Juli arrives at, 90–93
  kitchen renovation at, 255–256
  Krämer as chef at, 91, 92
    in late eighties and early
    nineties, 115–129
  Lutaud as chef at, 92–93
  Lutaud's departure from,
    111, 112

Michelin stars and, 4, 63, 93, 107, 124, 138, 155, 157, 164, 231–234, 282

Neichel as chef at, 61–66, 89, 102, 113, 138, 141

origin of name of, 55–56

popularity of, 22–23

proposed closing of, 11, 23, 150, 271–272

reviews and ratings of, 61–62, 119–120, 124, 129, 153–154

road leading to, 42–43, 86

Sagristà as chef at, 107, 123, 147

staff meals at, 248–251

stagiares at, 247–254, 262, 264

structure of menu, 46–47

tapas introduced at, 126, 160–161, 279

Vinay as chef at, 92–94, 101–103, 113, 138

Web site, 128, 162, 275, 277

workshop (the Taller), 5, 156–157, 165–174, 176–177, 183

Entre llibres i fogons (Between Books and Ovens) (Santamaria), 243

Escabeche technique, 105

Escoffier, Georges Auguste, 24, 132, 138–140, 180

Escribà, Antoni, 125, 192

Escribà, Christian, 17, 28–29, 125, 195

Euphron, 136

Farré, Ingrid, 177, 209

Fast Good, 243

Ferran (*see* Adrià, Ferran)

50 nuevas tapas de Ferran Adrià, Las, 160, 161

Flavors of the Riviera (Andrews), 4

Foams and airs, 30, 114, 126–127, 158, 189–194

Fodor's Guide to Barcelona, 56

Fombellida, Tatus, 142

Food Arts magazine, 22

Food for Thought/Thought for Food (ed. Hamilton and Todolí), 225–226, 276

Franco, Francisco, 59–61

Fuster, Valentín, 208–209

Gagnaire, Pierre, 124, 181

García, Dany, 6

García, Lluís, 48

García Santos, Rafael, 153

Gaudí, Antoni, 19, 132

Gault, Henri, 139, 140

Gault/Millau magazine, 61–62, 124, 140, 282

General Catalogue, 201–202, 269, 270

Gerez, Toni, 103, 123, 147

Gill, A. A., 49, 220

Girardet, Fredy, 9, 130, 140

Gopnik, Blake, 223

Granollers, Pere, 142

Groening, Matt, 166, 226

Gudrais, Elizabeth, 214

Guérard, Michel, 9, 82, 83, 132, 139, 140, 155, 237

Guide Gault/Millau, 124, 153

Guillén, Montse, 81

Hacienda Benazuza, 161, 201

Haeberlin, Jean-Pierre, 140

Haeberlin, Paul, 140

Hamilton, Richard, 56, 225, 276

Hamilton, Roderick, 56

Harvard University, 212–215

Hattori, Yukio, 205–206

Index

Henry, Pascal, 222–223
Herrera, Miguel, 166
Hesser, Amanda, 203
Horta i Almaraz, Miquel, 131,
    149–150
Hospitalet de Llobregat, 69–70
Huber, Luki, 199
Hughes, Robert, 224
Humbert, Alex, 139
Hüschelruth, Manfred, 58
Hydrocolloids, 125, 187

Inedit beer, 200
INICON, 226–229, 236
Ishida, Hiroyoshi, 205–206, 280

Janin, Annick, 93, 94, 100,
    102, 120
Jones, Rick, 188
Jujol, Josep Maria, 132

Kamozawa, Aki, 29
Keller, Thomas, 18, 29, 47, 188,
    190, 280
Kellogg, Ella Eaton, 179
Kirby, Colin, 251–254
Komm, Anatoly, 29
Krämer, Yves, 89, 91–93
Kreis, Fritz, 58
Krines, Claudia, 228–229
Kubelka, Peter, 226
Kurti, Nicholas, 180, 181

Laffont, Robert, 82, 112, 144
La Varenne, François Pierre, 138
Lavazza coffee, 14, 199–200
Lay's, 200, 237
Léon, Jean, 3

Lewis, Ross, 144
Loewy, Raymond, 267
López, David, 220
Lowe, Belle, 187
Lozano, José, 53, 54, 58, 63, 64,
    101, 197, 198
Lubow, Arthur, 16, 204
Lucini, Angel Liberal, 80, 84, 85
Lutaud, Kristian, 3, 66, 93, 94,
    100, 103, 104, 106–109,
    111, 112, 125, 126

Madueño, Pedro, 272
Maillard, Louis Camille, 178
Manière, Jacques, 140
Mans, Claudi, 211
Mantovani, Bruno, 215–218
Marin, Jorge, 79–85
Marinetti, Filippo, 24, 47, 178
Mariscal, Javier, 280
Marshall, Agnes B., 186
Marsical, 128
Martin, Agnes, 224
Massanés, Toni, 132, 207, 208, 210
Massialot, François, 131
Matthew, Kristen, 175
Maximin, Jacques, 9, 112, 124,
    132, 141
McCracken, John, 224
McGee, Harold, 181
Medina-Campeny, Xavier, 16,
    127–128, 166, 191, 204, 256
Meneau, Marc, 141
Mercader i Bruges, Josep, 1,
    142–143
Mibu, Tokyo, 205–206
Michelin stars, 4, 63, 93, 107,
    124, 138, 155, 157, 164,
    231–234, 282
Millás, Juan José, 273
Millau, Christian, 139, 140

Miralda, Antoni, 226
Miró, Joan, 19–20, 56
Molecular gastronomy, 175–177,
    181–182, 189, 213, 259
Mondavi, Robert, 276
Monk, Thelonius, 69
Monty, Henri, 188
Moore, Catherine, 57
Moore, John Peter, 57
Morales, Rafa, 152
Moret, Xavier, 42, 76
Motel Ampurdàn, Figueres, 1–2
Moy, Miquel, 74–76, 250
Müller, Otto, 56
Myhrvold, Nathan, 30
Myungsun "Luke" Jang, 253

Natura (Albert Adrià), 160
Naylor, Tony, 200
Neichel, Jean-Louis, 43, 61–66, 89,
    93, 102, 113, 138, 141, 282
New York Times Magazine, The,
    22, 204
Noma, Copenhagen, 23
Normosis, 229–230
Noto, Antonella, 21
Noto, Bob, 21
Nouvelle cuisine, 24–25, 32, 82
    basic principles of, 140
    beginnings of, 138–139
    defined, 138
    development of, 139–140
    Ferran and, 9, 143–145
    origins of, 139
    reaches Spain, 9, 143–145
Núñez, Montse, 162

Oliver, Raymond, 140
Olympic Games, Barcelona
    (1992), 129

Oringer, Ken, 156–157, 213
Outhier, Louis, 140

Parellada, Ramon, 89
Pasteur, Louis, 178
Perrin, Jacques, 222
Petrini, Carlo, 210
Physiology of Taste, The
    (Brillat-Savarin), 120, 226
Picasso, Pablo, 56
Pipeline (Schechter), 32–33
Point, Fernand, 139, 140
Postres de El Bulli, Los (The
    Desserts of El Bulli) (Albert
    Adrià), 160
Puck, Wolfgang, 47
Puig, Fermí, 81–86, 89, 94,
    95, 99, 100, 102–106,
    114, 144, 154,
    232–235, 238
Puig-Pey, Marc, 152, 209, 251
Pujol, David, 10, 18, 115, 270

Rabaso, Ramon, 76
Rafa's, Roses, 115
Ratatouille (movie), 82–83
Raurich, Albert, 15, 164, 251–253,
    264, 278
Redzepi, René, 23
Restaurant magazine, 23
Revel, Jean-François, 165, 247
Ribaut, Jean-Claude, 150
Robuchon, Joël, 130, 154–156,
    217–218, 237, 282, 285
Roca, Joan, 6, 28, 215,
    235, 241
Rodríguez Zapatero, José Luis,
    220, 241
Roellinger, Olivier, 227
Roigé, Eduard, 151

Rostang, Jo, 131–132
Roteta, Ramón, 142
Roura, Elena, 209
Ruscalleda, Carme, 28, 215,
    241, 243
Russin, Ted, 187–188

Sagristà, Xavier, 87, 107, 108, 116,
    123, 162
Sagués, Artur, 108–109
Saltz, Jerry, 48
Santamaria, Santi, 10–11, 121,
    230–246
Savater, Fernando, 224
Savoy, Guy, 83
Schechter, Peter, 32–33
Schilling, Hans, 51–56, 58–59,
    61, 63, 64, 89, 90–93, 102,
    105–106, 116, 122, 123,
    138, 149, 197, 282
Schilling, Margareta (Marketta)
    Schönova, 51–59, 61, 63–65,
    89–92, 94, 100, 102, 108,
    114, 116, 119–120, 122–123,
    138, 149, 197–198, 282
Science in the Kitchen
    (Kellogg), 179
Secretos de El Bulli, Los: Recetas,
    téchnicas y reflexiones (The
    Secrets of El Bulli: Recipes,
    Techniques and Reflections)
    (Adrià), 158–159
Semler, George, 56
Sen, Miguel, 229–230
Senderens, Alain, 140
Shatner, William, 191–192
Siejas, David, 200
Silva, Jean-Pierre, 162
Singla, Marc, 27, 152
Smith, Graeme, 225

Solé, Juan, 185
Soler, Isidre, 27, 121
Soler Lobo, Juli, 75, 81–82, 85–97,
    100–106, 108, 113, 114,
    116, 119–123, 127, 143,
    149, 150, 198, 199, 202,
    220, 233, 237, 242, 251,
    255, 264, 269, 272
Sophon of Acarnania, 137
Sotirides, 136, 137
Spain Gourmetour magazine,
    22, 246
Spanish Civil War, 59
Sparks, Katy, 5
Spherification, 29–31, 182–185
Spieker, Thomas, 198
Stone Barns Center for Food &
    Agriculture, 276
Subijana, Pedro, 141, 142, 144
Subirós, Jaume, 108

Talaia Mar, Barcelona,
    152–153, 156
Talbot, H. Alexander, 29
Taller (El Bulli), 5, 156–157,
    165–174, 176–177, 183
Terradas Muntañola, Esteban, 151
Texturas, 185
This, Hervé, 177–178, 180–181,
    186, 229
Thomas, Elizabeth Cawdry, 181
Thuriès, Yves, 125
Time magazine, 23
Todolí, Vicente, 45–46, 119, 176,
    225, 276
Torreblanca, Paco, 6, 108,
    125, 126
Troisgros, Jean, 139
Troisgros, Pierre, 139
Trotter, Charlie, 29, 235

Up Till Now (Shatner), 191–192
Urdiain, Benjamin, 233

Vásquez Montalbán, Manuel, 62,
    120, 142
Vázquez Sallés, Daniel, 262
Vehí, Manel, 263
Vergé, Roger, 140
Vinay, Jean-Paul, 42, 64, 86, 92–94,
    100–107, 113, 120, 138

Wakuda, Tetsuya, 235
Wan, Jiandi, 214
Weber-Lamberdière, Manfred, 72
Weil, Pierre, 229
Weitz, David, 213–215

Winkler, Heinz, 190
Wolan, Lee, 258

Xanthan gum, 29, 185,
    188, 259
Xatruch, Eduard, 172, 251,
    254–255, 257, 264, 265,
    275, 278

Yorio, Kim, 18
Yuki, Setsuko, 206

Zipprick, Jörg, 155, 204, 226–229,
    236, 239
Ziryab (Abu al Hasan), 137